THE *CHANGING DIMENSIONS* OF U.S. AGRICULTURAL POLICY

A. Desmond O'Rourke

THE *CHANGING DIMENSIONS* OF U.S. AGRICULTURAL POLICY

PRENTICE-HALL, INC., Englewood Cliffs, New Jersey 07632

Library of Congress Cataloging in Publication Data

O'ROURKE, ANDREW DESMOND, 1938-
The changing dimensions of U.S. agricultural policy.

Bibliography: p. 221
Includes index.
1. Agriculture and state—United States.
2. Agriculture—Economic aspects—United States.
I. Title.
HD1761.07 338.1'0973 77-11164
ISBN 0-13-127936-X

Printed in the United States of America

10 9 8 7 6 5 4 3 2 1

Prentice-Hall International, Inc., *London*
Prentice-Hall of Australia Pty. Limited, *Sydney*
Prentice-Hall of Canada, Ltd., *Toronto*
Prentice-Hall of India Private Limited, *New Delhi*
Prentice-Hall of Japan, Inc., *Tokyo*
Prentice-Hall of Southeast Asia Pte. Ltd., *Singapore*
Whitehall Books Limited, *Wellington, New Zealand*

CONTENTS

PREFACE

U.S. agriculture has been changing internally for many decades. Farms have become fewer, larger, and more mechanized. Final products have undergone processing, packaging, merchandising, and other marketing services. Great industries have grown up to serve farmers' supply and marketing needs, and at least once in a decade, some great external upheaval, such as depression or war, has rocked agriculture to the core, and often set it off on a different path than in the previous decade. In that sense, the dimensions of government policy for U.S. agriculture have also continually changed. We have had more than one abrupt swing from efforts to brake overabundant production to frantic drives to fill sudden shortages. When supplies were plentiful and prices low, only the agricultural sector was concerned about agricultural policy. When problems of supply or other emergencies arose, agricultural policy suddenly became everybody's business.

Much of the surge of interest in U.S. agricultural policy in the 1970s has been the result of just such cyclical swings. Supplies have been short. Prices have risen (and fallen) dramatically, as demand and supply varied. Government has continued to try gamely (if not always successfully!) to prejudge the next sudden turn of events. However, there have been a number of unique changes in the dimensions of U.S. agricultural policy in the 1970s. Continued population growth has given new credibility to the prophets of world famine. The decision by centrally planned nations like Mainland China, Russia, and Eastern Europe to supplement their domestic supplies by purchases from other countries has enlarged world market demand for agricultural products. The sudden increases in energy prices have enriched oil producing countries and severely hampered world agriculture, which had come to rely increasingly on petroleum-based power. At the same time, increasing concern (sometimes almost hysteria) about the quantity, quality, distribution, and use of natural resources has led to many new restrictions on farm operations.

In the past, U.S. agriculture was asked to provide farmers with a good living and consumers with plentiful supplies at low prices. Now it is being asked to meet expanded world trade needs and to be the world's reserve in case of famine. Some people wish to use it as a trade or ideological weapon. Policy makers are in a quandry as to how U.S. agriculture can fill these diverse roles.

This book, then, leads you from the origins and formation of U.S. agricultural policy, through past triumphs and reversals, to the present challenging situation. It attempts to provide you with a broad understanding of the major forces affecting policy, the groups seeking to influence or control it, the economic and social setting, the problems that have evolved, and the solutions offered by economic analysts. The text examines the present structure of the production, input, and marketing sectors of U.S. agriculture through which policy must be exercised and shows how recent legislation has affected this structure. It explores the changing links between U.S. agriculture and trade and aid. It looks at the relationship of agriculture to poverty in both urban and rural areas. One chapter discusses the changing goals and values of farmers and other citizens, what future goals might be, and the sort of agricultural policy such goals would imply. In order to give you a feeling for the complexity of U.S. agricultural policy making, I have concentrated on concepts and issues and have omitted details which can be gained better from official publications of the United States Department of Agriculture or from more advanced textbooks, such as Professor Luther Tweeten's *Foundations of Farm Policy* or *American Farm Policy, 1948–73* by Professors Willard W. Cochrane and Mary E. Ryan.

I have tried to avoid a few errors that have tended to creep into even the best analyses of U.S. agricultural policy. One is an excessive focus on the farmer. While agricultural policy works mainly through the activities of farmers, recent events have demonstrated that U.S. agriculture is vital to the welfare of all citizens. A second error is a tendency to conveniently disregard the imperfections in our economic and political system. Agriculture, like the rest of the U.S. economy, has both concentrations of economic power in a few hands and a large number of small, relatively powerless firms. The political system also has its concentrations of power in parties and lobbies, and at the same time diffusion of voting power. The results of the real system need not parallel what one might expect from a perfectly competitive, truly democratic society. A third problem in policy writings is that even the scientist trying to be objective and impartial may slip into advocacy of a view that satisfies his personal values. Where I advocate a particular point of view I have tried to make it clear that it is *mine*. However, as in all policy analysis, the reader must be constantly on the alert for the author's biases. Finally, in their policy analyses, economists have a tendency to concentrate on economic factors to the exclusion of important physical, social, and political elements which may at times be more critical.

However, good intentions should not be confused with virtue. A book on such a vastly complex subject as the agricultural policy of a large and diverse nation must be limited by the author's knowledge and perspectives. On some of the most critical policy issues, scientific studies either disagree or are not available. I have tried to examine past and present controversies fairly and have called the results as I see them. Above all, I have tried to give you the flavor of the big issues and the incentive to pursue critical inquiry in greater depth.

While the book is organized into 10 chapters and is suitable for a one-quarter or one-semester undergraduate course, an instructor or reader may conveniently change the order of study as required. For example, some prefer to begin with past policies and examine how present policies evolved from that base; others prefer to look at most recent experiences first. In either case, each section is followed by a review of key words and central concepts and a series of questions, which both clarify and provide subtle insights into topics discussed in the text. Chapter ten is Suggestions for Further Reading; it includes references cited in the text.

This book owes much to the pioneering policy analysts of the economics profession, not all of whose contributions can be recognized individually. They, like me, have depended heavily on the enormous output of facts, statistics, and analyses from the many services of the U.S. Department of Agriculture. I owe much to the intellectual stimulation of colleagues and students at a number of institutions both in the United States and in Ireland, and particularly the Department of Agricultural Economics at Washington State University. My wife, Sheila, lovingly assisted in many ways to make this book possible. Gerry, Dara, and Danny accepted with resignation the missed opportunities for softball, football, swimming, and other youthful diversions. To them all, my deepest gratitude.

A. Desmond O'Rourke

one

INTRODUCTION

For much of the 1950s and 1960s, U.S. farmers tended to see themselves as victims of their own productivity—taken for granted by consumers, neglected by government, and constantly losing faith in themselves. By a series of quirks of fate, suddenly in 1973 and 1974, U.S. agriculture became a dashing knight in shining armor, the only hope for saving the world from hunger, poverty, and disease. This reversal caught farmers, farm organizations, the federal farm bureaucracy, Congress, the president, and the American people off guard. Attuned to chronic farm surpluses and relatively low food prices, they had difficulty in adjusting their notions of agricultural policy to the new situation. (See, for example, the trend of wheat stocks and prices since 1960, Figure 1.1.) The people asked two main questions. (1) Is the new situation and the new prosperity likely to continue? (2) If so, how can agricultural policy be adapted to meet that changed situation?

It was clear to all parties that policies for a depressed agriculture would be inappropriate in the future if prosperity was to be continuous, or even if there were to be rapidly alternating periods of prosperity and depression. However, policies for a prosperous era would be equally inappropriate if agriculture were to sink back into chronic

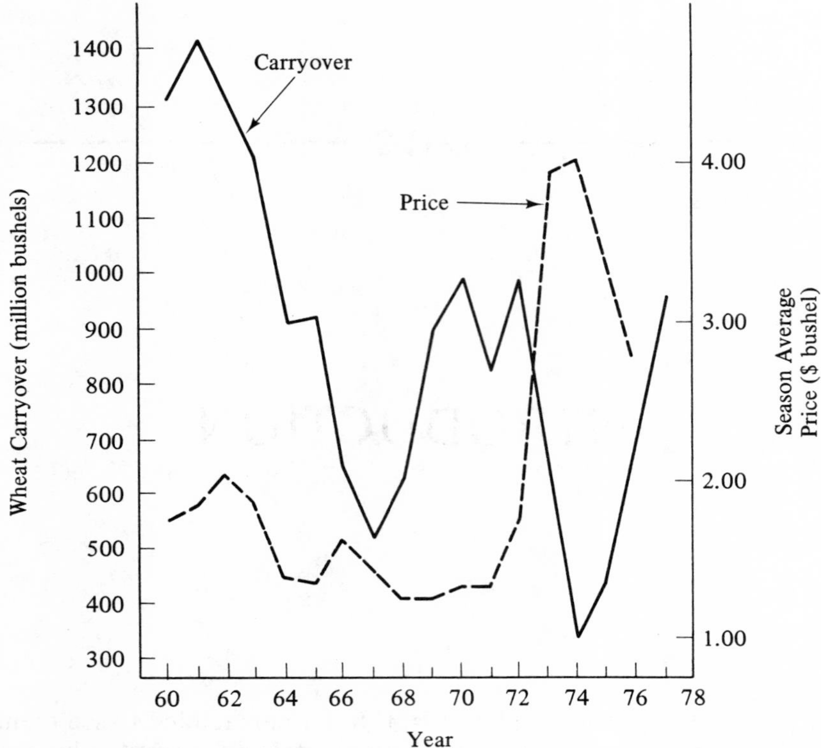

Fig. 1.1. Wheat beginning season carryover and season average price, 1960–76. *Source*: USDA, *Handbook of Agricultural Charts.*

depression. It might then prove difficult to persuade the American people to restore previously discredited policies. In addition, it was clear that many new or formerly latent national and international issues would have to be taken into account in future policy changes and that U.S. agriculture might be made to serve new masters. This book attempts to give the reader some insight into both the permanent and changing elements of U.S. agricultural policy and some basis for evaluating the impact on the nation and the world of current laws and future proposals.

A FEW DEFINITIONS

Since this is not intended as a technical treatise, the definitions will be kept simple and brief. By "policy" I mean the intent of the government to influence the lives of its citizens. Note that policy need not actually influence our lives. Many laws are permanently or occasionally ineffective (an example often cited is Prohibition). In turn, policy need not be written into law to affect the lives of citizens. For example, government agencies have in the past been accused of discrimination in employment or in the granting of loans. Thus, the customs of a bureaucracy in administering the law may alter the intent and impact of policy. Policies may be national or local in scope, apply to all commodities or only specific commodities, be intended as temporary or permanent. Policies may be instituted by different levels of government—federal, state, or local. In this book, we will be concerned mainly with federal policies.

The term "agricultural" linked with policy suggests government intent to influence the lives and the practices of farmers. However, limiting a study of agricultural policy to what affects the farmer would ignore the reality of modern American agriculture, which is a complex international economic system in which the farmer and the farm still play a key role. However, modern agriculture could not exist without the fertilizers, farm machinery, and agricultural, chemical, and other input suppliers. Its marketing is dependent on trucks, railroads, ships, grain elevators, cold storage, retail chains, restaurants, etc. Internationally, it is sensitive to Chinese tastes, Cuban politics, and European weather. Domestically, it is affected by price freezes, tax cuts, food stamps, consumer boycotts, and the latest dietary fads. The products of agriculture—food and fiber—impinge on all our lives. Government policy for agriculture, in turn, has spread its tentacles wherever food and fiber in any form go. Therefore, a discussion of agricultural policy may range over many issues held together by a common link back to the farm or farmer.

This approach differs from that of many previous writers who have seen agricultural policy as concerned with the welfare of farmers. As the number of farmers shrank, "agricultural" was redefined to include farmers and other rural dwellers. However, the assorted food and raw material crises of the 1960s and 1970s have surely brought home to us that while agricultural policy may affect the individual farmer more than any other citizen, the aggregate effect on farmers is small compared to that on all citizens. Agriculture is an important and essential aspect of all our lives.

Just as it is difficult to divorce the agricultural from other aspects of life, so it is difficult to isolate the economic effects of agricultural policy from the political, social, and cultural aspects. However, in most cases, the intent of agricultural policy has been to affect economic variables such as prices or incomes of farmers rather than their social or cultural habits. Accordingly, our focus will be primarily economic.

WHY STUDY AGRICULTURAL POLICY?

Because agriculture has such a pervasive influence on all our lives, self-interest alone would prompt an interest in policies that affect agriculture. However, there are many other reasons why a study of agricultural policy is particularly pertinent.

1. It changes the world. An increase in the price of wheat will push up the price of feed grains. This will affect the profitability of feeding cattle. If cattle numbers are reduced, beef prices will rise. This will push up the price of pork. Pork eaters may cut back on consumption, so the demand for applesauce (to eat with the pork) may slacken. The price of fresh apples may be affected, and so on. Retailers, consumers, foreign buyers, or aid recipients may be affected both directly and indirectly by a one-time change in the price of wheat. It will affect costs and revenues, profits and losses for many businesses that never handle wheat. Government has the power to influence the price of many commodities over a long period. In particular, the agricultural policy of a nation as large and powerful as the United States has economic and other impacts all over the world.

2. Agricultural policy has emerged as a prominent weapon in international ideological and power struggles. With the Russians we may be trading food for peaceful relations; with the oil-producing nations, food for oil; with developing countries, access to U.S. markets for their cooperation in other international activities. Since the 1940s, the nations of the world have increasingly banded together for common economic (EEC), ideological (COMECON), or military (NATO) purposes. Some of these new power groups have tried to frame an agricultural policy protective of members and antagonistic to nonmembers.

3. Agricultural exports have become of major importance to the favorable balance of trade and balance of payments of the United States. This was particularly evident between the years 1972 and 1974. As a result of the actions of the international oil cartel, the cost of U.S. oil imports rose from $5 billion to $26 billion. However, an increase in agricultural exports from $9 billion to $22 billion went a long way toward covering this increase.

4. Worldwide economic growth since World War II and the consolidation of international economic power groups have made U.S. agriculture more vulnerable to influences from abroad. This calls for a new international awareness on the part of U.S. agricultural policy makers.

5. Worldwide population growth has heightened concern about actual or potential shortages of resources to feed the world and to maintain or improve the present standard of living. The United States plays a major role both as a provider and user of resources. United States agriculture is both a major user of nonrenewable resources, e.g., oil, and a major supplier of food to the world. It is at the center of the controversy over whether it will be necessary to exhaust the world's nonrenewable resources to prevent the next generation from starvation, or whether resources must be protected at the expense of present suffering. Agricultural policy may at times have to face these grim choices.

6. At the same time, recent experience suggests that what was once considered "the" farm problem—low and uncertain returns to farmers—may still be very much with us. Can a starving world be fed if farmers are abandoning their farms for more certain income opportunities elsewhere? Should the government choose to shore up farm prices for a war on world hunger, just as it now does to boost domestic oil production?

7. As the foregoing suggests, agriculture frequently finds itself the center of warring interests. An existing policy (or lack of a policy) may help the corn-producer and hurt the hog-producer. It may delight the environmental protectionist and infuriate the advocate of growth. Some may seek a goal of equal opportunity in agriculture; others, equal welfare. Government has tended to play the role of resolving these conflicts. But what happens when government itself is firmly on one side of a conflict (for example, when farmers demand that government "get out of agriculture")? If government's role should be limited, where should those limits be set? Do we want government help when times are bad but resent interference when times are good?

8. Apart from its practical applications to world, national, and firm problems, a study of agricultural policy offers fascinating examples of how men and institutions interact in pursuit of welfare as they see it—a study which takes us through generations and across national borders. Agricultural policy is often the center of age-old conflicts between farmer and consumer, between town and country, between native and foreigner.

THE POLICY PROCESS

The development of public policy is an ongoing process. The main stages of the process are recognizable though not necessarily always occurring in sequence: (1) problem recognition and definition, (2) formulation and development of a policy proposal, (3) policy decision, (4) policy implementation, and (5) policy review and revision.

The problem may be a nationally recognized emergency like a food shortage, or an issue brought to public attention by pressure groups or consumer advocates, such as low incomes in sheep ranching. However, the problem does not actively become a policy issue until either the executive or legislative branch of government recognizes that government has a role to play in problem solution. Definition of the problem involves questions such as: "Are we concerned about all livestock producers or only sheep producers?" "Are we concerned primarily with sheep raised for wool or for meat?" "Are we concerned about all sheep ranchers or only ranchers with small flocks?" All interested parties exert pressure to have the problem defined to meet their own particular needs.

Formulation of a policy proposal may begin in either of the houses of Congress, in the executive branch, or with a private individual or organization. Frequently, two or more proposals may be presented simultaneously by groups who define the problem differently. At this stage, they may decide to adapt and compromise, or to fight it out. The original proposal may be rewritten many times before its sponsors deem it capable of being passed into law.

The actual policy decision may involve passage of a new law where a majority vote in the houses of Congress and presidential acquiescence are required. Or government administrators may formulate new rules under the authority of an existing law. Or the courts may be called on to pass judgment on a new conflict under existing law. Most new policy decisions depend on the will of Congress; most extensions of existing policy on the executive branch of government.

Policy implementation is largely the responsibility of the executive departments of government. Since no law can regulate for all possible circumstances which may arise, government departments have varying degrees of flexibility in how they will interpret any law. This flexibility is curtailed to some extent by the need to return to Congress annually for funds to carry out the provisions of the law. However, the personnel and mood of Congress change over time. The older a law becomes the more "creatively" can it be interpreted. Not infrequently, in later years a law may be implemented in a manner clearly at odds with the original intent of its sponsors.

Policy review and revision tend, like policy formulation, to be piecemeal and a reaction to problems rather than a continuous, coordinated process. Almost all civilizations have shown this tendency toward proliferation of disconnected laws. Only occasionally in history has a powerful ruler, or an extreme revolution, brought about a systematic review of existing law. It is easier to revise and amend in small steps than to seek to formulate a major new law.

Agricultural policy is no exception. There does not exist a single, coordinated body of agricultural policy, but a series of disconnected laws and interpretations of laws which affect agriculture. Even professional policy analysts in general content themselves with reviewing individual polices, and avoid the massive task of evaluating the total agricultural policy package.

Key Words	Central Concepts
Policy	The intent of the government to influence the lives of its citizens. Policies may be ineffective.
Agricultural policy	Policies affecting the agricultural system composed of supply and marketing firms, as well as producers and consumers of farm products.
Aggregate effects	The small effect of agricultural policy on farmers relative to its effects on all citizens.
Interaction effects	A change in the farm price of one product affecting costs, revenues, and profits of handlers of many other products.
Ideology	The support for certain political views which alter attitudes toward agricultural policy.
Exports	Agricultural exports enable the U.S. to pay for oil and other imports.
International	U.S. agriculture is influenced by economic factors in other countries.
Resources	U.S. agriculture uses some nonrenewable resources to produce renewable resources such as food and fiber.
Conflicts	Different groups seek different (often conflicting) goals for agricultural policy.
Policy process	Policy as generated, approved, and revised in recognizable steps.

QUESTIONS

1. What factors might prevent the government from carrying out the intent of its agricultural policy?
2. Describe national and international factors which might influence U.S. agricultural policy toward grain.
3. Why was much agricultural policy originally concerned with the welfare of farmers? Why has this been changing?
4. How might an increase in the price of fresh pears affect demand for (a) fresh apples; (b) hay?
5. Why might countries wish to protect their domestic market from low-cost foreign imports?

6. Is it strictly correct to say that exports of agricultural products pay for imports of oil?
7. Give an example of an economic power group abroad whose actions affect U.S. agriculture.
8. Is the world running out of nonrenewable resources? Search your library for opposing viewpoints.
9. Can a government be both a party to and an arbitrator of policy conflicts?
10. Can any part of the policy process be free from conflict?
11. Does a new policy also require a new law? If not, cite exceptions.
12. Why has a single, coordinated body of agricultural policy failed to emerge in the United States?

two

THE CAST OF CHARACTERS

In any human drama, there are heroes and villains who are principally responsible for the outcome of events. There are the unconcerned and the apathetic, only occasionally stirred to decisive action. There are stage managers and costume designers and lighting experts who color the environment seen by the casual observer in the audience. The more skillfully they do their jobs the more the desired attention is focused on the center stage, and the less obvious is their influence. There are plots which work themselves inevitably toward a planned conclusion: Macbeth must see the witches' prophecies fulfilled. And there are plots where only some *deus ex machina*, as the Romans called it, some divine intervention, can snatch the hero from danger at the last moment, just as the U.S. cavalry saved many a trapped wagon train from the teeth of a disaster.

Without stretching the simile too far, one can find many parallels between the process of policy development and the development of a stage drama. In this section, we look at the major characters involved in the development and implementation of agricultural policy.

Our goal is to enable the reader to distinguish between the dramatic illusions and the real forces and institutions shaping our agricultural policy.

A GOVERNMENT THAT GROWS

Change is endemic to human affairs. Even a little thought will show the relevance of this truism in every part of life. No miracle drugs or spa waters or mountain air can arrest for long the inevitable aging and death of all creatures great and small. Even to the most stable of human organizations change has come, sometimes with the devastating suddenness of plague or fire or fierce invasion; sometimes in stealth like the gradual drying up of the rich valleys of the Nile, Tigris, and Euphrates. For individuals, change may be the result of broad national movements or some personal tragedy, ill health, disablement, loss of employment, senility, etc. Throughout most of recorded history, individuals and nations have adjusted to change or been overcome by it.

Government—Knight or Dragon?

Modern government, however, has assumed the enormous task of foreseeing and offsetting the effects of change both for individuals and for society as a whole. If the Mississippi overflows, the government rushes in with emergency rescue services; it finances the cleanup, the restoration of roads and homes and jobs. There are inquiries into why the disaster occurred. Was adequate warning given, were adequate precautions taken? Was human error partly to blame? Were dikes inadequately maintained? Further, how can such a disaster be prevented in the future—by building more dams upstream, by draining the river, by diverting its course, by larger dikes, or even by forbidding further building in the flood plain? The government knows that if disaster strikes in the same spot again, the citizens will not blame the mighty Mississippi but the ineffectual government. For citizens and pressure groups have come to expect the government to buffer them from the consequences of change. All too often, leaders promise what they cannot delivery, and citizens believe what is promised.

Modern government finds itself constantly doing battle with many-headed, ferocious but ill-defined dragons which threaten to defile its maiden citizens. The bigger and more wealthy the government, the more dragons with which it does battle at any time. While local government struggles with water, sewage, unlicensed solicitors, and stray dogs, the federal government fights poverty and crime at home and evil doers abroad; defies gravity on earth, weightlessness in space, and presures in the deep sea; defends civil rights, justice, international peace; and so on. The U.S. and other rich nations set a pattern for national government which leads many poor nations into bankruptcy and despair. For without clean water and other basic services, no nation can long seek more sophisticated goals.

Unlike the knights of old, big government is careful never to slay all dragons. Citizens are an ungracious lot who, seeing dragons slain and stability restored, would quickly forget their saviours. After all, who ever paid a knight to stand around idly in case a dragon might come along. Some of the dragons, like poverty and inflation, are not about to be slain easily anyway. And for every dragon beaten back a new one emerges to fill its place. We were just getting pollution in hand when the energy dragon turned his icy breath on us (fiery breath costs too much); or we began to reduce wheat surpluses when wheat shortages became a threat.

Government itself sometimes is difficult to distinguish from the dragons it purports to fight. As it charges to the rescue, the earth heaves and cracks, tossing citizens in every direction. Various devices such as cost–benefit studies and environmental impact statements have been used to check that well-intentioned government is at least bringing a net benefit to citizens. However, control is exercised only imperfectly. In recent years, we have had the odd sight of a government setting up agencies to protect the citizen from other government agencies.

The Economics of Change

The essential economic aspect of change is that change redistributes economic opportunity. An obvious example is the alteration of a highway route. Existing retail stores may find the flow of traffic greatly reduced, while new stores may spring up along the new route. Even though the highway builders' original intent may have been to reduce a traffic hazard, economic opportunities will have been altered. In order, then, to understand public policy, we need to know what are the current major forces of change in our community or country. We need to know how government is attempting to arrest or adapt to change. We need to know how economic opportunity is likely to be altered by the underlying changes and by government's efforts to influence them. It is frequently unrecognized or poorly understood changes which make existing policies ineffective and which must be uncovered before desirable future policies can be formulated.

Great events are often used as a reference point for analysis of major streams of change. The world wars, the Wall Street crash of 1929, Pearl Harbor, the launching of Sputnik, the U.S. success in putting the first man on the moon in 1969—all stand out in the memory of many people. However, some of the most powerful forces of change ferment for many years before they boil over into the public consciousness. There may be a lag of decades between initiation of change and public recognition of its consequences.

Much of the changed environment for U.S. agricultural policy is due to changes in other countries which were little noticed in the United States. For example, the détente between the U.S. and the great Communist powers, the USSR and Mainland China, was a belated recognition of the new power realignments among smaller nations that had been forming since World War II. The U.S. was instrumental in forming NATO and SEATO and the OEEC (now OECD), but these have been bypassed by the European Economic Community and other economic unions with many goals other than mutual security. Many of the newly independent states found common bonds in their Arab or African links, or in their dependence on export of a major raw material. The full implications and possibilities for joint economic, military, and political action have not yet been exploited, but the fear of isolation is an incentive to every nonaligned nation to join some mutual aid group.

Domestically, the forces of change have been probed much more diligently. Yet even here, there is not always much relationship between the amount of publicity an issue receives and its lasting impact. For example, academic scientists and business leaders had been talking about a coming energy crisis for years without receiving any attention until the Arab boycott of 1973 shocked the press into paying attention. In contrast, where government preferred the minimum of publicity and no other pressure group was willing to force the issue, highly significant changes, like devaluation of the dollar or preparations for détente, were instigated with the minimum of public knowledge. One of the key battlegrounds in forming the public consciousness about issues is the mass media. Government, with its vast publicity apparatus, is an active promoter of its interpretation of current change, which issues to play up, which to play down. Nowadays, few issues spontaneously grab public attention. The careful analyst can usually trace back "new" issues to well-organized public relations campaigns by government or other pressure groups. The student of public policy, then, must be constantly on the alert to distinguish between the amount of publicity and eloquence of arguments behind an issue and its correctness and lasting importance.

The Economic Role of Government

Government's growing involvement in the affairs of its citizens is reflected in the trend of federal expenditures. While these had tended to grow with population during the first 150 years of the Republic, growth as a result of deliberate government decision to influence change began only in the 1930s. In the first two years of Franklin Delano Roosevelt's (F.D.R.'s) presidency, federal government expenditures doubled to $6.5 billion, doubled again by 1941, and reached a staggering $100 billion as the allies mounted their victory offensive in 1945. Federal government expenditures shrank to their lowest postwar level of $33 billion in 1948. It took almost twenty years of steady growth before they again topped $100 billion in 1966, only five more years to exceed $200 billion, and four years to reach $300 billion in the fiscal year ended June 1975. Federal government expenditures as a proportion of Gross National Product have shown the same upward thrust since 1930 (Table 2.1). Apart from the temporary aberration caused by World War II, the federal government's relative impact on national economic affairs has continued to climb, with the sharpest rates of increase being in the early thirties and late sixties. Clearly, fighting dragons is a costly affair. Other major developed nations have shown a similar growth trend, in some cases even more advanced, in the influence of national government on total economic activity.

Table 2.1 United States Federal Government Expenditures as a Proportion of Gross National Product, Selected Years, 1930–75

Year	*Percentage*
1930	3.8
1935	9.0
1941	10.6
1945	46.4
1948	12.8
1966	14.5
1971	20.1
1975	22.7

Source: Federal Reserve Bulletin, miscellaneous issues.

While the federal government is the giant in terms of dollar expenditures and influence, expenditures by state, city, and county governments have also grown as their influence on the lives of citizens has grown. For example, in the period 1967 to 1971, local governments accounted for 27 percent and state governments for 16.3 percent of all government expenditures. Local government accounted for 57.2 percent and state government for 21.6 percent of all government civilian employment. Citizens have tended to resist efforts to increase local taxes to fund these expenditures. As a result, governments at all levels are increasingly in partnership, with the federal government providing authorization and raising taxes, while the lower levels of government help to execute the programs.

Government Expenditures on Agriculture

It is very difficult to give a precise measure of the trend of government expenditures for agriculture. Not all the expenditure budgeted for the Department of Agriculture is used for the execution of agricultural policy. For example, the Food Stamp Program, which began as a device to utilize surplus food, has grown into a multibillion dollar aid to low income citizens, most of them *off* the farm. In turn, many parts of other government programs have a direct bearing on agriculture, for example, the Departments of Commerce, Labor, and the Treasury, and agencies such as the Food and Drug Administration, the Federal Trade Commission, the Environmental Protection Agency, etc. By almost any of the traditional measures, a person will tend to underestimate the proportion of government expenditures devoted to the wide range of agricultural problems dealt with in this book.

In the *Economic Report of the President for 1975*, the administration introduced a new classification of government expenditures by function. The agricultural function accounted for less than 1 percent of planned expenditures in the 1974, 1975, and 1976 fiscal years, compared to over 3 percent in 1969. In contrast, outlays by the Department of Agriculture accounted for more than 3 percent of federal expenditures in the 1974–76 fiscal period, reflecting the extent of USDA expenditures for nonagricultural functions. The chief agricultural programs for many years have been the price support and income maintenance policies supervised by the Agricultural Stabilization and Conservation Service (ASCS) and its predecessors. A combination of changes in government programs after 1969, and subsequent improvement in world market prices of many agricultural products, permitted a reduction in these traditional programs. The Emergency Farm Bill of 1975, which was vetoed by President Ford, would have imposed on the federal government a new open-ended commitment involving expenditures in direct relation to how far actual farm prices fell below the official target prices. For example, in the case of wheat, each 50-cent deficit per bushel would cost the federal government $1 billion. Agricultural expenditures have fluctuated widely since the 1930s, as agricultural prices and incomes have fluctuated and as government's willingness to buffer change has varied. As long as there is continued instability in agricultural prices and as long as Congress is willing to come to the farmers' rescue, we can expect federal government expenditures on agriculture to continue an erratic course.

Key Words	Central Concepts
Dramatic illusion	The student of policy needs to distinguish between the claims of partisan groups and the underlying reality.
Change	The present is only a momentary condition. Individuals and nations must constantly adjust to change.
Fighting dragons	Government tries to buffer its citizens from the ravages of change. Sometimes government itself becomes the problem.
Redistribution	Change alters economic opportunity.
Mutual aid	Nation states have joined with their neighbors in economic, military, and political unions.
Public relations	The art of bringing one's point of view before the public.
Federal government expenditures	The cost of national government keeps rising.
Agricultural expenditures	These include part of the expenditures of the Department of Agriculture and some expenditures of other departments.

QUESTIONS

1. What changes have affected your income in the last five years? What changes do you expect to affect your income in the next five years?
2. Describe a secret emergency operation by a government agency.
3. The U.S. has frequently been called the richest nation in history. Can it afford to solve all its problems by taxation and government spending?
4. Give an example of how government itself can cause economic problems for its citizens.
5. What do you consider to be the major forces of change in your community right now?

6. Find out about the origin, development, and present role of the Organization for Economic and Cultural Development (OECD). Your librarian can help.
7. The U.S. government is reported to have spent $1 billion in 1975 on publicity. How does this affect you as a reader or viewer of the mass media?
8. What would be the likely effect of a sudden sharp reduction in government expenditures?
9. Why do you think state and local governments have more employees than the federal government?
10. What expenditures by the Department of Commerce could be considered agricultural?
11. Why has it been difficult to predict the future level of government agricultural expenditures?

THE UNITED STATES DEPARTMENT OF AGRICULTURE—MUDDLING THROUGH

The United States Department of Agriculture (usually called by its initials, USDA) was created over a century ago (1862) when the role of the federal government in the everyday affairs of citizens was minimal. In particular, the belief in government as an agent for betterment of economic affairs was mute. In its first eight decades, the USDA only slowly expanded its original roles of scientific inquiry and education. The Morrill Act (1862), setting aside land for educational purposes, was the forerunner of the land-grant system of major universities. The Hatch Act (1887) authorized federal grants to states for research, while the Smith-Lever Act (1914) set up a federal–state extension service. From these three acts came the unique and much imitated system of federal, state, and local cooperation in agricultural teaching, research, and extension. Every state has its land-grant university, state agricultural experiment station, and extension service network; every county its extension agent. Both are linked financially to the USDA, which in research and extension also runs its own large programs to complement (and sometimes compete with) state programs.

USDA as an Action Agency

The Depression (particularly severe in agriculture) posed a challenge to the USDA which could not be met by the traditional dependence on teaching, research, and extension. Under F.D.R.'s New Deal programs, the federal government asserted its right and duty to intervene in whatever way would bring rapid economic recovery. The extent of intervention proposed in agriculture was commensurate with the level of distress. The USDA, almost overnight, found itself in charge of massive action programs which would affect directly the operations and returns of most of the farmers in the nation. An entire new bureaucracy had to be developed to oversee these action programs. It rapidly overshadowed the original educational system and continues to do so to this day.

The USDA has remained one of the largest departments of the federal government in terms of budget, employment, and impact on citizens. It develops, administers, and polices farm policy through a number of centrally directed agencies. It has its finger in direct payments, indirect supports, regulation, standards and grades, research, extension, education, imports and exports, storage, market supervision, market information, food stamp and other consumer welfare programs, marketing orders and other producer programs, forestry and wildlife both commercial and recreational, and on and on. With almost 100,000 full-time employees, perhaps a similar number of part-time employees, and over 100,000 farmer committeemen of the Agricultural Stabilization and Conservation Service (ASCS), the USDA has a major impact not only on agricultural policy initiatives but also on how policy will be exercised. If we add the state and county research, extension, and education systems, it is clear that when these groups join forces to defend existing agricultural programs or to develop new programs, their combined impact is impressive.

Titular head of this national network is the secretary of agriculture, who is appointed by and derives his authority from the president of the United States. Most presidents have, in fact, delegated to the secretary of agriculture a large measure of independent responsibility for agricultural affairs. The secretary is, first of all, a political extension of the president, with special responsibility for promoting and defending an official administration viewpoint on agriculture. However, at certain times, he may be called upon to promote and defend administration policies in general, He is also a member of the cabinet and a presidential adviser, competing for the ear of the president, particularly on issues where the interests of agriculture conflict with those of other departments or executive agencies. He is also chief administrator of a large bureaucracy with many competing agencies; but as a temporary appointee he may have great difficulty in asserting his policy ideas over those of the permanent bureaucracy. Finally, the secretary leads the administration's and the department's delegation to Congress for funding of the annual appropriations and interacts officially and unofficially with members of Congress throughout the year to gain approval for administration programs.

Both the secretary of agriculture and the USDA require great political skill if they are to maintain established programs, replace obsolete programs, and develop new programs. Their executive authority derives from the president, a political office holder, but their budget authority comes from Congress, also political office holders. Congressmen and senators are frequently at odds with each other and with the president over both broad goals and details of policy. Awareness that agricultural policy must constantly run this political gauntlet has done much to shape the modern structure of the USDA and its approach to agricultural programs.

Organization of the USDA

An organization chart of the USDA for 1974 gives a sampling of the major responsibilities and activities of the Department (Figure 2.1). In that year, the secretary and under secretary were assisted by five assistant secretaries with responsibility for (1) conservation, research, and education; (2) international affairs and commodity programs; (3) marketing and consumer services; (4) rural development; and (5) departmental administration. The director of agricultural economics headed the department's economic research, statistics, and policy analysis activities. Like all modern government agencies, the USDA frequently shuffles divisions, titles, and duties. However, it is clear that in the modern USDA, the research, extension, and education activities are heavily outweighed by the action programs. In addition, the department maintains all the trappings (investigation, communication, intergovernmental, and legislative) of a modern bureaucracy.

The growth of action agencies within the USDA began in earnest as a result of the Federal Farm Board fiasco of 1929. The board attempted to support farm prices by direct market purchases but went broke in the process. Its experience convinced policy makers that if farm incomes were to be maintained by price supports, there would have to be effective restrictions on production. The Agricultural Adjustment Act of 1933 (popularly known as the "Triple-A") set up the Agricultural Adjustment Agency within the USDA to manage the new price support and production control programs. As well as the headquarters staff in Washington, D.C., the Triple-A relied heavily on systems of community, county, and state committeemen elected by farmers themselves. It also hired permanent staff at each level. This widespread participation of farmers in the execution of the Triple-A was the political price that the administration had to

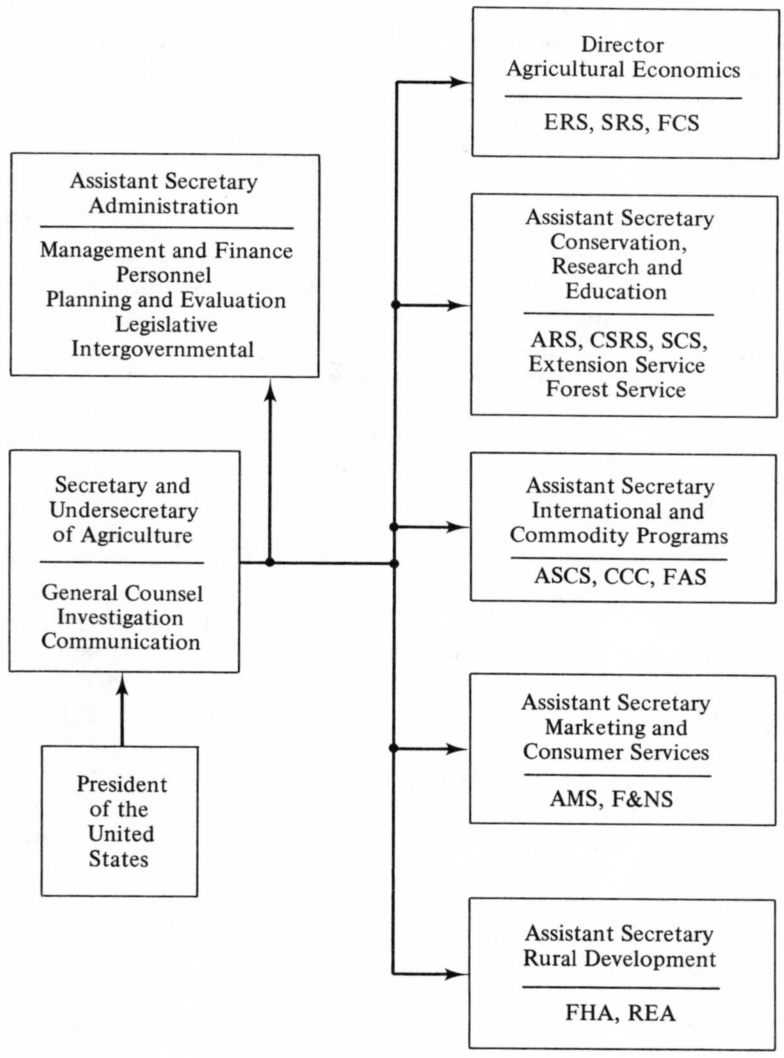

Fig. 2.1 Organization of main functions and services of the U.S. Department of Agriculture.

pay for growers' acquiescence in programs which interfered with their traditional freedom to produce.

This same ideological base of grassroots democracy has persisted through the successor agencies of the Triple-A, the Production and Marketing Agency (PMA) in 1945, the Commodity Stabilization

Service (CSS) in 1952, and the Agricultural Stabilization and Conservation Service (ASCS) in 1961. These name changes coincided with efforts of Congress or the administration to reject certain aspects of existing programs and impose new directions. However, the ASCS continues to hold a unique strategic position in influencing agricultural policy through its ability to represent farmers and bureaucrats simultaneously.

Charles M. Hardin says of it, "In summary, the AAA–PMA–CSS–ASCS committee system appears like many other agencies to be a staunch supporter of the programs it has to administer, which come to be the bread and butter of its members. Because of its wide coverage and 'democratic' base, the committee system has been an exceptionally formidable force in maintaining and in strengthening the major characteristic of governmental agricultural price support and education policy over the years. Moreover, because of the overriding importance within agricultural policy of its program, the significance of the committee system's influence on policy dwarfs that of other agencies. . . ."

The Soil Conservation Service (SCS) of the USDA was originated during the Dust Bowl crisis of the 1930s when large areas of the midwest were devastated by drought, mismanagement, and the resultant soil erosion. Work originally carried out in the Department of the Interior was transferred to the new agency and expanded dramatically to meet a crisis situation. SCS, like ASCS, with which it should not be confused, built up its own nationwide operating network. There are now about 3,000 voluntary soil conservation districts, each with its farmer committees and its permanent technical staff. In general, individual farmers request conservation analysis, planning, and funding from SCS (in contrast to ASCS programs which are mandatory for all producers involved). The SCS has flourished through the years on the basis of its praiseworthy and noncontroversial purpose—conservation—and on its amenability to congressional milking for individual districts. Recent concern over preservation of land, water, and other natural resources has strengthened its role and broadened its activities.

To add to the confusion of initials, agencies, and roles, the ASCS also has its soil conservation program, instituted initially as a means of achieving the production controls which had been thwarted when the first Agricultural Adjustment Act was declared unconstitutional. Farmers were paid for reducing their acreage of soil-depleting crops—which happened also to be crops in surplus supply, and for following soil-conserving practices. This ASCS program, the Agricultural Conservation Program (ACP), later came to emphasize soil conservation and was a congressional favorite because it channeled funds directly to the districts of individual congressmen.

Marketing and Consumer Services originally emphasized marketing goals such as the provision of information, inspection, and regulation of farm and off-farm marketing activities in order to improve returns to farmers. For example, under the Packers and Stockyards Act (1921) attempts were made to improve the efficiency of the sale, processing, and distribution of livestock. However, in recent years, consumer services have come to absorb over half the USDA's annual appropriations. More specifically, the Food and Nutrition Service, which controls food distribution, food stamp, and school breakfast and lunch programs, spent over $5 billion in the 1975 fiscal year. What began as minor programs to absorb surplus farm products have become major national welfare programs. This has created many problems for the USDA, which still relates more comfortably to its traditional farmer clients than to welfare recipients.

Other action agencies of the USDA which have reached into almost every rural community are the Farmers' Home Administration (FHA), a lender of last resort to many farmers; the Rural Electrification Administration (REA); and the Forest Service, which has supervised the multiple uses of federally owned forest land. The FHA is the successor to the highly controversial Federal Security Administration (FSA) which met depression conditions in agriculture head on by attempting to resettle impoverished farmers. The FSA's programs disturbed so many political feathers that its powers were greatly curtailed once emergency conditions had passed. The REA's programs, though now largely maintenance in character, continue to be at odds with privately owned utilities, both in philosophy and on specific issues. The Forest Service has an important bearing on the availability of grazing land for Western agriculture. In addition, it appears to share the invaluable plus of public goodwill toward its programs.

One super-agency within the USDA does not fit the normal mold. The Commodity Credit Corporation (CCC), which controls and directs price support, loan procurement, storage, disposal, and export of farm commodities under government programs, has a permanent federal charter. The CCC board consists of the secretary of agriculture and six other members appointed by the president with the advice and consent of the Senate. In carrying out its functions, it uses primarily ASCS personnel and "customary channels, facilities, and arrangements of trade." Despite the lack of its own bureaucratic empire, the policies of the CCC in managing accumulated stocks of farm commodities have often been a dominant force in United States and world agriculture and trade.

USDA Research

The research establishment within the USDA has had a continued struggle to maintain its relative share of total appropriations because its effects are intangible or difficult to measure. However, despite strong support from the American Farm Bureau, the land grant system, and farm agribusiness, the main research services usually command less than 5 percent of the USDA budget. The largest, the Agricultural Research Service (ARS), maintains laboratories, field stations, and personnel all over the United States, heavily involved in problem solving research. The Statistical Reporting Service (SRS) and the Economic Research Service (ERS) follow different paths. While SRS maintains established data collection and reporting systems on the statistics of agriculture, ERS bears the burden of most of the federal economic research effort on both long-term agricultural problems and short-term policy issues. The Cooperative State Research Service (CSRS) channels federal funds to state experimental stations, as does its extension counterpart the Federal Extension Service (FES) to state extension services. Both federal research and extension services must walk a tightrope between providing national guidance on relevant problems and avoiding the appearance of usurping executive or congressional powers.

International programs of the USDA are diffused among a number of agencies. The Foreign Agricultural Service (FAS) supervises the activities of agricultural attachés in U.S. embassies abroad. The attachés are responsible for promoting U.S. agricultural exports. The FAS itself has a major influence on the operation of government sponsored exports of agricultural products under various titles of the PL480 (popularly known as Food for Peace) program. Technical assistance to foreign agriculture is largely the responsibility of the International Agricultural Development Service (IADS). Because its programs appear to help foreign countries to compete with U.S. agricultural products, IADS has never achieved the budget or popular support of FAS. A third important element of U.S. foreign agricultural policy for 30 years has been food aid, mostly now carried out under the PL480 Program. The importance of food aid has tended to wax and wane as U.S. agricultural surpluses and foreign food shortages have come and gone. The upheavals in world agriculture in the 1970s have made trade, technical assistance, and aid the center of interest for many national and international agencies concerned more about world hunger and peace than about narrow agricultural interests. The international programs of the USDA are likely to change greatly in character to meet these new concerns.

The present structure and powers of the USDA are heavily dependent on the legacy of the 1930s. In general it has been easier to continue than to establish programs. New programs have only been possible where a broad spectrum of political support was assured. Even the level of funding and direction of programs have been subject to the whims of powerful executives and politicians. What the USDA is today is not the result of any master plan for agriculture, but of the give and take of the political process. What the USDA *may* become in the next decade is likely to be the result of further marginal changes, unless some powerful forces emerge to sweep away present programs. The USDA will continue to have a major influence on the shape of U.S. agricultural policy. *The* issue of U.S. agricultural policy in the next decade may well be whether the USDA is capable of leading U.S. agriculture to meet the worldwide demands which may be imposed upon it.

Key Words	Central Concepts
USDA	United States Department of Agriculture, the department primarily responsible for agricultural policy.
Morrill Act (1862)	Authorized setting aside of land for educational purposes.
Hatch Act (1887)	Authorized federal grants to states for research.
Smith-Lever Act (1914)	Set up a federal-state extension service.
Action agency	Describes the role of the USDA in administering government programs for agriculture. This has replaced research, extension, and teaching as the USDA's primary responsibility.
ASCS	Agricultural Stabilization and Conservation Service of the USDA. Has a central bureaucracy in Washington, D.C., and a nationwide network of state and local farmer committees.
Secretary of agriculture	Titular head of the USDA, he is a political appointee of the president.
Appropriations	Money set aside by Congress to fulfill the goals of legislation.
Executive authority	The right to take action on behalf of the administration through power derived from the president.
Federal Farm Board	Set up in 1929 by President Hoover, primarily to stabilize farm prices by buying up excess supplies.
Agricultural Adjustment Act (1933), AAA or "Triple-A"	Authorized a system of price supports and production controls to fight the effects of the Great Depression on U.S. agriculture.

Great Depression	A massive setback to the U.S. economy, dramatically heralded by the Wall Street crash of 1929. Recovery began in 1933 but was only completed under the stimulus of World War II demand.
Grassroots democracy	A popular term to describe farmer participation in the ASCS and other government agricultural programs.
Soil Conservation Service (SCS)	Has its own network of districts and farmer committees.
Commodity Credit Corporation (CCC)	Has a permanent federal charter to organize the acquisition and disposal of farm commodities and to issue loans against them.
Public Law 480 (PL480) (1954)	Agricultural Trade and Development Act. Financed alternative means of providing aid to needy countries and reducing surplus stocks.
Technical assistance	Helping other countries by showing them how to use modern technology.

QUESTIONS

1. How much emphasis does the modern USDA give to its educational role?
2. Why was it important to have farmer participation in Triple-A programs, and how has this been organized?
3. What conflicts are involved in the differing roles of the secretary of agriture?
4. Why should the name of a government program be of importance to the administration, Congress, or farmers?
5. What are the differences and similarities between the ASCS and SCS?
6. Suggest reasons why the USDA might be uncomfortable in administering general welfare programs.
7. Why was the organization of the USDA unprepared for the dramatic growth in the influence of international factors on U.S. agriculture?
8. Should the same government agency formulate *and* administer agricultural policy?

OTHER EXECUTIVE AGENCIES— CLAIMANTS TO THE THRONE

While the Department of Agriculture has in the past taken the lead in the executive branch of government in proposing policy for agriculture and has jealously guarded its jurisdiction over laws aimed at agriculture, other executive agencies have pressed their claims for a say in agricultural policy making.

These pressures have derived from four main sources: agencies set up in response to national crises; agencies created to meet long-term national goals; agencies intended to improve efficiency, co-ordination, and management within the executive branch; and finally, redefinition of the areas of responsibility among existing agencies.

Many of the temporary agencies set up to meet national emergencies wield considerable power during their short lives. The Office of Price Administration (OPA) of the 1940s and the Cost of Living Council (CLC) of the early 1970s both had responsibility for controlling prices, immediately putting them in conflict with USDA policies to support food and fiber prices. The Federal Energy Adminstration (FEA) was set up to meet the emergency caused by the Arab oil boycott of 1973 and the subsequent "energy crisis," as shortages of other power sources emerged simultaneously. The FEA had temporary control over the allocation of power to agriculture.

In 1975, the FEA became the Energy Research and Development Administration (ERDA), and thus became a permanent part of the executive branch with special responsibility for supervising the achievement of the nation's long-term energy goals. In any future energy crunch, it would reassert its authority over allocations to agriculture. In contrast to the ERDA, the Council of Economic Advisers (CEA) was originally created for the role it still plays of advising the president on broad economic policy to secure full employment. Thus the CEA looks at the overall economic impact of programs and expenditures by all government agencies including the USDA.

Perhaps the most controversial of all new agencies has been the Environmental Protection Agency (EPA) set up with the long-term goal of protecting the environment from the fallout of modern business, industry, and trade. The EPA has been particularly concerned about regulations to reduce the harmful chemical residues which enter the nation's air, soil, and water and are absorbed by humans by breathing, contact, or the eating of contaminated food. Agriculture has been a major user of chemicals for fertilization, pest control, and crop management; a major polluter of air, soil, and water; and a contributor to hazardous residues in food. The EPA has argued successfully that its responsibility for all of the environment supercedes the USDA's responsibility for agriculture. The EPA has tended to issue orders first and let the courts decide on the merits of any appeals by agriculture against the orders. However, it appears that due to pressure from Congress and the nation's farmers, the EPA will in the future consult more closely with the USDA before imposing new limits or bans on chemicals used in agriculture.

The chief agency responsible for management efficiency in the executive branch is the Office of Management and Budget (OMB), which in a sense acts as the president's watchdog over the myriad executive departments and permanent and temporary executive agencies. As our government grows larger, the possibility for duplication of effort, counterproductive policies, waste, and inefficiency increases geometrically. In addition, the natural tendency of each bureaucratic nucleus to attempt to extend its programs would, if uncontrolled, cause an explosion in total government expenditure. OMB keeps this growth within budget limits acceptable to the president in any given year.

The USDA has always faced conflicts with other government departments because it has claimed special jurisdiction not only over the people in agriculture but also over all rural dwellers. The USDA tends to argue that agriculture and rural problems are special; other government departments say they are not. For example, the U.S. Department of Labor has attempted to extend the Occupational Safety and Health Act (OSHA) to agriculture. The USDA has sided with farmers in suggesting that rules designed to protect employees from the impersonal decisions of industrial managers are not appropriate for one-man farm operations where the employer is the main employee. The USDA has final authority over the provisions and revisions of marketing orders and agreements, which are essentially legalized restraints of trade designed to improve the profitability of farm operations. The Anti-Trust Division of the Department of Justice regards such restraints of trade as undesirable in principle and unjustified when farm prices are high or incomes low. It is particularly skeptical of the growth of giant cooperatives which have been encouraged by the USDA. One could cite many other actual and potential sources of conflict between the USDA and other government agencies.

Who Shall Control Agricultural Policy?

A more serious conflict has emerged from the turmoil of the early 1970s—not over the minutiae of agricultural policy but over where control should properly belong. The growth in U.S. agricultural exports; the possibilities of worldwide famine; the role of food in U.S. relations with developed, developing, and centrally planned countries; the use of food as a diplomatic weapon; the impact of agricultural prices on domestic inflation and on the balance of payments—all have moved agricultural policy to center stage and brought demands for its removal from the influence of a farmer-oriented USDA. The State Department, with its responsibilty for relations with foreign countries; the Treasury, with its concern for economic stability; the Department of Commerce, with its oversight of business and industry; Health, Education and Welfare, with its concern about the effect of inflation on its clients; the Federal Reserve Board, which manages the nation's monetary system; the Council of Economic Advisers; the National Security Council; and others are determined to exercise influence on the future direction of agricultural policy.

A new cabinet-level Agricultural Policy Committee, set up by President Ford in 1976, appeared to give the USDA prime responsibility in this government activity. The secretary of agriculture was made chairman, and two of his assistant secretaries were made responsible for preparing policy statements and position papers and for continuous monitoring of agricultural policy issues of concern to the Agricultural Policy Committee. The secretaries of state, treasury, and commerce appeared to be assigned lesser roles. However, the tendency of administrations to tinker with the formal systems by which top-level policies are made suggests that agriculture's role will continue to be under challenge on many issues.

In its first few decades, the USDA tended to come into conflict with other departments on the periphery of its activities. More recently, conflicts have centered on the autonomy of the USDA in its major programs. It has had its power trimmed by presidential fiat (for example, export prohibitions) at the instigation of other departments and nonfarm interests. It is possible that this power may be trimmed even more in the next decade either by presidential reorganization or by act of Congress. In order to survive, the USDA may have to accommodate greater input from many other government agencies in the process of developing future agricultural policy.

Key Words	Central Concepts
Temporary agencies	Set up to meet national emergencies.
ERDA	Energy Research and Development Administration, replaced the Federal Energy Agency (FEA) in supervising ogvernment energy programs.
CEA	Council of Economic Advisers to the President.
EPA	Environmental Protection Agency; has responsibility for limiting harmful use of the nation's air, soil, and water.
OMB	Office of Management and Budget acts as the president's watchdog over government departments and agencies.

OSHA	Occupational Safety and Health Agency within the Department of Labor. Its intrusions into farm operations caused widespread protest among farmers.
Anti-Trust Division	This division of the Department of Justice attempts to prevent or remedy monopolistic business practices.
Balance of payments	An accounting of flows of funds to and from a country in a selected period.

QUESTIONS

1. What circumstances have caused other government departments and agencies to challenge the USDA's dominant role in agricultural policy?
2. Do you think agencies set up in national emergencies can operate effectively?
3. Does creation of umbrella agencies such as ERDA and EPA with conflicting goals ensure counterproductive policies?
4. In what ways may the USDA and OSHA clash over areas of influence?
5. Can you suggest ways in which the goals of different government departments and agencies might be given due consideration in the formulation of United States' agricultural policy?
6. Who represents the consumer in interagency wrangling over U.S. agricultural policy?
7. How has the power of the USDA relative to other agencies changed during the 1970s?

THE HOUSES OF CONGRESS—DILAPIDATED

Almost all the present body of government policy related to agricultural affairs came into being with either the approval or the acquiescence of the houses of Congress, the second branch of our tripartite government. The future shape of agricultural policy will almost certainly be heavily influenced by the unique structure, organization, and procedures of the U.S. legislative system. There are many important differences in makeup and in attitudes between the Senate and the House of Representatives. Each state elects two members to the Senate every six years. In effect, Rhode Island has as many Senate votes as New York or Texas. Representatives must stand for reelection to the House every two years. Their electoral districts are determined by population, so that the more populous states have more members of the House. In combination, the houses of Congress have the power to make laws, to raise taxes, and to appropriate tax funds for approved uses. Today the executive branch requests most of the changes in laws and the taxes and appropriations. While the growth in the federal government (already noted) has been at the instigation of expansionist executive agencies, it has been facilitated by an acquiescent Congress.

The mass media focuses continually on the tensions and disagreements between the executive and legislative branches, especially when the president's party does not have a majority in Congress. However, it is important to separate the posturing of each in public from the desired policies they are pursuing. The president is chosen by a nationwide electorate; legislators by their local district. The president is limited to two four-year terms, while his political appointees (such as the secretary of agriculture) serve at his discretion, often less than one term. Congressmen and senators may continue to be re-elected without limit. Influence in Congress is related to length of tenure (seniority). Particularly those from one-party districts can achieve seniority and the power that derives from it. Within the executive branch, all power is exercised in the name of the president. He can, in theory if not always in practice, enforce his wishes on his subordinates. Within both the houses of Congress, power is parcelled out among numerous committees which act as filters for any proposals which might eventually be voted on by the entire House. Individuals can carve out an island of power for themselves by gaining positions on key committees. Seniority, or sponsorship by a senior member, is critical to gaining membership on the more powerful committees. Chairmanship of such committees is reserved for the most senior members and confers exceptional influence over the entire program of legislation covered by that committee. When accompanied by differences in party affiliations and underlying political philosophies, there can be very real difficulties in resolving disagreements between the president and Congress on the direction of government policy.

In 1975, the Senate had 18 permanent committees, 4 select committees, and 2 special committees, ranging in size from 7 to 26 members. The House of Representatives had 22 permanent committees and 3 select committees, ranging in size from 12 to 55 members. In addition, there were 7 joint House–Senate committees. The actual number, size, and jurisdiction of committees can vary widely from year to year. Depending on the judgment of its chairman, each committee can itself hold hearings and debate issues or can delegate the work to subcommittees.

Making Agricultural Legislation

Much of the actual work of the Congress is conducted by myriad subcommittees. For example, the House Committee on Agriculture in 1975 had six commodity subcommittees—cotton, dairy and poultry, forests, livestock and grains, oilseeds and rice, and tobacco—and four operational subcommittees covering such areas as conservation, marketing, departmental oversight, and rural development. Proposed legislation is usually considered in the relevant subcommittees before being considered by the full Agriculture Committee. Any farm bill that passes the full House Agriculture Committee tends to be a ragtag collection of narrower subcommittee interests.

The next hurdle is the subcommittee on agriculture of the Appropriations Committee, which assesses if and how much public funds should be made available to finance the proposed activities.

For many years the chairman of this committee, Jamie Whitten (D. Mississippi), exercised personal vigilance over agricultural legislation. Many political appointees or senior bureaucrats were roasted at appropriations subcommittee hearings for proposals that ran counter to the conservative rural philosophy and policy prescriptions of Chairman Whitten. Without his subcommittee's recommendation, no agricultural program could get the funds needed for operation.

While the full Appropriations Committee can, in theory, overturn the subcommittee's decision, the subcommittee's recommendation is usually rubber-stamped by the full Appropriations Committee. After approval by the Appropriations Committee, the Rules Committee can then submit the legislation to the full House for debate and a decisive vote. However, the Rules Committee may attempt to prevent legislation it does not like by keeping it from reaching the House floor.

If approved by the House of Representatives, the legislation then goes for consideration by the Senate and through approximately the same steps to a final Senate vote. The Senate Agricultural Committee does not have commodity subcommittees, but the geographical diversity of its members' districts tends to encourage representation of commodity interests. The Appropriations Subcommittee on Agriculture in the Senate is a strategic pressure point for changes in legislation or funding. However, as in the House, legislators continue to be subject to persistent persuasion from other legislators; from the president or his appointees; from farm groups, lobbyists, the media, constituents, etc., as long as provisions, wording, or funding can still be changed to the benefit of an interested party. The change in even one word can mean millions of dollars in gains or losses to a particular group.

When versions of the same bill have been passed by both the full House and the Senate, the differences are reconciled by a joint (conference) committee drawn from both houses. The revised version, which may be significantly changed in intent or provisions, is then resubmitted to both houses. If passed, it is signed by the speaker of the House and the president of the Senate, and is sent to the president of the United States for signature. If he does not sign or veto the bill within ten days, the bill automatically becomes law. In the case of a veto, Congress can override the veto by a two-thirds majority of both houses. Even then, the president may thwart a version he does not like by impounding funds appropriated or by footdragging in executing a bill's provisions.

The Law Making Maze

No mere cataloging of the procedures by which a bill becomes law can recreate the give and take, the pressures and tensions, or the strengths and weaknesses of the congressional system. Simultaneously many bills will be moving through the maze of subcommittees and requiring majority votes to move to the full committees and on to the House floor. The sponsor of a bill must be able to swing the necessary votes at each stage by personal persuasion, by friendship, by clever use of the media, by horse-trading, by drawing on party or regional affiliations, by utilizing favorable lobbies and neutralizing critics—in fact by every conceivable type of personal interaction. Timing may often be of the essence. For example, a president may be able to veto many spending programs similar to those passed in previous years because they would be "inflationary." Congressmen, in particular, must be aware of the impact of the bills they sponsor and of their congressional voting record on the biennial re-election effort. An unpopular stand may antagonize their home district voters, financial supporters, the party organization, or vocal pressure groups, whose support is vital to re-election. Yet, in many cases it may be necessary for a representative or senator to support programs of other legislators in order to gain their support in passing a measure he or she strongly favors. For example, liberal labor Democrats supported passage of the 1973 farm bill in the House, in order to get support for a new minimum wage bill.

Is Agriculture's Influence on Congress Declining?

During most of the 1960s and early 1970s, many commentators reported on the diminishing power of farm interests in the houses of Congress. Because of population shifts toward urban areas and the resultant redistricting, fewer legislators depended on the farm vote for political support. This ignored the fact that many growing segments of the economy were still vitally concerned with agricultural policy, oil and fertilizer companies, farm machinery and automobile companies, agribusiness, exporters, the transportation industry, etc. Perhaps the true situation was that agricultural programs still had very powerful friends but that the influence of farm producers was diminished. The key agricultural committees and subcommittees were still led by southern or western Democrats or midwest Republicans from predominantly rural areas, just as they had been during the heyday of the farm bloc in Congress in the 1920s and 1930s. However, while agricultural or rural interests could no longer guarantee a majority in either house, many rural congressmen and senators continued to acquire the seniority and power which gave them influence over all aspects of congressional business, defense, welfare, education, urban affairs, etc., and thus considerable leverage in getting the agricultural legislation they wanted.

The realignment may have taken a new twist in the 1970s. Committee reforms in early 1973 dispersed the key agricultural chairmanships more widely across the nation (appearing particularly to weaken the southern presence). However, the forces of change throughout the world political and economic systems caused many groups (not usually concerned with agriculture) to look closely at their impact on U.S. agricultural policy. In turn, many congressmen and senators from the major industrial states saw new relevance to their constituents in the nuances of agricultural policy.

Congress, a Living Institution

The houses of Congress are a living institution. Almost any characterization may be rendered out of date by reforms within or by changes in the world outside. Harvey Mansfield suggested that "Congress acts on economic matters nearly always in a piecemeal fashion, from limited perspectives. . . . It is congenial to regulatory and distributive types of actions, involving pressure groups and patronage groups and moves incrementally." This certainly has been true of agricultural policy in the past. However, the discipline of a congressional budget and the world pressures on U.S. agriculture may force Congress to develop a more coordinated agricultural program compatible with overall U.S. domestic, foreign, economic, and social goals.

This will not be easy as long as Congress and the executive branch have widely different goals. For example, in the case of agricultural trade, while the executive branch has been involved in numerous bilateral and multilateral discussions to expand world trade, Congress has often been protectionist in sentiment. Agreements reached by negotiators in the executive branch can be rejected or blocked indefinitely by Congress. The separation of powers can lead to suspension of the power of the United States to act decisively in international affairs. Even in domestic affairs, while the executive branch has a tendency to prefer strong centralized departments and agencies, Congress likes more sprawling, limited, and malleable agencies.

Richard E. Neustadt has argued that while Congress and the president fight over who is to control the great executive agencies, these tend to escape effective control by either. Charles Hardin tends to believe that the broad operations of the USDA have escaped control in this way. However, if the contest for dominance over U.S. agricultural policy between the great executive agencies becomes heightened, Congress may be called upon to make some critical decisions about the future of the USDA. Even professional Congress-watchers frequently have difficulty in predicting the outcome of an upcoming vote. Accordingly, any effort to predict long-term changes in the Congressional system is extremely hazardous. One can be sure that it will remain critical to the future direction of agricultural policy.

Key Words	Central Concepts
Houses of Congress	The two legislative bodies approved by the Constitution of the United States.
House of Representatives	Representation is accorded to states on the basis of population. Representatives are elected every two years.
Congressmen	Members of the House of Representatives.
Senate (Senators)	The second legislative body (and its members), elected every six years.
Seniority	Length of tenure in a post. In Congress, ability to get re-elected confers seniority. Power and influence in Congress are allocated on the basis of seniority rather than merit.
Committees	Most of the workload of both houses of Congress is divided up among numerous committees and subcommittees.
Geographical diversity	The tendency of agricultural committee members to be drawn from regions with different interests.
Conference Committee	Reconciles different versions of a bill passed in both houses.
Presidential veto	When the president says "no" to a bill passed by both houses of Congress.
Veto override	A presidential veto can be squashed by a two-thirds majority vote of both houses of Congress.
Lobbying	A broad term covering legal means of persuading congressmen or senators to accept one's views on pending legislation.

Farm vote	The phenomenon of voters associated with agriculture uniting for or against candidates or issues.
Farm bloc	A group of congressmen and senators from farm states who consistently voted for farm-related legislation in the 1920s and 1930s.
Living institution	An institution with the ability to change continuously.

QUESTIONS

1. How does the U.S. Senate differ from the House of Representatives in number and election of members? How does this affect members' performance?
2. What alternatives to seniority might one suggest for Congress?
3. Describe the process by which an agricultural bill originated in the House of Representatives becomes law.
4. Does the commodity orientation of congressional subcommittees prevent the development of a comprehensive and internally consistent agricultural policy?
5. In what ways can Congress thwart its own laws?
6. In what ways can the president and his administration thwart congressional intent?
7. How might you legally influence pending legislation?
8. Is agriculture's influence on Congress declining? Discuss.
9. Could a new farm bloc be formed in today's Congress?
10. In what ways do congressional operations permit executive agencies to escape effective control?

FARMERS AND THEIR ORGANIZATIONS—FOLLOW MY LEADER

It is no accident that farmers enter our story so late. While agricultural policy is aimed at farmers and often justified on their behalf, theirs is only one of many powerful voices affecting its direction. As the number of farmers has declined, they have faced an uphill fight to keep their interests prominent with both the executive and legislative branches of government.

The Diversity of U.S. Farmers

Perhaps the outstanding feature of modern U.S. farmers is their lack of common interests. This is not surprising given the wide differences in size, organization, geographic location, commodities produced, growth, etc. (See Table 2.2 and Figure 2.2.) United States farms may be part of multinational conglomerates, single-unit commercial enterprises which are the sole support of a farm family; tax-shelter operations using farm losses or investments to reduce tax liabilities on other income; part-time farms where a family requires additional off-farm income for its support; or hobby farms where a home in a rural setting is an adjunct to a nonfarm job.

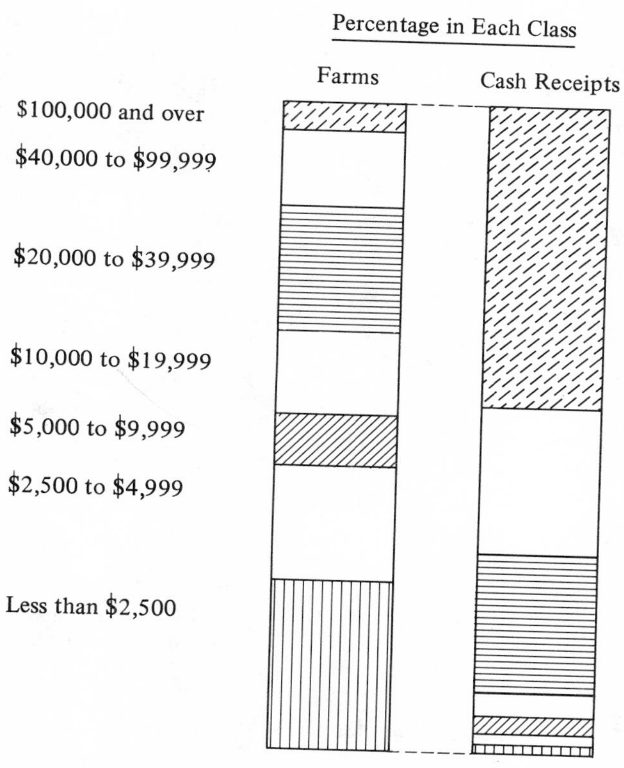

Fig. 2.2. Number of farms and cash receipts by sales classes, 1975. *Source*: USDA, *Agricultural Outlook*, Nov. 1976, p. 20.

Another difference among farmers is in land tenure. The farmer may be a landlord, leasing his land for use by others. Or he may be the lessee. When, as frequently happens, government program benefits are capitalized into land values, the landlord will gain and the tenant lose. Where the tenant is a sharecropper, the landlord too may be vitally concerned with current price of the output. In the more usual case, the farmer will be an owner–operator, perhaps with some leased land, where what is left over after paying current obligations will be the reward for his land, labor, capital, and management skill.

The nature of farming and farmers is continually changing. The increasing demand for land for urban development, highways, recreation, and other competing uses, and changes in tax laws which have made many surviving farmers subject to income, capital gains, estate, and other taxes have forced the farmer to become as much a manager of real estate as of crop production. Farm labor has declined dramatically in numbers, become unionized, protected by health and safety laws, and eligible for government welfare programs. Capital needs have risen rapidly, creating a barrier to entry for many potential farmers and a need for more external financing for existing farmers. The larger the farm, the more complex the modern management problem becomes.

Table 2.2 Cash Receipts of U.S. Farmers, 1965 and 1975

Commodity	1965 ($ billions)	1965 (%)	1975 ($ billions)	1975 (%)
Cattle and calves	8,942	22.7	17,482	19.5
Feed grains	3,693	9.4	12,513	14.0
Dairy products	5,038	12.8	9,866	11.0
Food grains	2,042	5.2	8,347	9.3
Hogs	3,607	9.2	7,948	8.9
Oil crops	2,173	5.5	7,920	8.8
Vegetables	2,618	6.7	5,370	6.0
Fruit and nuts	1,650	4.2	3,548	4.0
Broilers and farm chickens	1,304	3.3	3,005	3.4
Eggs	1,785	4.5	2,812	3.1
Cotton (lint and seed)	2,330	5.9	2,372	2.6
Tobacco	1,186	3.0	2,155	2.4
Other	2,997	7.6	6,225	7.0
Total	39,365	100.0	89,563	100.0

Source: USDA, *Agricultural Outlook*, November 1976, p. 18.

The fate of farm families cannot be separated from that of the farmer; they do much of the farm labor and share the farm income or lack of income. For the farmer, failure in his job means the loss of his property, the uprooting of his family, and an often frustrating search for adequate alternative means of livelihood. Preventing the uprooting of farm families has been one of the long-term goals of government policy. Yet in the four decades since the first Agricultural Adjustment Act of 1933, the number of U.S. farm families has fallen from 8 million to 3 million. One could argue either that without government programs for agriculture, the drop would have been more severe or that other types of government programs would have slowed the decline more. However, history suggests that most government programs widened the gap between large and small farmers and hastened the exit of small farms.

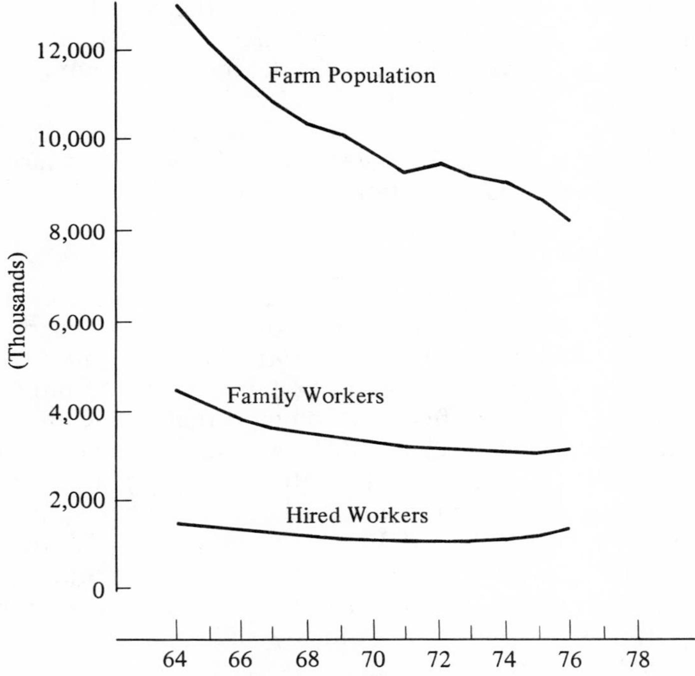

Fig. 2.3. Size of farm population, number of family workers, and hired farm workers, 1964–76. *Source*: USDA, *1976 Handbook of Agricultural Charts.*

The net effect has been that rural areas have bred and trained a steady stream of young people for future city life (Figure 2.3). The cities have gotten an infusion of qualified labor when needed, and the rural areas have alleviated their surplus labor problem. But both have suffered from unpleasant side effects. Overcrowding in many cities worsens the problems of slums, crime, pollution, etc.; depopulation in many rural areas tends to reduce both the quantity and quality of essential services available to farm families. Children in rural areas frequently receive poorer health and educational care because of the manner in which such programs are funded. Mothers receive less adequate prenatal and maternity care. In a wide range of public and private services—roads, railroads, and canals; police, fire, and ambulance; churches, theaters, sports facilities, diversity of shopping services, legal, accounting, and personal services; and even in the level of competition between local businesses, many rural communities have been in secular decline. The multiplier effect within a rural community of an increase in agricultural income has been shown to be quite significant. Despite the recent immigration of disenchanted city dwellers, the number of dead or dying rural communities is mute evidence that four decades of agricultural policy have not given sufficient boost to agricultural income to offset creeping community decline. In turn, a decline in the quality of life in a rural community leads to a decline in the quality of life of farm families and increases the relative attractions of urban living.

Hired Farm Workers

Until the 1960s, when organization attempts erupted in violence and nationwide political agitation, the forgotten man of agricultural policy was the hired farm worker. In part, this was accidental. Until World War II the transition from hired farm worker to farm tenant to owner–operator was sufficiently common that the interests of all three could be considered identical. However, the spread of agricultural mechanization and the substitution of other inputs such as chemicals for farm labor led to a decline in the number of hired farm workers from 4.3 million in 1930 to 1.1 million in 1972. Increasing capital requirements for entry into agriculture cut off opportunities for farm workers to become farmers. The sophisticated operations of modern farming demanded more highly skilled workers. Unskilled labor was in demand only for peak needs.

Many of these unskilled laborers were migrants, moving northward with the harvest, but unwanted in the nation's farm regions when harvest was through. Antagonisms created by race, language, and cultural differences between migrants and the permanent inhabitants of the areas through which they moved, and their efforts to unionize, contributed to their difficulties. Government policy over previous decades of consistently exempting agriculture from social legislation to protect the employment, health, or income of workers made correction of the problems more difficult in the sixties. The post-World War II admission of Mexican *braceros* provided a flood of cheap labor to southern farms. In 1966 when this was made illegal, "wetbacks" (illegal aliens) with the aid of sympathetic farmers continued to evade immigration officials. Government has been slow to introduce programs for hired worker protection to agriculture comparable to those for the rest of society. This has led to prolonged and acrimonious protests, including a number of secondary boycotts such as those for California lettuce and grapes, which became national political issues.

General Farm Organizations

In contrast to hired farm workers, farmers for almost a century have had a plethora of general, regional, and commodity organizations to represent their common interests. The five best known general farm organizations claiming national status, and the popular abbreviations of their names, are: the American Farm Bureau Federation (AFB or Farm Bureau), the National Grange (Grange), the National Farmers Union (NFU), the National Farmers Organization (NFO), and the National Council of Farmer Cooperatives, which does not have direct farmer membership but is a loose federation of farmer cooperatives.

Since our purpose is to examine the role of these organizations as national policy spokesmen for farmers, we omit detailed histories of each, which are readily available elsewhere, and concentrate on their common origins, growth, and maturity. The oldest, the National Grange, began as a secret fraternal society in 1867 and mushroomed as a vehicle for agrarian discontent in the 1870s. It has never recaptured the dominant role it enjoyed a century ago. The National Farmers Union of today is a successor of a farmers' movement begun in 1902 with a major goal of self-help for farmers through combined business enterprises. The Farm Bureau is a federation of state bureaus, the first of which was set up for educational purposes by the Chamber of Commerce of Binghamton, New York, in 1912. Its federal constitution was approved in 1919. The National Farmers Organization is a modern version of a long line of short-lived farm organizations that believed in self-help through direct action; they questioned the value of government help. The National Council of Farmer Cooperatives is the successor to an organization first organized in 1923 to give cooperatives a unified national voice.

The relative strengths of the general farm organizations are difficult to assess, depending in part on the nature of the issues in contention, the political party in control of Congress and the White House, the size and distribution of membership, and the political alliances they can draw on. Farm Bureau membership may represent a million farms, the NFU and Grange one-quarter million, and the NFO 100,000 or less. Membership fees have tended to be low; the first three have assessed only one dollar or less for the national executive. In contrast, the NFO assigns a hefty $22 out of an annual membership fee of $25 for its national program. Membership fees are a misleading guide to the financial strength of the organizations, tied in as they are with many large farm business enterprises with total gross receipts measured in billions of dollars. The Grange and NFO have lagged in terms of the size of their business empires, the former as a result of past costly failures, the latter because of attention to other goals.

The Farm Bureau is the nearest to a truly national organization, with bureaus in 49 states. Its greatest membership is in the Midwest and South. Geographical dispersion can be a disadvantage in framing a national policy platform because different regions or commodities may have conflicting goals; for example, while wheat farmers demand free trade, dairy farmers call for protection. Grange membership is concentrated in two dissimilar regions, the Northeast and the West, so that it too has difficulty in taking unified stands on many national issues. The NFU has been quite concentrated in commodity terms (heavily to wheat) and geographically in the central belt running from Arkansas through the Great Plains to Minnesota and Wisconsin. It has been able to speak out boldly in favor of a national farm policy of government intervention and supply management similar to that followed by Presidents Kennedy and Johnson, and yet finds the free market policies of Presidents Nixon and Ford (in changed circumstances) compatible with its members' welfare.

Only during the farm depressions of the 1920s and 1930s have the rival farm organizations been able to submerge their ideological differences in joint action. Since the 1940s, on any scale of ideologies—economic, political, or social—at least one of the farm organizations would be at odds with the others. For example, on two issues of great concern to farmers, the desirability of market intervention and the type of intervention, farmers alone, government alone, or some combination of both, the Farm Bureau, NFO, and NFU would lie in contrary corners of the policy spectrum, the Grange somewhere in the middle. The Farm Bureau tends to be vociferously conservative and free enterprise oriented, the NFO self-help oriented, the NFU much more willing to press for government aid.

In addition to regional and commodity differences, the ideologies of farm organizations have grown apart because of differences in social status, political leanings, grassroots values, and leadership goals. Ross B. Talbot and Don F. Hadwiger suggest that farm organizations tend to be heavily influenced by a governing minority which is responsive to a participating plurality (still a small percentage) of active members. The continuity in office of the national leaders and their control over organization, funds, communication, and education gives them considerable leverage in influencing the ideology of their organization. Their present ideologies have led the farm organizations into controversial alliances. The Farm Bureau's alliances with the U.S. Chamber of Commerce, the National Association of Manufacturers, the American Medical Association, and other agribusiness groups have antagonized farmers brought up in the agrarian tradition. The NFU's links with the AFL–CIO disturb the strong anti-union bias of many farmers who regard themselves more naturally as employers. The Farm Bureau's ties with the extension services have been as anathema to the NFU as the national agricultural committee system of the ASCS has been to the Farm Bureau.

Despite their inability to agree for long, the general farm organizations singly and together have many important achievements to their credit. The Grange won many state and national victories over the apparently invulnerable railroads, culminating in the establishment of the Interstate Commerce Commission in 1887 and the passage of the Sherman Antitrust Act of 1890. The local farm bureaus stimulated the passage of the Smith--Lever (extension service) Act in 1914 and have been major supporters of extension and research activities since then. The Farm Bloc coalition of farm organizations and politicians was responsible for a series of major laws during the 1920s and for winning farmer support for the New Deal policies of the 1930s.

However, in recent years there have been few issues on which the general farm organizations have been able to present a united front. Many political commentators maintain that this inability to agree on a common platform has tended to paralyze the agricultural committees in Congress whose members depend on different farm groups for support. However, as we have pointed out, farmers are only one of the groups continually pressing their view of agricultural policy on Congress. In turn, the success of the Farm Bureau, NFU, and others in business ventures, insurance, marketing, etc., has given them an alternative to political success. The return of agriculture to the center of national policy debate may pose a new challenge to organizations which have become set in a mold created by past forces. While their grip on the farmers' business activities may continue to grow, their influence on agricultural policy will increasingly come under challenge.

Commodity Organizations

Ironically, the forces which threaten the general farm organizations may help some of the farm organizations with special (and therefore more unified) commodity interests. Organizations such as the American Cattlemen's Association, the American Sheep Producers' Council, the International Apple Institute, and similarly titled groups represent their chosen commodity with varying degrees of flair, sophistication, and success. At certain times, their political influence may be more powerful than that of the general farm organizations because of their ability to put intense pressure on one issue, one region, or one group of politicians. At all times, they keep a jealous eye on activities of government, suppliers, or marketers likely to affect their commodity.

However, even the commodity organizations frequently show the divisiveness that hampers so much farmer political effort. There is a tendency to select leaders and follow policies acceptable to the larger commercial farmers, large handlers, supply companies, and other groups influential in that commodity. Individual farmers may lack any active commitment to the goals of the organization. In turn, the opportunity for regional and sectional differences in goals is great. However, just as the general farm organizations have secured their financial future by building business empires, the commodity organizations rely on a per unit checkoff to ensure their continued financial viability. Most farmers are aware of the need for defending their commodity from myriad hostile forces, so that they accept this checkoff as a normal business cost. Clearly, the commodity organizations will continue to be a strong political voice for farmers.

Key Words	Central Concepts
Diversity	Farms differ widely in size, location, product mix, and interests.
Multinational conglomerate	A firm engaged in many different business activities in many countries.
Tax shelter	An operation entered into for the tax savings or loopholes available.
Land tenure	The rules governing how land is owned or used.
Capitalized values	Suppose a farmer can grow soya beans which yield a net income of $50 per acre in perpetuity. If the farmer requires a 10 percent return on investment, the capital value of the land to him is about $500 per acre. Now suppose he receives a government allotment to grow cotton which yields a net income of $100 per acre. The capital value of the land to him is now about $1,000 per acre. The benefit of the allotment has been capitalized into land values of $500 per acre.
Farm families	Generally refers to families living on farms. Their numbers have declined as the number of farmers declined. Contrast with the concept of "family farm" discussed on page 60.

Multiplier effect	The process by which an increase (decrease) in the income of one sector of a community leads to a sequence of increases (decreases) in other sectors.
Agricultural mechanization	The replacement of labor and draft animals by machinery and powered equipment.
Farm organizations	Two types: general, accept farmers or farm family members; commodity, only those producing or marketing a specific product.
Agrarian discontent	A recurring theme in agricultural history. After periods of depressed incomes, farmers and associated groups have launched vehement protests against the factors considered responsible.
Governing minority	Talbot and Hadwiger's term for the small inner circle which controls most farm organizations.
Interstate Commerce Commission (ICC)	Set up in 1887, primarily to regulate interstate railroads, at the instigation of the National Grange.
Sherman Antitrust Act	Set up in 1890 to control monopolies.
Checkoff	The deduction per unit of product used to finance commodity farm organizations.

QUESTIONS

1. Why do you think farm operations are so diverse?
2. Give an example of the different effects a direct payment of subsidy per unit of commodity would have on a landlord, a tenant, and a sharecropper.
3. Should nonfarmers be allowed to use farm operations as tax shelters? Give pros and cons. Could a ban on use of farm tax shelters be enforced?
4. How do both city and country gain and lose from rural migration?
5. Would you expect an increase in agricultural income to have a larger multiplier effect than a comparable increase in welfare payments? Explain.
6. Labor laws should treat farm laborers exactly like industrial workers. Discuss.
7. Would farmers be better off with only one large nationwide general farm organization?
8. Review and compare recent policy statements of the main general farm organizations.
9. Should general farm organizations make alliances with nonfarm groups?
10. How do the ancillary business activities of general farm organizations affect their policy goals?
11. Will an expansion of world issues in U.S. agriculture be likely to favor general or commodity farm organizations?

OTHER PARTICIPANTS IN THE POLICY PROCESS

So far the cast of characters has contained only the expected government agencies, the houses of Congress, farmers, and their organizations. However, two other less well-known groups wield in their different ways a very powerful influence on agricultural policy. These are the organizations representing agriculture-based or agriculture-related industries, and nonprofit organizations specializing in knowledge generation on national policy issues. As a reading of Wesley McCune's book *Who's Behind Our Farm Policy* would show, the interest of these groups in farm policy is a long-standing one.

Business and Agriculture

Typical of the agriculture-based organizations are the National Cotton Council, National Canners' Association, American Dairy Association, American Meat Institute, American Frozen Food Institute, and similarly titled groups. For many other industries, agriculture may be only one (not always the most important) part of their total activities. However, it is clear that agriculture's well being is of great interest to the Association of American Railroads, the American Trucking Association, the American Bankers' Association, the National Association of Food Chains, the American Limestone Institute, the American Feed Manufacturers' Association, and others. Together, the organizations named so far represent some of the greatest combinations of financial and corporate power (and of lobbying power) in the world.

Some of the general business organizations have also been involved in shaping agricultural policy through their continuous involvement in national economic affairs and in international trade issues. The National Association of Manufacturers and the U.S. Chamber of Commerce, as staunch supporters of enterprise capitalism, have generally favored reduced government intervention in agriculture and have been frequent allies of the American Farm Bureau Federation.

Business does not, of course, present a single unified approach to agricultural policy. The banking industry is particularly concerned with who finances the credit needs on which massive government programs run. For example, it would prefer the government to guarantee commercial bank loans for farming rather than make direct loans through government loan agencies. Railroad and trucking interests may be in competition for federal funds to improve the nation's highway system or the national railroad system. Both will seek to woo grassroots farm support in their lobbying efforts. For many years the American Limestone Institute has devoted most of its efforts to perpetuation of government subsidies for limestone use under the ASCS's Agricultural Conservation Program.

These and many other groups publicly adopt and widely circulate their openly partisan views. Such activity is clearly desirable in a democracy governed by majority rule. Not so clear is the role of a veritable netherworld of links between big business, government, foundations, and groups whose ostensible purpose is study, research, debate, and dissemination of new knowledge for the betterment of citizens.

Foundations and Agriculture

At the axis of this system are the two great foundations, the Ford and Rockefeller Foundations. Both are best known to the public and to scientists as patrons of university research not otherwise supported by public funds; both are the offspring of two of the nation's greatest and still prominent industrial fortunes, one based on automobiles, the other on oil. The board of trustees of each reads like a *Who's Who in America* listing. The activities of both are international in scope, being particularly important in developing countries. Their influence on agricultural policy is exercised in both direct and indirect (more subtle) ways, which we will examine in more detail.

A third foundation, the Farm Foundation, is a baby in dollar terms relative to the two Goliaths, but it attempts to play a pivotal role in agricultural research. Despite its name, the Farm Foundation was set up and still draws much of its support from oil, railroad, bank, retail, and other nonfarm sources. Instigated by Alexander Legge of International Harvester, the Farm Foundation aims "to improve rural life and rural living." For many years its operating principle was "to stimulate the efforts of other agencies, to multiply the Foundation's efforts, and to involve people in programs designed to benefit them." It achieved this by attempting to bring together in working committees researchers and extension workers in the USDA and in the Land Grant university colleges of agriculture. In 1975 the Farm Foundation appeared to be replacing this long-established policy of acting as a catalyst with a policy of funding specific solicited and unsolicited projects.

The Opinion Makers

A host of other groups, drawing their trustees and financing from the same corporate sources, influence agricultural and general economic policy not with funds (as do the foundations) but with knowledge and information generation. There is considerable similarity in the stated aims of these study groups. To quote from their own publicity releases: The Committee for Economic Development (CED), in its bylaws, initiates

> studies into the principles of business policy and public policy which will foster the full contribution by industry and commerce to the attainment and maintenance of high and secure standards of living for people in all walks of life through maximum employment and high productivity in the domestic economy.

The Brookings Institution is

> an independent organization devoted to nonpartisan research, education, and publication in economics, government, foreign policy, and the social sciences generally. Its principal purposes are to aid in the development of sound public policies and to promote public understanding of issues of national importance.

Resources for the Future, Inc., in its *1970 Annual Report* states it is

> a nonprofit tax-exempt corporation chartered under the laws of the state of New York, with headquarters in Washington, D.C. It was established in October 1952 with the cooperation of the Ford Foundation. Its purpose is to advance the development, conservation, and use of natural resources and the improvement of the quality of the environment through programs of research and education.

The Twentieth Century Fund,

> founded in 1919, and endowed by Edward A. Filene, devotes the major share of its resources to research, concentrating on objective and critical studies of major economic, political, and social institutions. It usually publishes the results of its research in book form.The Fund attempts to ensure the scholarly quality of works appearing under its imprint; the trustees and the staff, however, accord authors complete freedom in the statement of opinion and the interpretation of fact.

Other similar organizations, not listed in order of importance, are the Conference on Economic Progress, the American Assembly, the Tax Foundation, the National Planning Association, the American Enterprise Institute, the National Bureau of Economic Research, the

Foundation for Economic Education, the Conference Board, and the Foundation for American Agriculture. A recent development is the linking of U.S. organizations with comparable organizations in Canada, Western Europe, and Japan in international groups such as the Club of Rome (sponsor of the doomsday study, "Limits to Growth") and the British–North American Committee.

All these organizations stress their goal of improving the general welfare by study and education. They stress their independent, nonpartisan viewpoint and their objectivity, scholarly quality, and the "complete freedom" of the authors sponsored. They have ready access to the best academic publishers. They attract to their projects some of the most productive and influential economists and other social scientists. Their prestige is high in academic circles, with the business press, and throughout the mass media. They have ready and frequent access to congressional hearings and to senior government officials. When they make pronouncements on national economic or agricultural policy *they are listened to.*

While recognizing the scientific merit of much of the work of these study groups, a student must be wary of accepting uncritically the aura created by words like "nonprofit," "independent," and "prestige." A research group may not itself make any profits but its recommendations may have vast profit consequences for its financial sponsors; for instance, the recommendations of the Tax Foundation can have a large and continuing impact on corporate taxes or tax breaks. Independence, in turn, is a quality which can be guaranteed only by control of one's own source of funds, goals, and programs. The best test of a group's independence is the publication of findings which would damage the vested interests of the sponsoring corporations. However, it is often difficult to discover how these groups choose their priorities and whence they draw their funds. For example, many funds are filtered through larger foundations or other study groups. The Ford Foundation, in particular, has been involved in initiating, supporting, or funding projects for Resources for the Future, Brookings, Rand, the NBER, the NPA, and many other U.S. study groups.

Such centralized filtering of acceptable projects, scientists, and results is itself a denial of the independence so insistently claimed. Prestige is an equally elusive characteristic. Many of the groups under study secure at least a friendly media reaction by having a prominent press or television executive on the board of trustees. A prominent university president or senior scientist lends the imprimatur of the academic community to the board. Occasionally, a representative of a major union (usually the AFL–CIO) or of one of the more conservative farm groups may become a member of the board of trustees. However, corporate interests are usually in the overwhelming majority. Indeed, one could not without prior knowledge distinguish the board of trustees of these independent, nonprofit, objective study groups from the boards of directors of any major corporation. It is questionable how well farmers, consumers, taxpayers, or other noncorporate interests are represented in influencing the choice of policy priorities for study, the scholars selected for support, or the utilization of study findings.

The Threat to Objective Policy Making

This network of foundations and study groups exists basically on tax loopholes granted to private wealth. Society needs to constantly reappraise whether the good to which these tax exemptions are put outweighs the tax burden transferred to other citizens. If benefits are going primarily to the corporations which originally avoided taxation and not to society in general, it would seem appropriate to restore control of such monies to the constitutional authority of the executive branch or Congress. Where the network succeeds in concealing the true sponsors of research or publications, the objective evaluation of major policy studies is made difficult. Since policy involves political and social as well as economic issues, *who* says something and *why* is as important as *what* is said. Congress or the executive branch may be inefficient managers of research (as is often argued) but they are, at least in the long run, answerable to the voting public.

Universities have become subject to considerable influence from study and education groups. The universities, entrusted by society with responsibility for policy study and education, have been squeezed by lack of funds and manpower. However, the networks have cleverly used "competitive" grants to redirect the work of university researchers, to stifle criticism from university administrators hard pressed for funds, and to bleed some of the best talents from the university system. Thus, we have the ironic situation of private groups outbidding tax supported institutions with tax exempt dollars.

In agricultural policy, the bleeding has been severe. With the USDA research arm reluctant to publish sensitive policy studies and universities in general unwilling to fund policy research, foundations and study groups have come to dominate the field by default. They have tended to be much better geared to bringing their recommendations to the ear of policy makers. With their interlocking financing, the opportunities for a managed policy consensus are greatly increased. The risks are great that the interests of farmers and consumers, and of society in general, in a rapidly changing environment will not be adequately represented.

Key Words	Central Concepts
Agriculture-based	Industries totally dependent on agriculture for raw materials or markets, for example, food processing, fertilizer production.
Agriculture-related	Industries important to but not solely dependent on agriculture, like, banking and insurance.
Foundations	Organizations set up to finance charitable, educational, or other socially beneficial activities. The founders gain considerable benefits in asset management, tax avoidance, etc.
Patrons	Wealthy individuals or (more usually) organizations who grant funds for work in the arts, sciences, and so forth.
Opinion makers	In a democracy, power is exercised through one's ability to influence voters' or their representatives' opinions.
Nonprofit	An organization which does not seek to make profits which can be distributed to the owners. Confers tax benefits.
Objectivity	The ability to keep personal biases out of assessments of a particular issue. A rare (perhaps extinct) ability.
Centralized filtering	The process of having many projects evaluated by a dominant, central group.
Network of foundations and study groups	A group sharing common trustees, funds, projects, personnel, etc.

QUESTIONS

1. Would you expect agriculture-based or agriculture-related industries to be more continuous lobbyists in Congress?
2. Why does business *not* take a single, unified approach to agricultural policy?
3. Read the recent annual reports of the Ford and Rockefeller Foundations. On which activities do they cooperate?
4. How does the Farm Foundation maximize use of limited funds?
5. In what ways can descriptions like "independent," "nonprofit," "objective," and "nonpartisan" be misleading?
6. What results would you expect to follow the internationalization of foundations and study groups?
7. Discuss the merits of foundation patronage relative to direct government patronage.
8. Why is the brain drain from universities to private tax-exempt groups of relevance to U.S. agriculture?

three

ECONOMIC AND SOCIAL BACKGROUND

The body of laws and regulations that we call agricultural policy emerged from the economic and social turbulence of past decades. Prior to the 1930s, the prevailing economic philosophy was that of laissez-faire. Government was acceptable as a referee but never as a player in economic affairs. To understand why this was so we need to understand something of the world economy prior to the thirties.

THE ECONOMIC ENVIRONMENT OF AGRICULTURAL POLICY—INTO A NEW ERA

The British Empire and Laissez-Faire

Even though the United States threw off the political domination of the British empire in 1776, that empire, the greatest world power since the Middle Ages, continued to dominate world trade and finance for the next 150 years. By the 1840s, its economic interests were served by free trade and its political and military power affirmed that system. Britain imported raw materials from the colonies and economic dependencies, such as the U.S., to feed its industrial system (the most advanced of its time) and exported finished manufactured goods to colonies and other dependents. The views of its economists on money supply, competition, and trade were colored by the benefit of laissez-faire to the empire, especially after the repeal of the trade-restricting Corn Laws in 1846. In general, British economists emphasized perfect competition, micro problems, and the benefits of free trade. American studies of economics were dominated by the views of Adam Smith, David Ricardo, and Alfred Marshall.

As the United States expanded westward, the laissez-faire approach was evident in many ways, such as the preference for free trade between states and the opposition, for almost a century, to the establishment of a national bank. The government did emerge, however, in the role of referee to control forces like cartels or monopolies which might damage the assumed benefits of perfect competition. In the frequent economic slumps, the economic collapse of the unfortunates was regarded as a small price for the opportunities of free competition gained by the fortunate. By hard work, intelligence, and thrift, the unfortunates might also be successful in the next boom.

The end of World War I left the great European powers near bankruptcy. In contrast, the U.S. had gained considerable economic benefits and had suffered little of the physical destruction from the war. The automobile industry put the nation on wheels in the 1920s, changed the patterns of business and housing, and precipitated a nationwide real estate boom. Excessive credit expansion, despite the existence of Federal Reserve Banks, led to a stock market boom and collapse. A general economic slowdown became a panic, then a deep depression, which was to affect many parts of the economy until the outbreak of World War II in 1939.

The New Deal

Franklin Delano Roosevelt (F.D.R.) swept into the presidential office on the promise of using the full powers of government to get the country moving again. The New Deal economic program was the pragmatic reaction of practical men to widespread need. Economic theory, as it then stood, was of little benefit to policy makers. But even though the mighty British empire had crumbled, its economic principles (now known as the "classical theory") still reigned unchallenged.

A remarkable British economist, John Maynard Keynes, in 1935 published a book *The General Theory of Employment, Interest and*

Money, which set out to show that classical theory was only relevant in a special case and that a more general theory was needed to explain the workings of a modern industrialized economy. Keynes attempted to build a macro theory at a time when macro statistics to support his case were often lacking. He showed that government could, by spending more than it earned, give a boost to a depressed economy. Governments attempting to do this already listened sympathetically to Keynesian logic. Their economic advisers, mostly raised in the classical tradition, frequently denounced deficit spending, government intervention, and the intellectual takeover of the Keynesian theory. Ironically, only 30 years later under President Kennedy the Keynesians finally captured most of the positions of influence in economic policy making in the U.S. Their supremacy seemed complete as the nation moved from stagnation to rapid growth in the 1960s, but the Keynesians ran into unexpected troubles when they attempted the politically more difficult task of slowing down excessive growth brought on by the Vietnam War.

While F.D.R. was not a deliberate follower of Keynes, many of his programs did involve the government in private economic affairs. Despite the waves they created, it is very difficult to show that F.D.R.'s New Deal brought the sort of recovery it promised. Much of the economy remained depressed until the advent of World War II.

U.S. Agriculture, Depression, and War Years

American agriculture was particularly hard hit by the Depression. During the years 1929–33, prices *paid* by farmers fell 33 percent, while prices *received* by farmers fell 50 percent. Many farmers had borrowed for expansion during and after World War I and they were no longer able to meet their debts. To poverty was added the threat (and frequently the reality) of foreclosure. While the new policies stabilized ownership, the gains in farm income were slow. Measured in terms of a parity price index (1910–14 = 100), the index of prices received by farmers rose from 65 in 1932 to 77 in 1939. Of course, one could argue that without New Deal efforts to boost the general economy and direct government intervention in agriculture, farm prices would have been even lower than the 1932 level in 1939. (This pinpoints one of the problems in evaluating economic policies: Once a particular action is taken, one cannot actually measure what might have been without that action.)

The outbreak of war in Europe in 1939 provided the boost to farm demand which had been missing during the 1930s. Depression-generated agricultural policies did not respond rapidly to the sudden change from concern about overproduction and depressed prices to the need for greater production. However, this is understandable in view of the general uncertainty about if, when, and how the U.S. might enter the conflict. The Japanese attack on the U.S. fleet at Pearl Harbor was the signal F.D.R. needed. Once again, agriculture's fate was altered by forces outside itself. U.S. agriculture during the war was called on to make up much of the food and fiber supplies lost overseas in the ravages of war, or not produced because of resources diverted to the war effort. Government became deeply involved in stimulating rather than curbing production. The system proved to be as startlingly *successful* in increasing production as it had been *unsuccessful* in curtailing unwanted production during the 1930s. The key was the timely melding of advances in farming research and technology with an aggressive farm supply industry and a skilled and adaptable farmer population.

Postwar Slowdown of the Great Farm Machine

As the war neared an end, most economists were concerned that the drying up of war-related demand would lead to a postwar slump. However, a spending boom triggered by pent-up demand for consumer goods, and food shortages among both victors and defeated kept agriculture producing at close to full capacity. The outbreak of the Korean War in 1950 led to a further major U.S. "war" effort overseas. Prices thus remained at relatively high levels for almost ten years, 1942–52.

When the Eisenhower administration took over in 1953, its general political stance was to restore stability to a nation which had gone through a decade of exceptional turbulence. General economic policy was one of balanced budgets, reduced federal expenditures, and the withdrawal of government from agriculture. In a situation where domestic demand was growing only slowly, the productive potential of U.S. agriculture could not be curtailed. Even though Secretary of Agriculture Benson gradually reduced the level of price supports, surpluses mounted and would have been even larger, had not much surplus food been exported under overseas food aid programs. Government became a manager of stored surpluses and of export sales and disposals. Since U.S. economic power dominated the Western world, other countries were not in a position to protest the use of exporting to reduce U.S. farm problems. Government seemed incapable of disentangling itself from the agricultural maze.

After World War II, freer trade between countries (particularly in industrial goods) had been espoused as an aid to rapid economic recovery and as a preventative of future international conflict. The European Economic Community and the European Free Trade Area, founded in 1958, added some new wrinkles to this concept. Both these groups sought economic growth as an antidote to past and future destructive European wars. A further goal was to unite in the face of U.S. economic domination. The EEC, in particular, adopted a protectionist attitude toward trade with nonmembers. To offset this, the U.S. under President Kennedy sought a gradual reduction of restrictions on international trade, but progress was slow partly because of the continued protectionist attitude of Congress. Trade expansion in the 1960s tended to come in bilateral deals between countries. While much progress was made in freeing trade in industrial products, gains in agricultural trade under one deal were frequently offset by losses in access to traditional markets.

Agriculture—Out of Step with the General Economy

Agriculture in the 1960s demonstrated that it could stagnate in the middle of general economic prosperity, as efforts continued to curb the productivity of the great U.S. farm machine. Increased productivity again became the cry in the 1970s as U.S. agriculture was called on to meet food deficits throughout the world. Agriculture showed it could be prosperous in the middle of general economic "stagflation," as the combination of stagnant economic growth and inflation is called. The very rise in the economic strength of the EEC, Japan, and the Communist bloc countries, which had challenged the competitiveness of the U.S. in industrial markets, provided increasingly lucrative bilateral deals for U.S. agriculture and separated its fortunes further from that of the general economy.

In many ways the conventional economic wisdom of the 1970s proved inadequate for the changed circumstances, as had previous economic philosophies. Classical economists had sought economic growth in the conquest by military force or economic domination of foreign markets which would absorb the mother country's output at full employment levels. The Keynesian revolution focused on seeking solutions by government intervention in the domestic economy. Each was adequate for its time—the classical to a dominant imperial power, the Keynesian to isolationist nations. The neo-classical synthesis, combining the best elements of classical and Keynesian economics, was adequate as the post-World War II world groped its way toward a new prosperity. It provided no adequate policy solutions to the tangled web of international economics, more and more dominated by power bloc politics. Yet spurred on by Keynesian logic, governments have become embedded in many aspects of economic life far beyond the current expertise of economic theory or application. The unresolved issue of the 1970s is that government may *not* have the intellectual depth to solve national and international economic problems, but feels compelled, like the punch-drunk over-the-hill pugilist, to keep on flailing, because that is the only way it knows to tackle them.

The Agricultural Roller Coaster—A Summary

This brief summary of the U.S. agricultural economy since the 1930s indicates the roller coaster ride that farmers and policy makers have faced as they alternated between policies to curtail production and policies to expand production. The latter policies generally resulted from international forces, World War II, the Korean War, famine in India, or more general world food shortages. As these temporary forces faded, the productivity of U.S. agriculture rapidly reasserted itself, often before policies had adjusted sufficiently, and farm prices plunged. Not surprisingly, even in the early seventies, conventional wisdom was that chronic surplus was the normal or usual state of U.S. agriculture and that the removal of thirties-style government programs of price supports would severely hurt U.S. farmers. This was the view of the National Advisory Commission on Food and Fiber appointed by President Johnson, which reported in 1967. A Science Advisory Committee, which reported in the same year, on the world food problem, while recognizing the need for extensive self-help measures to increase food production in developing countries did not see a major role for U.S. farmers in meeting those food needs. Yet only six years later, U.S. agriculture was once again the savior of a hungry world. This should teach us that (1) U.S. agriculture is subject to the influence of very large external shocks; (2) even the nation's best scientists have not been very successful in predicting the timing or extent of such shocks; and (3) until our predictions become more reliable, U.S. agriculture must retain the flexibility to survive and prosper on both the up and down swings of the roller coaster.

Key Words	Central Concepts
Laissez-faire	A French phrase meaning "to leave alone" or "not interfere." Used here to refer to absence of government intervention in the economic life of the nation.
British Empire	At various times controlled vast land areas on all five continents. Power was based on its lead in industrial development and on military might.
Colonies	Settlements of a country's citizens on foreign soil, retaining allegiance to the mother country.

Perfect competition An economist's abstraction of how markets work, given many buyers and sellers, freedom of entry, full market information, etc. Perfect competition is often regarded as an ideal to be aimed at by society. This bias has been passed on to generations of economists by labeling all other forms of competition "imperfect."

The New Deal Popular term to describe the many programs initiated by President Franklin Delano Roosevelt (F.D.R.).

John Maynard Keynes British economist who demonstrated that government spending could be used to fight recession.

Deficit spending Government spending more than it collects in taxes in any year.

Balanced budget Spending equals taxes.

Foreclosure The repossession by a lender of property used as collateral on a loan that has fallen into default. Widespread foreclosures on farm property took place during the Depression.

Technology The application of science to practical affairs. A key factor in increased agricultural production.

European Economic Community (EEC or EC) By the Treaty of Rome (1958), France, West Germany, Italy, the Netherlands, Belgium, and Luxembourg pledged themselves to work toward economic and eventually political union. The United Kingdom, Denmark, and Ireland joined the expanded community in 1973.

Productivity The ratio of output to a given input. Higher productivity of labor can be achieved by utilizing more or better equipment per worker.

Isolationist Avoiding involvement in the affairs of other countries. U.S. policy tended to be isolationist until the U.S. entered World War II. It has been the opposite since then.

Agricultural roller coaster Describes the rapid swings of the agricultural economy from periods of supply control and low prices to periods of all-out production and high prices.

World food problem The fear of population growth outracing food supplies. May be acute in some developing countries.

QUESTIONS

1. Discuss the relationship between the British Empire, the political theory of laissez-faire, and the economic theory of perfect competition.
2. Why did American colonists rebel against political but not economic domination by the British Empire?
3. How much influence did Keynes' general theory have on F.D.R.?
4. In what ways did Keynesian policies fail in the 1960s?
5. Have wars helped the U.S. economy and U.S. agriculture?
6. Is there an alternative to war as a means of expanding demand for U.S. exports?

7. What factors kept government in agriculture when depression conditions and wartime emergencies ended?
8. Compare rates of growth of farm income and nonfarm income from 1950 to the present. What does this tell you about the links between the agricultural sector and the rest of the economy?
9. Can government deliver all, half, some, or none of what it promises? Why do you think so?
10. Why do you think U.S. farmers are concerned about policies to stabilize farm prices and incomes?

THE SOCIAL ENVIRONMENT— THE VANISHING FARMER

Economic policies are rooted in the social environment of their times. Economists too easily forget that their conception of how economic affairs work is based on assumptions about how society as a whole works. The Great Depression perplexed economists partly because so many people were no longer so concerned about responding to marginal returns or marginal utility as theory said they should, but were concerned about human survival. Worsening economic conditions led to poverty of income, poverty of assets, banking failures, absence of credit—in fact a collapse of the bases on which rational man makes economic decisions. The normally conservative farming community was a lively part of the widespread doubts about the viability of the American social order and the desirability of experimenting with other social orders such as communism and fascism, which were being widely tried in Europe. The New Deal policies of F.D.R. were designed as much to buttress the prevailing social order and nip unrest in the bud as to meet any specific economic goals. (Remember Keynes' *General Theory* was published only in late 1935.)

Many economic commentators have questioned the rationale of agricultural policy makers in the thirties in promoting "parity" as a key goal. However, this concept, implying as it does social equity between farmers and nonfarmers, was an essential element in winning the farmers' support for the experiments with the social order being tried by F.D.R. As farmers looked at the decline of farm prices relative to other prices despite equal or increased work effort, they were questioning not commodity markets but the equity of the existing economic system. (Remember, too, that the alternative systems, notably communism and fascism, had not as yet shown the heinous excesses to which they could go.) The New Deal agricultural policies had sufficient success to hold farmer support until war demand brought a new era of prosperity. Since then, farmers have tended to return to their more usual economic and social conservatism (for instance, a strong loyalty to the status quo).

Parity as a goal of farm policy has survived for over 40 years. Parity is an excellent rallying cry, attractive to most farmers but ambiguous enough to satisfy many different viewpoints. Originally, parity was defined in terms of a price equivalent to the average level of prices enjoyed during 1910–14, a past period of prosperity for U.S. agriculture. Parity has also been defined in income terms, first as the income of farmers which would equate the income of nonfarmers, and then as the income of farmers from farming which would equate income from nonfarming activities. During the 1940s, the USDA was authorized to develop a measure of parity in terms of living standards. However, because of serious conceptual and measurement problems, this measure was not made operational. A further concept, the "parity ratio," defined as the index of prices received by farmers divided by the index of prices paid, is closely watched. Even though these various parity concepts have been denigrated by a generation of economists because they are poor statistical measures and no longer relevant to modern agriculture, farmers and farm groups rediscover their attachment to parity each time agricultural prices dip.

Social Trends

The massive intervention of government in agriculture probably did more to slow or strengthen long-term social trends than to create new trends. For example, the decline in the number of farms, farmers, and farm workers persisted before and after the Great Depression, only slowing during the 1930s as economic opportunities off the farm dried up. The spread in ownership and use of the automobile, electricity, telephone, radio, etc., slowed in the 1930s but was almost certainly boosted by government programs to pave farm roads, bring electricity to rural areas, and improve farm living conditions. Wartime gave these trends a further boost as the nation geared up for maximum agricultural production. Thirty years later, farm homes differ scarcely at all from nonfarm homes in ownership of the accoutrements of modern living.

Not all the results of these developments have been beneficial. The improved roads and motor vehicles which increased access of farm communities to markets also led to the absorption of the business of smaller market towns by larger regional centers. Continuing depopulation wiped out many of these smaller communities and left many others hanging to life by a thread. As a result, rural communities face an uphill struggle to provide "parity" of services, educational, medical, commercial, professional, etc., with those available in most urban communities.

The Great Migration

The wartime production drive of agriculture unleashed the pent-up power of research and technology. The switch to machinery, chemicals, etc., released a vast pool of labor. Particularly in the poorer communities of the South, outmigration from agriculture was of a volume which, had it been across national borders or as the result of war or other calamity, would have been considered one of the most dramatic migrations of history. During the two decades 1940–60, the net outmigration from the South was 3.5 million, 81 percent black, much of it from agriculture (William H. Nicholls, 1972). Outmigration from agriculture has continued into the early seventies, without any perceptible loss in total output. However, by the mid-seventies it appeared that supply technology, product demand, and labor needs were at least temporarily in balance.

An important aim of government economic policy in rural areas has been directed toward compensating for the effects of population losses. Efforts have been made to locate industry in rural areas, perhaps most successfully in the South. Many programs, ranging from Eisenhower's Rural Development Program to Johnson's War on Poverty to Nixon's Revenue Sharing, have recognized the increasing role of the federal government as the "super" tax collector which then funnels funds back to states and rural areas. Government has become the major employer in many rural areas, both directly in its civil service programs and indirectly through defense contracts, highway funds, and activities channeled through state or local governments. As a result of all these activities, about half of all farmers now also earn from off-farm employment. The absorption of women into the labor force and the availability of jobs for farm wives off the farm also have been critical in enabling many farm families to remain in farming.

The Family Farm

The fate of the "family farm" has remained a central issue in agricultural policy. In the 1930s, the concern was for the economic, social, and spiritual welfare of many families facing destitution if their farm unit failed. Later, as family farms continued to disappear in good and bad times and their land was consolidated into larger holdings, anxiety increased about the takeover of agriculture by large conglomerate corporate farms. Some of these conglomerate farms had their roots in the eastern banks and not in the soil. Farmers in many states tried (and in some cases succeeded) in passing laws to limit the growth of corporate or conglomerate agriculture.

Many family farms (farms where family members provide most of the farm labor) are inefficient and will continue to disappear. However, efficient family farms are still the dominant form of farm operation in terms of acreage owned, output, and productivity. The commercial farmers who produce most of the national agricultural output tend to be large and heavily capitalized; independent of their neighbors and community; but dependent on organizations, supply and marketing co-ops, agribusiness, etc., capable of providing the specialized services they need. George S. Tolley has argued that capital is no longer replacing labor, but that "low level" management is being replaced by management with superior skills. He foresees the number of farms continuing to decline until the 1980s but rising in the 1990s as demand for farm products grows. He also anticipates a reversal of the increasing average age of farmers as younger, better managers enter farming.

Changing Rural Communities

Rural communities face similar changes in identity as farm families become a minority of the rural population. Symptomatic of the invasion of rural society by nonfarm interests are the shifts in land use. Walter W. Wilcox, W. W. Cochrane, and Robert W. Herdt show that in the decade 1959–69, 2,400 thousand acres of rural land each year shifted to other uses: recreation, wilderness areas, parks and wildlife refuges (1,225), urban development (750), reservoirs and flood control (275), and airports and highways (150). This invasion has been most noticeable near major cities but has been persistent even in low population states like Idaho and Montana.

Rural areas have lost much of their individuality. The unique local supply–market systems for perishables, dairy products, etc., have given way to national supply–market systems. As a result, the price discrepancies between urban and rural areas or between different regions have tended to disappear. Incursions of the mass media threaten to eliminate the survival of independent rural or agrarian philosophies, and are forming farm and rural, town and country into a single mold. The social uniqueness of farming, farmers, and rural communities, which had been a rallying cry for past agricultural policy, is becoming less and less relevant in the last quarter of the twentieth century.

Key Words	Central Concepts
Social environment	A broad term used to describe the beliefs, values, concerns, attitudes, and behavior of society at any time.
Communism	Both a theory of common ownership and enjoyment of the fruits of property and a political system based on that theory. In practice most Communist regimes favor state ownership of all productive goods.
Fascism	A system of government with power vested in an autocratic dictator and militaristic regimentation of citizens.
Depopulation	Continuing heavy losses of population by a region. Most often involves younger, more talented, and more active persons.
Outmigration	The movement of people from rural to urban areas. A source of much social distress.
War on Poverty	Popular term for a series of programs promoted by President Lyndon Johnson to help alleviate poverty.
Family farm	A farm owned by one family which provides most of its own labor requirements (excluding harvest). The definition tends to change as average farm size increases and farm numbers decline.
Rural communities	Small towns and the surrounding farm communities.
Local supply–market systems	Markets where what can be produced locally is produced and sold locally.
Agrarian philosophy	A viewpoint on life derived from special regard for the importance of farm and rural activities.

QUESTIONS

1. Social conditions at any time have an important influence on economic policies. Explain.
2. How does the large-scale intervention of the government in U.S. agriculture differ from state-run agriculture under Communist regimes?
3. Examine changes in the parity ratio since the 1930s. What do they tell you about the relative standard of living of farmers and farm families?
4. Can a separate agrarian philosophy survive in an urban dominated society?
5. What social changes resulted from the mass migration of rural people after 1940?
6. Should the social consequences of the disappearance of many family farms be of greater concern to policy makers than the economic consequences?
7. Review evidence of the influx of urban dwellers into rural areas and the possible future effects on our economy.

four

HOW ECONOMISTS EXPLAIN FARM POLICY NEEDS

All scientists tend to explain what is happening in the world around them in terms of their own discipline. Over the years, economists have drawn on the prevailing economic theories and tools of measurement to explain what *has* happened in U.S. agriculture, to predict what *may* happen, and to *evaluate* the likely impact of alternative policies. This section trys to show the main threads of thought among U.S. economists over the decades which have influenced agricultural policy. Of necessity, this has had to be selective, because so much has been written, particularly in commodity terms, on U.S. agricultural policy. However, it indicates that economists often disagree violently in explaining the same phenomenon, that the prevailing wisdom tends to change over the years, that the past is explained more easily than the future (which is more relevant to policy development), and that economists (like generals) are too often caught out fighting the last war.

ECONOMISTS—LEARNING ON THE JOB

Much of the economic justification for the advent of government in agriculture in the 1930s was drawn from static market supply and demand theory or the theory of the firm under perfect competition. It was relatively short run in nature, partly because the most pressing problem was avoiding imminent disaster.

The Federal Farm Board, set up in 1929, saw its role as one of mopping up surplus output in a given period so that prices would not fall below an acceptable minimum (Figure 4.1). The Federal Farm Board aimed to raise price from P_1 to the higher P_2 level by buying up surpluses. Its effort failed because the demand curve did not, in fact, remain stable after 1929. As employment and incomes shrank, the demand curve for many commodities shifted rapidly to the left (Figure 4.2). As a result, surplus removal failed to hold up market price. The more responsive demand for any product was to income changes, the more rapid was the leftward shift in demand.

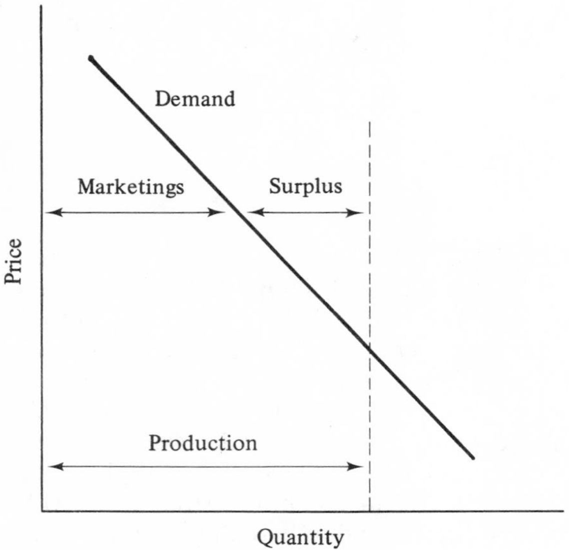

Fig. 4.1. Agricultural problem as viewed by the Federal Farm Board.

While prior to 1930 economists had developed statistical studies of the demand and supply of many commodities, the reliability of such studies or their application to policy problems was not well understood. Even to this day, the long-run influences on supply and demand have been inadequately studied. The Federal Farm Board operated with only a fraction of the economic knowledge now available to policy makers. When it failed to halt the downward price slide, it argued strongly for mandatory production controls.

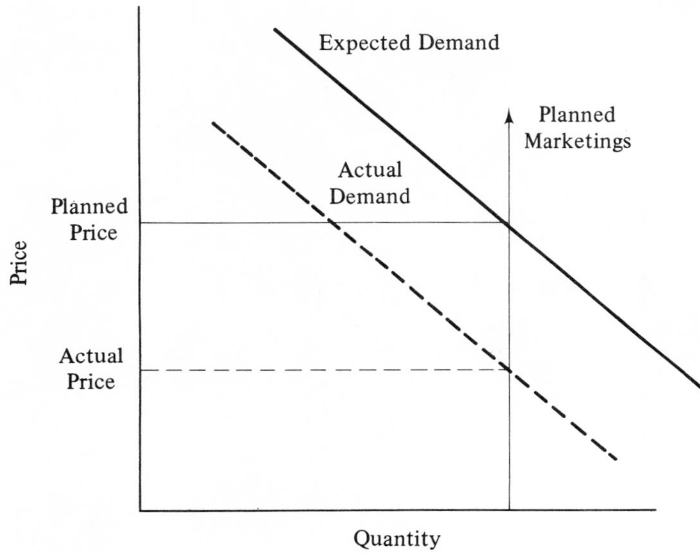

Fig. 4.2. Agricultural problem actually faced by the Federal Farm Board.

First, the board believed that only by coupling such controls with price support operations could farm prices be kept from falling. Second, the traditional view of the farmer was of a small, atomistic competitor who saw price as a given factor in any time period (Figure 4.3). Each individual farmer would want to produce up to the level of output Q_1, where marginal cost = price (MC = P) and his profits were at a maximum. Voluntary production controls, marketing cooperatives, etc., had failed to persuade the farmer to cut back production below Q_1. Only government could now secure that objective.

Cost of Production or Parity Goal

Prior to the passage of the 1933 Agricultural Adjustment Act (Triple-A), there was considerable controversy over whether government efforts should be aimed at covering farmers' costs of production or providing an equitable price (as in the parity concept). The idea that a farmer should be paid the cost of his production appears simple and fair. However, as Figure 4.3 shows, marginal and average costs vary with output. In addition, marginal and average costs vary among farmers. One could arbitrarily establish the average cost of production for an efficient farm producing at normal output. A guarantee of that level of price would then be a carrot to the more efficient farmers and a stick to the less efficient. The more usual bureaucratic approach tends to be a maze of target cost-of-production levels to take account of special regional, soil, climatic, disease, or other factors.

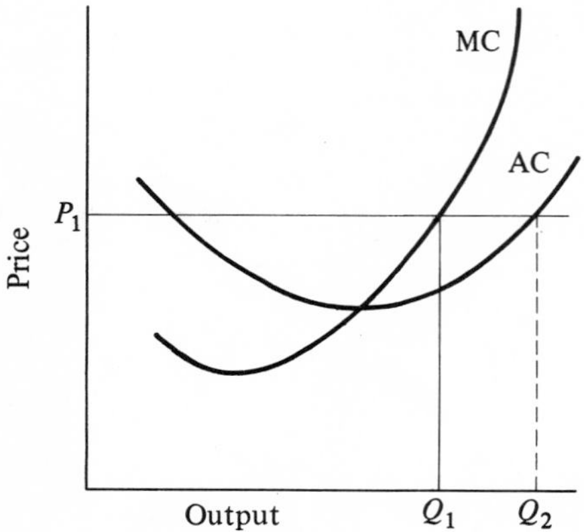

Fig. 4.3. Demand and cost curves for the individual farmer.

Parity price emerged as the chosen tool of government in restoring the relative purchasing power of the farmer. By using the years 1910–14 as a basis for comparison, when farm prices were significantly above the level of the early 1930s, the targeted parity price would ensure a profit to most farmers whether they were low-cost or high-cost producers. During the 1930s, government loans or price supports were not at full parity but at a level usually within the 52 to 75 percent range of parity. Accordingly, the more efficient farmers tended to benefit most and the less efficient continued to go out of business. In the early 1940s, price support levels moved upward as the government sought to increase production. T. W. Schultz, in his book *Redirecting Farm Policy*, blasted the use of parity price to increase production or to improve farm incomes. "Prices," he argued, "have a function, and that function is to direct and regulate economic processes." Prices drawn out of the air (or out of the past) will not reflect demand or supply conditions and will distort economic processes. By employing the expertise of economic analysts, Schultz maintained, the USDA could set forward prices for each season which *would* reflect supply and demand conditions. Improving farm incomes should be regarded as a problem separate from increasing production, since the price needed to draw forth the needed production nationally would not in itself give many small farmers an adequate income.

Schultz was pointing to the distinction between aggregate and farm impact of price. In the aggregate, the industry supply curve for a commodity and the aggregate demand curve will tend to intersect at the equilibrium price (P_1). An actual price above the equilibrium (P_2) will discourage consumption and encourage production (Figure 4.4). At a price above equilibrium (P_2) more will be supplied (AC) than will be demanded (AB). Prices will tend to fall. The new level of prices will cause further supply and demand interactions, with the general tendency being toward an equilibrium where quantity actually supplied equals quantity actually demanded.

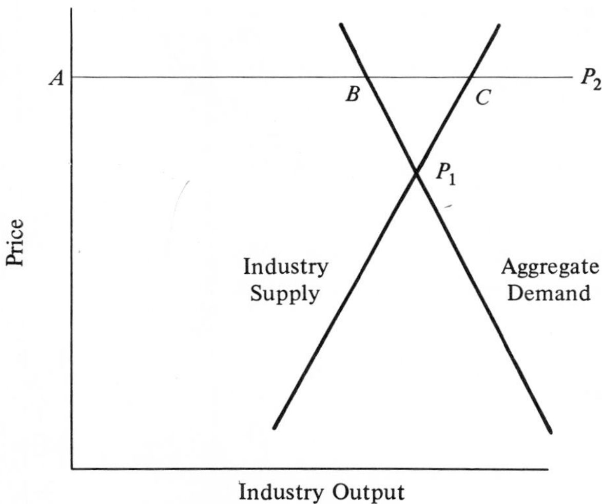

Fig. 4.4. Hypothetical effect of price set above equilibrium.

In contrast, at the farm level (Figure 4.3), the farmer must accept a price determined by outside market forces. Beyond output Q_1, total profits will fall. Beyond output Q_2, the farmer will incur losses, not profits. Yet there is no guarantee that even the maximum profits $Q_1(P_1 - \text{AC})$ generated by a particular enterprise will yield the farmer an adequate income.

Farm Policy Conflicts

Farm programs of the 1930s such as the soil conservation programs had both aggregate and farm-level economic objectives. In the aggregate, they were initially related to taking land out of production. In addition, at the farm level they were aimed at increasing the productivity of the soil. Insofar as such activity did increase productivity, it also tended to lower the average fixed cost per unit and might, depending on the costs of certain practices, also lower the variable cost per unit. Proponents further argued that it increased farm incomes; however, it also increased output, so that it was at variance with aggregate efforts to reduce farm output. Similar conflicts between the farm and the aggregate impacts arose in many government farm programs.

Much of the early efforts of research and extension were aimed at improving the cost situation of the individual farmer. The market system *off* the farm was not considered. Agronomists, farm management economists, animal scientists, horticulturists, and others worked to reduce unit costs of production. They assumed that any output increasing effects on the individual farm would not alter the market price. The rapidity with which farmers were able to apply research results and extension advice often proved this assumption to be short sighted.

This narrow and short-sighted view of agriculture's economic problems occurred despite the availability of economic expertise. The Federal Farm Board included on its staff two prominent agricultural economists, John D. Black and Mordecai Ezekiel (father of the "cobweb theorem"). Under Triple-A, the USDA recruited many excellent economists who were able to focus on aggregate effects of farm policies. However, the commodity orientation of much of farm policy meant that work was still partial, for instance, in terms of the effects on one commodity or group. Little outstanding work was done in economic assessment of the effects on the whole of agriculture and on the whole economy of all farm policies.

A few agricultural economists had been heavily involved in the cooperative marketing efforts of the 1920s and the marketing orders and agreements of the 1930s. Their recommendations were frequently in disagreement with those of their production-oriented colleagues. Once again, part of the disagreement arose from looking at farm problems from different viewpoints, one macro, one micro. Even the macro viewpoint suffered from its own brand of myopia. In the short run, marketing controls would boost prices but lead to increased production, which would eventually depress prices.

The fact that government farm programs in the 1930s did not achieve their economic goals was due as much to the inherent conflict between goals and the absence of good economic guidelines as it was to the failure of government to apply the prevailing economic knowledge.

Key Words	Central Concepts
Static theory	Theory of market behavior at one point in time.
Demand curve or schedule	The relationship between quantity demanded and price under given conditions.
Demand shift	A new relationship between quantity demanded and price following a change in conditions—a sharp decline or increase in income.
Long-run influences	In a period longer than a year, market conditions can be expected to change. The policy analyst must be on the alert for such changes.
Atomistic competitor	Each competitor alone is too small to influence total market supply, demand, or price.
Cooperative	An association of farmers for the purpose of joint supply, production, or marketing activities. Each shares equally in ownership.
Bureaucratic approach	A separate rule for each situation or variation thereof, managed by an unwieldy and inflexible system.
Forward price	A cash price agreed on prior to time of sale or delivery.
Aggregate impact	The impact of an entire group.
Equilibrium	The stable point toward which a system leans. In price theory this is the point where the supply and demand schedules intersect.

QUESTIONS

1. Why did static market analysis fail to interpret correctly the demand problems of U.S. agriculture in the 1930s?
2. What could the Federal Farm Board have done to raise farm prices had it known the true situation?
3. What long-run influences have affected the demand for butter, sugar, fresh oranges?
4. Can atomistic competitors maximize profits other than by chance?
5. Compare "parity price" with "costs of production" as a target of agricultural policy.
6. If parity is a desirable goal, why do governments offer and farmers accept a target price below parity?
7. Explain how the farm income problem is distinct from the problem of encouraging increased production.
8. Discuss the conflicting farm-level and aggregate effects of subsidizing fertilizer inputs.
9. Why might production-oriented and marketing-oriented economists give conflicting advice?
10. Give an example of how short-run regulations may have adverse long-run effects.

ECONOMISTS COME TO GRIPS WITH THE PERSISTENT FARM PROBLEM

Despite all the efforts of government, in the 1930s the farm sector continued to have difficulty in maintaining a level of prosperity relative to other sectors of the economy. The symptoms of the disease were low prices and incomes, wildly fluctuating prices, farm foreclosures, rural depopulation, and declining demand. Many of the prominent agricultural economists of the thirties were intimately involved in formulating options for policy makers and in current criticism of specific outcomes. For example, the Brookings Institution financed a series of studies by prominent economists examining the work of the Agricultural Adjustment Agency as it affected various commodities.

Most of the economists involved in the genesis or framing of Triple-A policies, John D. Black, M. L. Wilson, Henry C. Taylor, and others, did not see their recommendations as emergency measures, but as permanent policy for adjustment of agriculture to changing economic conditions. However, no one could claim sole credit for the package of policies which eventually emerged. They had the support of the administration, Congress, the Farm Bloc, farm organizations, and most farmers. It was only when war had boosted agricultural prices to predepression levels that the Farm Bureau began to attack much of the AAA administrative machinery and that economic criticism of the entire AAA package emerged.

Critics of New Deal Policies

T. W. Schultz's book, *Redirecting Farm Policy*, has been mentioned. Schultz pinpointed the inconsistency of goals and of the means being used to achieve those goals. John D. Black of Harvard, possibly the most prestigious agricultural economist of his time, published a book eight months earlier, in May 1942, in which he too attacked the parity concept and argued that production control programs had increased neither total revenue from farm products nor net revenue. He argued that the farm income problem could be solved by reducing the number of farmers, increasing average sizes of farms, and expanding consumption. Black favored the Keynesian approach of increased government spending to avoid a postwar depression. He assumed that agriculture would fare about as well as the general economy.

In 1952, another Harvard economist, John Kenneth Galbraith, published a book *American Capitalism* with the subtitle, "The Concept of Countervailing Power," in which he gave a different insight into government's role in agriculture. Under perfect competition, he argued, market power was kept in check by competition. If firm A's price was high, a reduction in price by firm B would force firm A into line. If both firms colluded to keep prices high, excess profits would draw new entries into the market. However, for much of the economy, oligopoly, not perfect competition, was now entrenched. Oligopolists did not compete by price, but by nonprice methods. Their power could not be controlled by antitrust methods or by government takeover.

Fortunately, where sellers get power, there is a tendency for buyers to get countervailing or offsetting power. Strong corporations induce strong unions; strong manufacturers induce retailers to grow strong. Countervailing power does not arise naturally in the case of either vertical integration or weak, numerous firms, and it works worst in times of excess demand or inflation. Where it does not work, government can do much to make it work. In fact, much of the AAA legislation, the Wagner Act, minimum wage laws, etc., are designed to give some weak group countervailing power.

In a special chapter on agriculture, Galbraith maintained that farmers had sought countervailing power by (1) breaking the market power of others, such as the Grangers, antitrust; (2) strengthening their own power, as with the cooperative movement; and (3) inducing inflation, by support of silver coinage, etc. All had failed. Only government aid could give agriculture the needed countervailing power.

George B. Stigler, in a famous article entitled rather sarcastically "The Economist Plays with Blocs," claimed that Galbraith's ideas were not "theory" but "dogma," lacking empirical evidence and internally inconsistent. Undaunted by the difficulties of collecting convincing empirical evidence, Galbraith has continued to theorize about the relevance (and frequent ignoring) of the role of power in economics. During the same period, farmers have continued to be concerned about their lack of market power, in particular where its main exercise by large buyers, in Galbraith's words, is "in keeping the seller in a state of uncertainty as to the intentions of a buyer who is indispensable to him." Extensive efforts have been made to get Congress to pass legislation giving groups of farmers power to bargain so that the results of the bargaining would become binding on all producers of the relevant commodity and on the other parties to the bargaining. A model act for fruits and vegetables was passed by the Michigan legislature in 1972, but high farm prices thereafter took much of the steam out of national efforts to get a federal bargaining bill passed.

Despite Galbraith's efforts, the mainstream of agricultural economic thought, perhaps best represented by T. W. Schultz in his 1945 book *Agriculture in an Unstable Economy*, and his 1953 work *The Economic Organization of Agriculture*, continued to see agriculture's problems in terms of inefficient use of resources which could best be corrected by recourse to the free market. If proper monetary and fiscal policies for the whole economy were followed, there should be no need for emergency measures (as in the 1930s) to rescue agriculture. Some of the Schultzian ideas were included in the ill-fated effort of Secretary of Agriculture Brannan to replace the AAA network of carrots and sticks with direct income payments.

The Agricultural Treadmill

Professor W. W. Cochrane, in his 1958 book *Farm Prices, Myth and Reality*, took issue with the theory that agriculture was self-adjusting, either alone or with government aid. To support his thesis he dipped into essentially the same intellectual tradition as Schultz but came up with different answers. He defined the farm problem as both an income problem and an uncertainty problem. The income problem derives from the generally low level of farm prices; the uncertainty problem from the erratic changes in price of individual commodities. Cochrane used comparisons of incomes of commercial farmers with nonfarm income as evidence of relatively low incomes in agriculture. Unstable prices of many commodities represent the uncertainty problem. Cochrane went on to show that the aggregate demand for food was highly inelastic and the aggregate supply also highly inelastic (Figure 4.5). Due to technology, the supply curve tended to move to the right more rapidly than the demand curve,

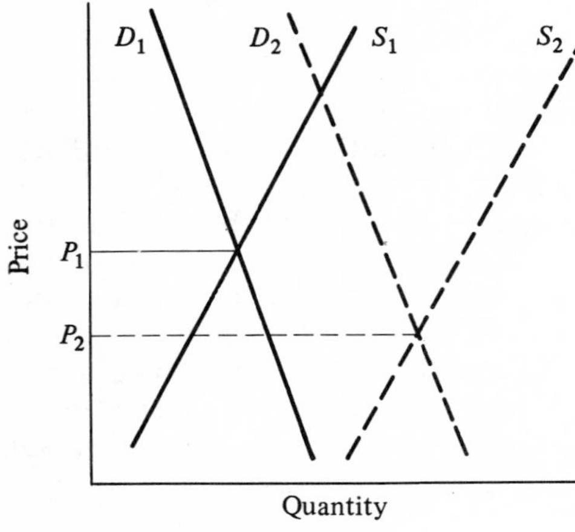

Fig. 4.5. Hypothetical position and shifts over time in the aggregate supply and demand curves for U.S. agricultural products.

leading to a downward drift of price. The reason why farmers do not obey the free market principle of cutting back production when prices fall is related to their method of adopting new technology. Farmers are of three types with respect to new technology: (1) early adopters, (2) followers, and (3) laggards. The *early adopters* gain cost savings or income increases from the new technology. The *followers* imitate them, but gain less as increased output depresses all market prices. The *laggards* are forced to adopt the new technology in order to survive. By this time, returns to the early adopters are back to where they started. They set off in hot pursuit of the next new technology, which *may* give them a brief advantage. This process of great activity to reach the same spot he called "the agricultural treadmill."

Cochrane concluded that, in light of his theories, past policy prescriptions had led agriculture down blind alleys. He foresaw that the public would no longer support expensive farm programs. His solution was mandatory supply control, limiting entry into production and adjusting the supply of each commodity to expected demand each year. Each farmer would in fact be given a share of a national sales quota. Cochrane did not have to wait long for an opportunity to promote his proposals at the highest levels of government. In 1960, he became chief economic adviser to Agriculture Secretary Orville Freeman in the Kennedy administration.

Key Words	Central Concepts
Countervailing power	The development of market power by one group tends to induce development of offsetting (countervailing) power in a rival group; big business–big unions.
Oligopoly	A market characterized by few sellers.
Inflation	An increase in the general price level.
Market power	Ability to influence supply, demand, or price.
Bargaining power	Ability to secure influence over terms of an exchange.
Brannan plan	Plan by Secretary of Agriculture Brannan to replace price supports for agriculture with direct payments. The plan was ignored by a hostile Congress.
Agricultural treadmill	Great activity by U.S. agriculture to stay at the same low level of income.
Mandatory supply control	Compulsory control by government.

QUESTIONS

1. Distinguish between the price, income, and uncertainty problems of U.S. agriculture.

2. Why did the American Farm Bureau change its mind about AAA policies for U.S. agriculture?
3. Did boosts to the general economy help agriculture in the 1930s?
4. Discuss the weakness of the theory of countervailing power.
5. Should farmers have the power to compel processors to bargain with a recognized farmer bargaining group?
6. Schultz and Cochrane made conflicting diagnoses and suggested different remedies for the problems of U.S. agriculture. Discuss.
7. How does adoption of new technology by agriculture differ from adoption of new products by consumers?
8. Could mandatory supply control ever work in U.S. agriculture?

THE PATIENT MAY NOT RECOVER

Cochrane's theory of the agricultural treadmill was a denial of the self-equilibrating power which a perfectly competitive sector should have. Many farm leaders and farm economists accepted his thesis that the competitive nature of agriculture, combined with a fatal affection for new technology, led it to overproduction and to chronic price and income problems. Had this not been the experience in the years prior to publication of Cochrane's book? About the same time, a number of studies suggested that a dismantling of farm programs and a return to the "free" market would drastically reduce farm prices and income. The patient's disease was diagnosed as "chronic disequilibrium." Cochrane offered one diagnosis and proposed the cure. Others were to follow.

Dale E. Hathaway, in his book *Government in Agriculture*, was particularly critical of Cochrane's treadmill theory. "The analysis," he said, ". . . appears to explain too much with too little, is not completely internally consistent, and is not always consistent with the observed facts." Hathaway did not think the theory was generally valid for all agriculture. Saying that an industry is competitive does not explain why farmers would continue to expand use of fertilizer, chemicals, etc., unless the expected revenue would exceed cost. On internal consistency, Hathaway insisted that Cochrane at one point claimed the adoption of technology would continue with either rising or falling prices, at another point that they would not do so in hard times. In terms of consistency with the observed facts, Cochrane did not account for the increased use of purchased inputs in agriculture—an equally powerful source of increased output. In addition to Hathaway's comments, further research has not demonstrated that leaders, followers, and laggards adopt farm technology in the neat, related sequence suggested by Cochrane. Cochrane's thesis, however, was politically acceptable to the needs of the day and gave intellectual respectability to the Kennedy administration's drive for mandatory controls on output.

The Theory of Asset Fixity

One of its most serious intellectual challenges was from the theory of asset fixity developed by Glenn L. Johnson, popularized in Hathaway's widely read textbook and further extended by later writers. In essence, the theory of asset fixity suggests that within a cerain range of changes in product prices, the farmer will not alter his use of fixed inputs, so that production will not be responsive to such price changes. Johnson tended to blame agriculture's problems on imperfections in factor markets as opposed to Cochrane's belief that the perfectly competitive environment of agriculture was a prime source of disequilibrium.

In his treatment of asset fixity, Hathaway pointed out that an asset has not just one price but two, its acquisition cost and its (usually lower) salvage value. A new unit of the asset will be added in production when marginal value product (MVP) exceeds acquisition price (P_A). A unit will be sold when MVP falls below salvage value P_S. However, the owner of either four, five, or six units of the asset in our example (Figure 4.6) falls under neither of those cases. A farmer who in a past season acquired four units of the asset can get more from using the fourth unit than from salvaging it. The fourth unit is in this sense trapped in production. The trap arises because product demand, and hence the MVP for each input, frequently shifts during the life of the input. The individual farmer may face MVP_1 when national crop is small and price high and MVP_2 when national crop is large and price depressed (Figure 4.7). Acquisition price and salvage value, being dictated outside agriculture by machinery companies, tractor dealers, etc., tend to remain stable or increase slowly. Hence, product price fluctuations which trap resources are not counteracted by offsetting forces.

This theory has interesting implications for the normal production theory when two or more inputs are combined. Hathaway demonstrates a case where both inputs are fixed. In that case, there are four possible points where the price lines can be tangent to the iso-value-product curves. Over the whole range of production this gives rise to four possible lines of expansion, depending on which

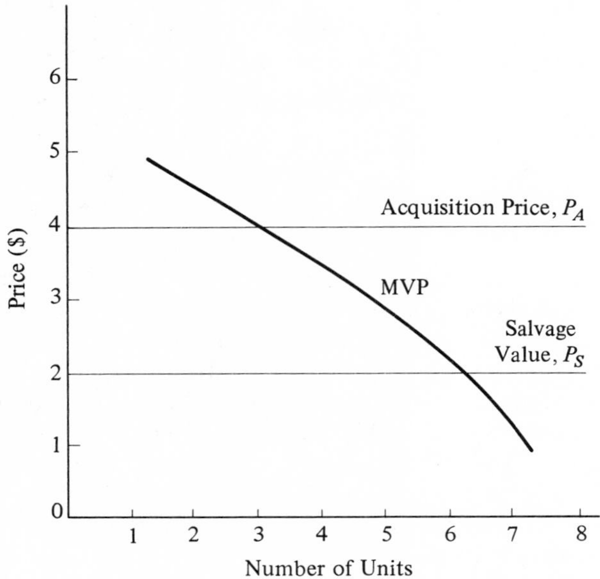

Fig. 4.6. Relationship of acquisition price, salvage value, and marginal value product for an asset employed in agriculture.

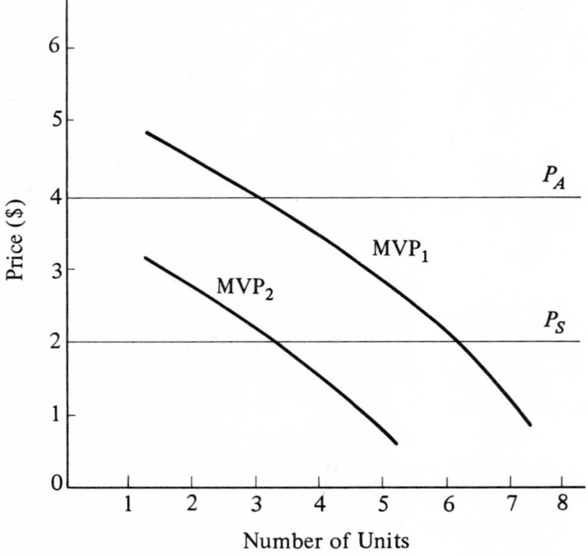

Fig. 4.7. How a decline in marginal value product traps assets in agriculture.

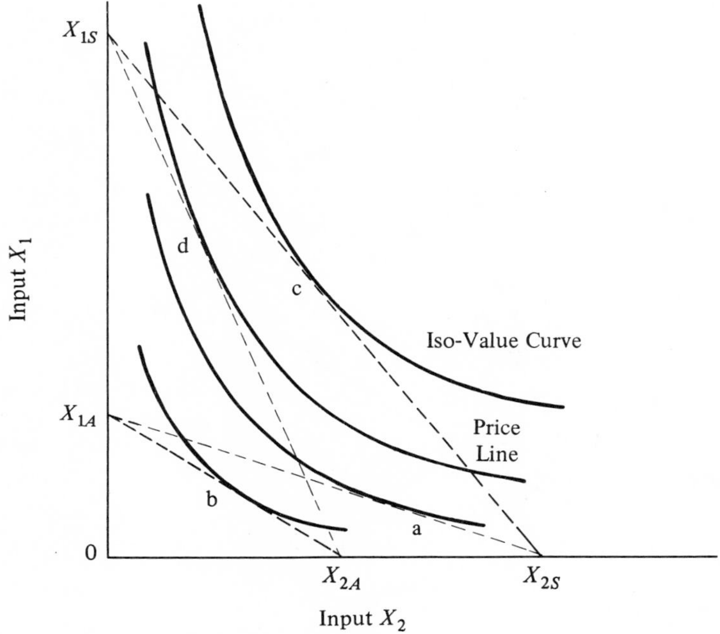

Fig. 4.8. Iso-value curves and price lines for a firm or industry employing two inputs.

price guide the producer follows. Figure 4.8 gives the situation for a given level of farm resources. Acquisition prices would lead a farmer to produce at b, salvage values at c. For different levels of resources, the corresponding expansion paths are shown in Figure 4.9. The high profit point on line c will always be above b with a and d at intermediate levels of output. Fixed asset theory suggests that it is difficult for the producer to operate at the maximum point on line b. Output will tend to be greater.

Hathaway further showed how to use the theory to determine profitable level of usage of two inputs (say X_1 and X_2). Both inputs face the same phenomenon—that MVP will equal acquisition price at a lower level of usage than where it equals salvage value (Figure 4.6). If we plot both inputs on one diagram we can draw a line e at the level of use of X_1 where MVP equals salvage value and a line f where MVP equals acquisition price (Figure 4.10). We can draw comparable lines, h and g for X_2. Our production surface is now divided into nine regions numbered in Roman numerals. From the way these regions are defined, we can make the following recommendations to a farmer whose present input mix is in a given region.

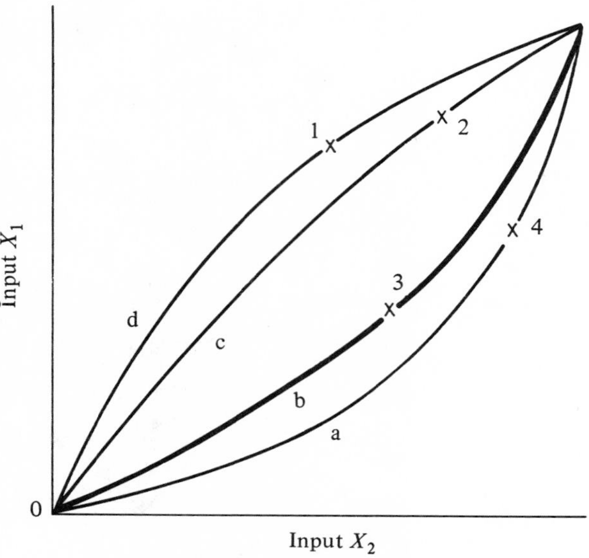

Fig. 4.9. Alternative expansion paths for a firm or industry employing two inputs.

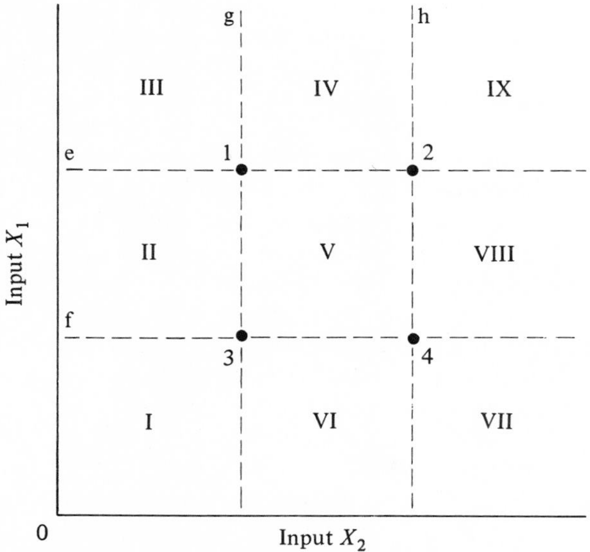

Fig. 4.10. Map of production surface for a firm or industry employing two inputs.

I Expand use of both inputs
II Expand use of X_2
III Expand use of X_2, reduce use of X_1
IV Reduce use of X_1
V No change will increase profits
VI Expand use of X_1
VII Expand use of X_1, reduce use of X_2
VIII Reduce use of X_2
IX Reduce use of both inputs

If a farmer were operating at point 3, where MVP of both outputs equals acquisition price, resources in agriculture would be earning the same as similar resources elsewhere, and the optimal resource allocation of perfect competition would exist. Region V is unique in that even though both inputs are earning less than acquisition costs, no change would occur, and the trapped resources would continue to earn less than they would elsewhere in the economy.

Point 3 is the only point where MVP equals acquisition price—where agriculture can be said to be in equilibrium. In Region V, though not at equilibrium, operations have no tendency to move toward equilibrium. Agriculture is in disequilibrium. In other sections the optimum adjustment may increase output even though one or more inputs are earning less than acquisition cost, or are producing above equilibrium output. Once again agriculture is in persistent disequilibrium.

The acceptability of the theory, Hathaway says, depends on whether acquisition cost and salvage value actually differ for enterprises on a farm, for a total farm, or for agriculture. He finds evidence of this for on-farm durables (trees, fences, etc.), off-farm durables (machinery, vehicles), farm-produced durables (breeding herds), labor, land, farm-produced nondurables (hay, etc.), and nonfarm-produced nondurables (fertilizers, sprays). Fixity of assets will be greatest for the agricultural industry in total, next for the farm in total, and least for individual enterprises. Hence, the aggregate supply curve may be quite inelastic, while commodity supply is more elastic.

Key Words	Central Concepts
Chronic problems	Persistent problems for which there are no apparent remedies.
Chronic disequilibrium	A market persistently removed from and unable to return to equilibrium.
Internal consistency	Absence of conflict within the parts of a theory.

Asset fixity	Assets staying in production even though their marginal value product is below their price.
Factor markets	Markets for inputs such as labor, fertilizer, etc.
Acquisition price	Purchase price of a new item.
Salvage price	Sale price of a used item.
Iso-value-product curves	Lines linking combinations of inputs which produce output of equal value.
Optimal allocation	The allocation that meets the goal of maximizing benefits to society. The marginal value product will equal the price of each input at this optimum point.
Durables	Goods whose services can be enjoyed for more than one time period.
Elasticity	The relative response of one variable to changes in another, for example, the response of output to changes in price of a product.

QUESTIONS

1. Could the theories of the agricultural treadmill and of asset fixity be true simultaneously?
2. How and why do resources become fixed in agriculture?
3. Why might the price of tractors *not* fall even though the demand for tractors fell?
4. Could sudden large product price increases find agriculture utilizing too few inputs?
5. How could a farmer determine the acquisition price and salvage price of a combine harvester?
6. Choose any two inputs. Develop a numerical example of the concepts illustrated in Figures 4.6 through 4.10.

LOCKED-IN PROBLEMS

The theories of the fifties and sixties depicted a U.S. agricultural industry in one way or another locked into persistent problems. In general, the criticisms of these theories have concentrated on broadening their range of application to the real world of the 1960s.

For example, Luther Tweeten, in his 1970 book, *Foundations of Farm Policy*, elaborated Johnson's model of asset fixity to take account of both objective and subjective elements of factor response to price. Using farm labor as an example he specified four (rather than two) prices relevant to the decision maker (Figure 4.11):

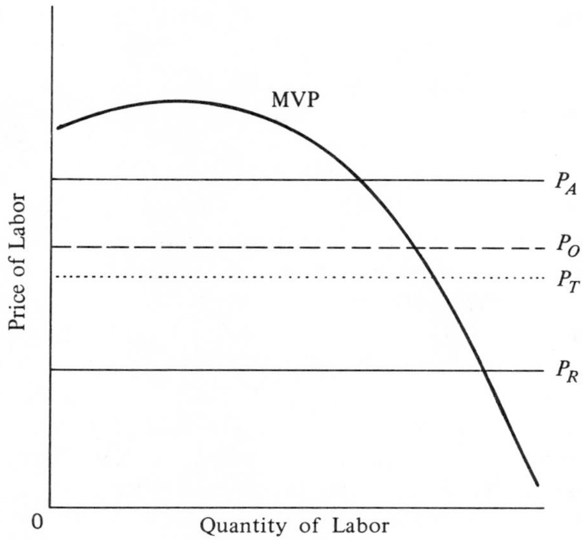

Fig. 4.11. Marginal value product and alternative prices of labor.

P_A Acquisition price equals farm wage rate

P_O Salvage price equals opportunity cost in other employment

P_T Salvage price minus the cost of transferring to other employment

P_R Reservation price, below which returns in agriculture must fall before farmers will give up their way of life

One can readily visualize circumstances where not just salvage price but salvage price adjusted for transfer costs or reservation price will be the trigger that persuades farm labor to leave farming. For example, farmers' love for the land is part of U.S. folklore. Farming has gotten under their skin. Hence, the concept of a reservation price is also known as the "endodermal" hypothesis. However, it is a different matter to show that folklore is a correct explanation of the decisions of a large number of farmers or farm laborers.

Tweeten re-examined the fixity of farm resources in terms of (1) their durability and (2) their relationship to MVP. His conclusions about the fixity of the five main categories of farm resources were:

Financial resources: Currency, bank deposits, bonds, etc., can be easily transferred out of agriculture.

Operating capital: Fertilizer, fuel, seeds, etc., are usually consumed within one season and thus have low fixity.

Durable capital: Farm machinery, tractors, etc., have a salvage value which tends to fall more rapidly than their productivity, but productivity itself can be expected to fall one-fifth in four years, so that even durable capital is not permanently fixed.

Real estate: Undoubtedly it has great fixity in the agricultural industry and in many cases low salvage value for other uses. However, one cannot blame real estate fixity for excess capacity and low returns. Its price is largely dependent on economic conditions in agriculture. So the MVP and price of real estate are affected by common factors.

Labor: As shown in Figure 4.11, labor may be fixed in agriculture within the range of prices P_A to P_R. Many studies show labor remaining in agriculture when its MVP is clearly below the current nonfarm wage rate. This situation may be due to inadequate information on nonfarm job opportunities, to the inefficiency of the nonfarm labor market in absorbing surplus farm labor, to subjective preference for life on the farm, or to discrimination against farm labor in other labor markets. Undoubtedly, certain types of farm labor, such as older, less skilled farmers away from developed urban labor markets, can be trapped in agriculture, as the asset fixity theory would suggest.

However, as Tweeten points out, asset fixity may explain "the lack of annual variation in farm input in the face of fluctuating prices but does not explain the 'nonexistent' secular low returns on farm resources." Some economists have argued that the real problems of agriculture are shortage of education and low absolute returns, not surplus of inputs and low relative returns. Because they lack the education, skill, and training needed in nonfarm labor markets, the opportunity cost of farmers in other occupations may be much lower than economists have argued. Labor markets may, in fact, be quite efficient, as evidenced by the considerable mobility of farm labor. Tweeten argues that the truth lies somewhere between the two alternative hypotheses. In addition, as more labor leaves agriculture, the remaining labor will tend to be less fixed by external market forces than by its own innate quality.

Chronic Disequilibrium

Hathaway, of course, was not willing to accept the theory of asset fixity as sufficient "to explain the large and persistent disequilibrium in output and earnings which is almost unique to agriculture." It required, he said, a combination of five factors to cause this unique situation:

1. U.S. agriculture faces a highly inelastic demand for its products.
2. Its products have a low income elasticity.
3. It experiences rapid rates of technological change which lead to output increases.
4. Its competitive structure leaves it vulnerable to price and income slumps.
5. Asset fixity tends to prolong these slumps because resources do not move out of the industry rapidly.

"The observed changes in United States agriculture in the post-World War II period appear to be consistent with the interaction that would be expected," said Hathaway. However, factors outside agriculture play a key role in determining *how fixed* resources may be, for example, nonfarm wages, fertilizer prices, new technologies. Once resources are fixed, they tend to lead to low earnings or capital losses. The conclusion one can draw is that remedial policies must take into account both farm and nonfarm factors affecting the farm problem. Among other goals, Hathaway stressed the crucial importance of full employment, the improvement of the mobility of farm labor through education, removing the output-increasing effects of price supports, and better research and extension information on farm problems, if these problems were to be alleviated. He did not, as had Cochrane, advance a ready made, guaranteed new farm policy.

WILL THE OLD PROBLEMS RETURN?

The passage of time and changed economic circumstances have moved the economic debate about farm problems out of the areas of greatest concern to Schultz, Galbraith, Cochrane, and Hathaway. In particular, the expansion of international demand has lessened the immediate need for implementation of the price support–production control programs and the fear of difficulties in adjusting to a free market. The chief question one must ask about the agricultural economy in the mid-1970s is whether it has moved to a new era or whether agricultural prosperity is always a temporary aberration in an otherwise unchanged situation. It is not difficult to visualize future situations in which the old arguments about whether agriculture is or is not competitive and self-equilibrating would be fought out among a new generation of economists.

The experiences of 1972 through 1976 suggest that U.S. agriculture temporarily solved the general farm income problem, but that greater dependence on international demand may tend to increase, not decrease, the uncertainty problem. Export demand for U.S. agricultural products tends to be buoyed by major worldwide growth in purchasing power and by favorable currency revaluations and increases in the raw product prices (gold, oil, copper, sisal) of our major customers. However, it is equally threatened by any reversal in purchasing power.

However, even consistently high farm prices are no guarantee of consistently high net farm incomes. High farm prices mean prices of farm inputs tend to be bid up. General price inflation reinforces this trend. Outputs of one farm may also be inputs to another farm. Costs rise more rapidly than prices so that net farm income falls as it has in many previous booms. If prices fall due to an excess of supply over demand, as did cattle prices in 1974, farmers find themselves back with the more familiar problems of surpluses, cost–price squeezes, and low returns. A period of prosperity in the grain economy may be one of depression in the livestock economy, and vice versa. In summary, very dramatic economic developments can influence but not remove permanently the income and uncertainty problems in agriculture.

Agricultural Economists Reappraise Themselves

The decade of the 1960s saw no great new theory of agricultural policy emerge. However, as in its other activities, the agricultural economics profession turned its talents to quantifying and testing empirically some of the theories and hypotheses which had been developed by earlier writers. If one could summarize such a large body of work in a few words, one might say that both the limitations and the strengths of past theories were exposed and questioned. It no longer became fashionable to expect *one* theory to explain a large and complex industry.

A large body of programming models, many emanating from Iowa State University and the Center for Agricultural and Rural Development (CARD, formerly CAED) there, tapped the increasing capacity of computers to simulate the operations of U.S. agriculture under various types of government programs. Almost all these models were unanimous in predicting sharp declines in U.S. agricultural prices if supply control programs were abandoned and agriculture returned to the free market.

However, the agricultural economics profession slipped into the error of believing its mathematical models because these had been able to expose some of the errors of previous theories. The mathematical models were simplified abstractions of the real world. They could be rendered inaccurate in prediction by a change in importance of a factor not given sufficient weight in the original model. Some very prestigious forecasting models failed dismally to predict the sharp price and income swings in U.S. agriculture after 1972. In response, the agricultural economics profession made great efforts to improve the concepts, scope, and accuracy of its mathematical models, to reduce the uncertainty surrounding options open to policy makers. Only time will tell how successful policy analysts have been in their revised, more sophisticated prognostications about the future.

Key Words	Central Concepts
Reservation price	If farmers do not get this price (wage) they will withdraw their labor.
Endodermal hypothesis	Farming has gotten under their skin.
Low absolute returns	The actual dollar returns to labor in farming are low.
Low relative returns	Returns to labor in farming have been low relative to returns to comparable labor in other industries. This does not seem to be true under modern conditions.
Inelastic demand	A percentage change in price of a product leads to a smaller percentage change in the opposite direction in the quantity demanded. Conversely, a percentage change in the quantity placed on the market leads to a proportionately greater change in price in the opposite direction.
Income elasticity	The relative response of quantity demanded to a percentage change in income. If income in the U.S. grows at 4 percent per year and the income elasticity for food is 0.2, the income effect will increase demand for food by (4 times 0.2) 0.8 percent per year.
Currency revaluation	A change in the official rate of exchange of a currency in terms of other currencies.
Mathematical model	Simplified representation of an economic system where levels and relationships are measured numerically.

QUESTIONS

1. Could the theory of asset fixity be applied to small retailers? to private homeowners?

2. Can you recall an acquaintance who chose to stay in the same post though offered a better paying job elsewhere? Describe the situation. Is this an example of the "endodermal hypothesis"?
3. In what ways does an aging tractor become less productive?
4. Can we blame real estate fixity for low net returns in agriculture?
5. Search for statistical evidence (census data, population studies) that farm labor lacks education, skill, and training relative to nonfarm labor.
6. When demand is inelastic, an increase in price will increase gross revenue. What will happen to net revenue? Give examples.
7. How is a national full employment policy related to the problem of asset fixity in agriculture?
8. Give an example of the output increasing effect of price supports.
9. Can agricultural prosperity ever become permanent? What does past experience suggest?
10. Is the agricultural economics profession subject to fads in its policy analyses, that is, sudden bursts of interest in a topic and equally sudden losses of interest?
11. What have been the most permanent concerns of analysts of U.S. agricultural policy?
12. Why are economic phenomena so difficult to predict?

A BRIEF GUIDE TO U.S. AGRICULTURAL POLICIES

Policy Targets, Beneficiaries, and Goals

Agricultural policies have proliferated and been amended, rescinded, and restored as times and administrations have changed. Before examining any one policy in detail it is instructive to take a brief tour through the main types of policies with which the U.S. has experimented. This will be particularly informative if the student attempts to trace through the likely effects of each type of policy on supply, demand, price equilibrium, countervailing power, price and income uncertainty, and evidence of chronic disequilibrium in agriculture. Almost all the programs to be discussed were based on the common underlying assumption that government intervention was necessary and desirable in agricultural economic affairs. The nature and extent of that intervention would, of course, differ between programs. Intervention would draw on the finances, personnel, and authority of the federal government where a vacuum existed in the private sector. The government would aid, not replace, private enterprise. The essential character of U.S. agriculture would thus remain unchanged.

While the language of most farm legislation has made it clear that the farmer was intended as the primary beneficiary of agricultural policies, the consumer's interests have also been a factor. The relative emphasis has tended to shift more strongly toward the consumer at certain periods (severe depression or high farm prices) and in certain types of legislation (food stamp programs, consumer subsidies, etc.). The interests of other beneficiaries, although real, have rarely been spelled out explicitly in the legislation. A few recurring goals run through the decades: (1) parity of prices and incomes for farmers with nonfarmers, (2) preserving the family farm, (3) relief from hunger and malnutrition at home and abroad, (4) stabilization of prices and incomes, (5) strengthening farmer bargaining power, (6) conservation of the land, (7) a farmer voice in the programs under which he would operate, (8) protecting consumer purchasing power, and (9) preference for domestic producers in the domestic market.

Major Classes of Agricultural Policy

Most farm policies since 1933 have come into law through the tedious congressional process, with its vulnerability to special interest pressure at every turn. Another group of policies has become operational by presidential fiat, frequently in times of specific emergencies. Finally, a number of policies depend for their legitimacy on legislation passed prior to 1933. There is not a single, integrated U.S. farm policy; instead a series of policies exists, piled one upon the other and often inconsistent in intent and effect. While the government may have its right foot on the throttle, at the same time it may have its left foot on the brake. Major types of policies and the systems developed to implement them have been:

1. *Price supports*: These have usually taken the form of government readiness to loan money on harvested crops at some minimum acceptable level. Loans are available to those who cooperate in other supply control or acreage conservation programs. The farmer remains free to sell in the market at prevailing prices. Government also on occasion has purchased supplies on the open market to meet aid or relief needs *and* help boost prices. In turn, government manipulation of stocks has frequently been blamed and occasionally been responsible for lowering market price to enforce compliance.

2. *Supply control*: Supply has been controlled primarily by inducing farmers to reduce planted acreage through loan guarantees or direct pay-

ments. Conservation has been used as justification for many acreage reduction programs. Acreage allotments have been allocated on the basis of farmers' previous production patterns. The ability of farmers to increase yields more rapidly than acreage was reduced often led to the need for a further escalation of supply controls. Marketing quotas were frequently used in addition to acreage controls when output was excessive. In 1956, farmers were encouraged to take some of their allotment land out of production and put it into the soil bank (either in an acreage reserve or in a conservation reserve).

3. *Marketing orders and agreements*: Marketing agreements to control the volume and timing of shipments to market were part of the original 1933 AAA. California experimented with such agreements successfully. The legislation governing most existing marketing orders and agreements was passed in 1937. Either can be instituted after a vote by participating farmers and with the approval of the secretary of agriculture. Agreements are binding only on the signatories—orders on all growers and handlers in the areas concerned. Orders may contain provisions for regulation of quality (grades, sizes, etc.), quantity, surplus control, unfair trade practices, containers, research, and promotion. Marketing orders have tended to be strongest on promotion and weakest on quantity control. They have been particularly important in dairy products and in fruits and vegetables.

4. *Trade restrictions*: Import quotas, tariffs, prohibitions, custom and health requirements, shipping regulations, etc., have been used since the mercantilist era to protect domestic agriculture or aid it in export sales. Most trade restrictions refer to foreign suppliers. However, they are occasionally used to block regional product movements. A feature of recent trade restrictions has been the exercise of presidential authority to control exports and reduce domestic prices.

5. *Soil conservation*: Historical accident played a major role in winning for conservation such a prominent place in U.S. agricultural policy. The Dust Bowl era of the 1930s drew attention to a real problem of many midwest farmers. The overthrow of the first Agricultural Adjustment Act led to the adoption of soil conservation in the 1936 Soil Conservation and Domestic Allotment Act as the device for securing acreage controls on commodities in excess supply. Always possessed with strong emotional appeal, soil conservation has found a new impetus in the modern concern over the environment and nonrenewable resources.

6. *Supply utilization programs*: These overlap both price support and consumer welfare programs. However, many are of a special nature such as emergency international relief, Red Cross programs, etc. Some aspects of the Marshall Plan (to help war-damaged countries to economic

recovery after World War II) and the PL480 (food for peace) programs were also conveniently designed to utilize supplies of surplus foods.

7. *Consumer welfare programs*: These have had a number of goals: to alleviate distress, fight chronic malnutrition, protect children's health, overcome temporary or permanent poverty, etc. They have frequently proceeded by moving surplus commodities outside normal trade channels. Such programs have included direct food distribution and the school lunch, subsidized milk, and food stamp programs. The latter three were originally instituted on a small scale but have reached their greatest level in the last decade.

8. *Exports*: One of the most effective means of removing supplies from normal market channels is to ship them abroad. This has been pursued in a number of ways: (a) by commercial sales, (b) by export subsidies, (c) by two-tier pricing, (d) through long-term loans to foreign purchasers, (e) through outright gifts, and (f) by barter sales for needed raw materials. Section 32 funds (from the 1935 amendments to the first AAA) can be used to aid export sales. The PL480 program, instituted in 1954, included a number of the above approaches to exporting. Subsequent administrations have used long-term credits to stimulate major export sales.

9. *Special government arrangements*: These have tended to arise where other countries have a major interest in the U.S. domestic farm policies. Examples might be the International Wheat Agreement and certain aspects of the sugar program. Most special arrangements tend eventually to become a part of regular farm policy and a precedent for similar action in other commodities.

10. *Science and technology*: Government maintains a very extensive team of scientists and research laboratories throughout the country examining means of bringing the benefits of scientific and technological discoveries to agriculture. The results are brought to farmers through the extension service and the Soil Conservation Service and by books, pamphlets, radio, and television.

11. *Infrastructure*: Government provides the basis for more productive economic activity through aids to rural electrification and other utilities, highways, provision of credit and crop insurance, market information and regulation, etc. Much of this infrastructure policy was conceived when farmers were numerous and yet too small to help themselves.

Appraisal of Major Policies

Agricultural policy, now in its fifth decade since 1933, has had many targets, potential beneficiaries, and specific goals. How have the main classes of policies fared in meeting the aims of their sponsors? There is little evidence that price supports have been effective for very long in approximating price equilibrium or in reducing income uncertainty. However, by their nature, they have tended to reduce price uncertainty, while the dollar benefits have accrued mostly to larger farmers. Price supports have had a tendency to approach equilibrium with a lag, but, in general, consumers have not been penalized and have probably enjoyed greater supplies than under free market equilibrium. Other than times of war or international emergency (for example, a world food scare), price supports have been ineffective in ensuring parity. They have, in turn, probably induced some overuse of resources in agriculture relative to the rest of the economy.

Supply control has been ineffective largely because the legislation has avoided mandatory controls, and has used a "carrot-and-stick" approach to encourage reduced acreage. At the same time, price supports and loan rates paid per unit of commodity have been a direct incentive to increase the application of other inputs to the reduced acreage until diminishing returns set in. In the years since 1933, marginal returns have tended to increase as the quality of inputs increased. Supply has not been successfully controlled. However, the stock of land has been kept at a high level of productivity. The acreage control approach has encouraged the use of new technology. As a result, U.S. agriculture has been able to react quickly when national or international needs required it.

Marketing orders and agreements have been effective in the short run in increasing the bargaining power of farmers. However, in the long run, the increased supply response has often offset any price gains due to marketing order provisions, because marketing order committees and the secretary of agriculture have avoided direct quantity control and, in particular, limitations on entry into production. Marketing orders suffer the weakness of all attempts at monopoly when substitute products exist. Processors can switch from order to nonorder states, consumers from order to nonorder products. Many observers see the greatest value of present orders as the statistics they generate (a valuable aid to efficient marketing) and the opportunity they offer for individual farmers to enjoy some of the strength of a common organization.

Trade restrictions tend to raise costs to consumers and raise returns to producers, again in the short run. In a system such as that of the EEC, where all agricultural products may be covered by trade restrictions which are closely linked with other agricultural policies, it is difficult for consumers to escape the added costs by substituting other agricultural products. However, in the U.S., where domestic agricultural and foreign trade policies are selective, substitution can take place. Much of the effectiveness of dairy price supports and trade protection have been circumvented by the switch to use of margarine and other milk product substitutes, although there have been some ineffective attempts to hinder this substitution by legislation.

Soil conservation programs have often been regarded as boondoggles for farmers—which, in fact, they have been. But they have been more. They have permitted and encouraged improvement of the national farm plant and farm reserve. They also set an easy precedent for agriculture in meeting more recent national concerns about scarce natural resources and environmental and ecological issues. Conservation in its effects has been similar to other government efforts to improve the infrastructure of rural America. For it is only when the quality of basic inputs is improved that a farm or community can expect increased production or consumption possibilities. Needs, costs, and benefits, like other infrastructures, must be constantly reassessed. Even highway miles and electrical generating plants have a point of diminishing marginal returns to society.

Supply utilization programs in their many guises have provided some relief to an overproductive agriculture. They have two main limitations. First, whether the food and fiber is given away to distant developing nations or to neighborhood American schools, someone (usually the government) must bear the cost of production and distribution. Taxpayers will only endure such costs for so long before rebelling. Second, it is extremely difficult to prevent giveaways either at home or abroad from depressing the market for local producers. The larger the scale of such giveaways, the more likely they are to disrupt local markets. Here again, there is a limit to how much charity producers can bear.

Special government arrangements with other nations on agricultural products have tended to be to the advantage of the United States during the U.S.'s period of economic and political hegemony, 1945–65. For example, the U.S. sugar program, by use of a quota system, artificially raised consumer prices of sugar in the United States to subsidize a domestic sugar-beet production and processing industry and rather arbitrarily allocated its sugar-cane needs over a number of developing countries. The sugar program was permitted to lapse in 1974, just when the developing countries were pressing for a series of world agreements to stabilize prices of raw products at a high level. Given the changed circumstances in the U.S. since 1965, neither U.S. consumers nor producers are confident that such international agreements will continue to be to their benefit.

Science and technology have been seen both as the heroes that allowed U.S. consumers to spend a lower average share of their income on food than any other people in the world, and also as the ogres which caused excess production and depressed prices to farmers. Tweeten has argued that "public policies to expand farm output through research and other means have not depressed farm gross receipts as much as many economists have supposed. It means that research and other efforts to raise farming efficiency have kept the U.S. competitive in foreign markets, and without these efforts export volume and export earnings would have been much lower." In other words, we cannot afford *not* to utilize new science and technology in agriculture.

So far this discussion has not revealed many benefits to consumers from agricultural programs. Even the large and controversial food stamp program, while helping some consumers, may bid up the price of food for all consumers. Direct provision of food to consumers may help to alleviate hunger and malnutrition, if access to food is the critical factor. However, it is clear that many other factors—culture, habit, lack of good dietary information, preparation time and facilities, etc.—are obstacles to improvements in nutritional standards. A system designed to boost demand for farm products is not geared to serve such needs.

This brief survey would be incomplete without drawing attention to some of the problems of agriculture which government has overlooked or neglected. Farm programs have tended to concentrate on land and commodities and not on personal needs. Despite rhetorical protests, families in farming declined dramatically. The displaced farmers, farm workers, and rural poor have usually been left to fend for themselves. The disproportionate benefit of most programs to the surviving larger operators has not been corrected. Agriculture has failed to win countervailing power in an economy of giants. The health of rural communities, which has been closely related to the welfare of farmers, has been tackled only fitfully. The official policies themselves may have had an impact quite opposite to their publicly stated objectives and contradictory to that of other national legislation. The lack of a uniform and internally consistent national policy for farmers has been frequently apparent.

Key Words	Central Concepts
Primary beneficiary	Most agricultural policy was designed primarily to help farmers.
Stabilization	Limiting variation in prices or incomes. It has proven difficult to agree on an acceptable range of variation. In addition,

	stabilizing prices does not stabilize income unless production is stabilized.
Domestic preference	Trade barriers designed to give U.S. producers an advantage over foreign competitors in the U.S. market.
Presidential fiat	Under the constitution and through enabling legislation of Congress, the president has power to give specific orders or make rulings on many issues.
Import quotas	Limits on the quantity of a product that may be imported.
Import tariffs	Absolute or percentage of value (ad valorem) taxes on imported goods.
Marshall Plan	Named after General George Marshall, this plan to help restore war-torn Europe was a model for much subsequent U.S. foreign aid.
Infrastructure	The facilities and services (roads, railroads, communications, etc.) which are prerequisite for a national industrial and commercial system.
Food stamps	Low income persons may buy food stamps of a given face value from the government at a discount. The lower the income, the larger the discount. Food stamps are accepted by stores as equivalent to currency. The government pays the discount.

QUESTIONS

1. Can government intervene to help agriculture without asserting control over some of its activities?
2. Give examples of congressional language suggesting that one goal of farm programs was to help consumers.
3. In what ways do farmers have a voice in farm programs?
4. Give examples of formation of agricultural policy by presidential fiat?
5. How do price support and supply utilization programs interact?
6. How do supply control and soil conservation programs interact?
7. Compare expenditures by the Red Cross and other private organizations with government expenditures for emergency relief.
8. What is the likely impact on foreign producers and consumers of subsidized U.S. agricultural exports?
9. Should large commercial farmers provide and maintain their own infrastructure needs?
10. Distinguish between the short-run and long-run effects of marketing orders.
11. In what ways are soil conservation programs compatible with environmental concerns?
12. Study changes in U.S. sugar quotas for foreign suppliers since the 1960s. Why did they change in that way?
13. Can U.S. agriculture afford *not* to continue to develop and use new technology?

A CHRONOLOGY OF U.S. FARM POLICIES 1933-76

A further way in which one can gain perspective on U.S. farm policies is by examining the historical sequence of events surrounding major pieces of legislation. A few issues stand out because of their longevity. For example, a Democrat occupied the presidency for the first twenty years of the period studied. Depression colored the first decade, affluence the last two decades. War, both cold and hot, persisted for the last three decades, having a distorting effect on agricultural production and trade. In the last decade, pockets of poverty in the U.S. and large-scale hunger abroad have become major policy issues. Table 4.1 (pp. 96–97) illustrates how the interaction of key personalities and major events have helped to shape agricultural policy.

U.S. agricultural legislation has tended to come in flurries early in the careers of new administrations. (See, for example, the short report by Rasmussen, Baker and Ward.) The Roosevelt programs of the 1930s left a legacy which still overhangs current administration efforts to change policy directions. Each secretary of agriculture in turn has had to brave established programs and prejudices to bring alterations in farm policy as new needs arise.

Henry A. Wallace, Roosevelts's secretary of agriculture, had the difficult task of moving agriculture from laissez-faire to government intervention in a few short months. He was a man of exceptional abilities and he succeeded. His programs were helped by the desperation of the problems faced. Wallace served as vice-president (1940–44) and secretary of commerce (1945–46), and he ran for president as leader of the Progressive Party in 1948.

The next secretary of agriculture, Claude Wickard of Indiana, had to put the Wallace farm programs into reverse in 1942 in order to meet expanded wartime needs. However, farmers were responding to calls for increased output. Clinton P. Anderson came to prominence as the young reporter in New Mexico who uncovered the Teapot Dome Scandal (the 1920s Watergate affair). He faced the difficult task of preparing the industry for reduced demand. He helped design postwar farm policy, but resigned to run successfully for senator in 1948, a move which, in retrospect, proved to be a wise one.

Charles F. Brannan became secretary of agriculture as the controversy over dismantling the price support system was at its height. He advocated a program of allowing markets to seek their own level and providing compensatory payments to give farmers parity of income. A republican-dominated congress threw the plan out unceremoniously. However, Brannan's ideas remained a viable alternative to existing programs for almost two decades.

Ezra Taft Benson had been a leader of the National Association of Farmer Cooperatives. He was also a member of the Council of Twelve of the Church of Jesus Christ of Latter Days Saints, a man used to securing consensus among different viewpoints. He attempted to reduce price support levels, but because controls were inadequate, enormous surpluses developed. His successor, Orville Freeman, backed Willard Cochrane's plan of mandatory controls. However, his efforts were successively defeated—the Cochrane Bill of 1961 to strengthen the USDA's powers, the efforts to include mandatory supply controls in the 1962 Food and Agriculture Act, and the 1963 wheat referendum. Freeman did succeed in instituting voluntary production controls at the cost of open-ended price support payments. So, while the surplus food problem abated, the budget deficit problem increased.

The Freeman-sponsored 1965 Food and Agriculture Act was extended in 1969 for one year. Clifford Hardin attempted in the 1970 Agriculture Act to move agriculture toward freer conditions. However, he now faced a democratic-controlled congress, which denied him the flexibility he sought in order to manage the farm programs. Again in 1973, Congress thwarted his successor's, Earl Butz, effort to eliminate excess farm income supports and broaden production allotments from a per crop to a total cropland basis. While market prices and producer flexibility in deciding what to produce were generally freed from government controls, important vestiges of allotments, quotas, supports, etc., for minor commodites remained in many programs. Since the inception of the 1973 act, a series of events, increased trade deals with centrally planned countries, concern about world food shortages, various crop failures in other countries, increased purchasing powers in OPEC countries from higher oil prices, and other stimulants kept demand and price of U.S. farm products at levels similar to those found in wartime. However, as stocks gradually returned to more normal levels in 1976–77, the price support provisions of the 1973 act became more and more operative. The Carter administration's new secretary of agriculture, Robert Bergland, and the Congress did not appear to think the time ripe for new initiatives, but concentrated on extending the more acceptable features of the 1973 act. After the buffeting of the turbulent early seventies, neither the administration nor Congress wished to be caught once again by surprise.

Table 4.1 Chronology of Agricultural Legislation, 1933–76

	President	Secretary	Major Farm Legislation	Other Important Events	
1933	Roosevelt	H. A. Wallace	Agricultural Adjustment	Depression	Worldwide protectionism
34	(Democrat)	↓	Act, 1933	↓	
35	↓				
36			Soil Conservation and Domestic Allotment Act, 1936		
37			Agricultural Marketing Agreement Act, 1937		
38			Agricultural Adjustment Act, 1938		
39					
1940					
1		Wickard		World War II	Wartime price and wage controls
2		↓	Stabilization Act, 1942	↓	
3					
4					
5					
6	Truman	Anderson		Cold War	
7	(Democrat)	↓		↓	Marshall Aid Plan
8	↓		Agricultural Adjustment Act, 1948		
9		Brannan			Brannan Plan rejected
1950		↓		Korean War	
1				↓	
2	↓	↓		↓	Emergence of U.S. and USSR as nuclear powers

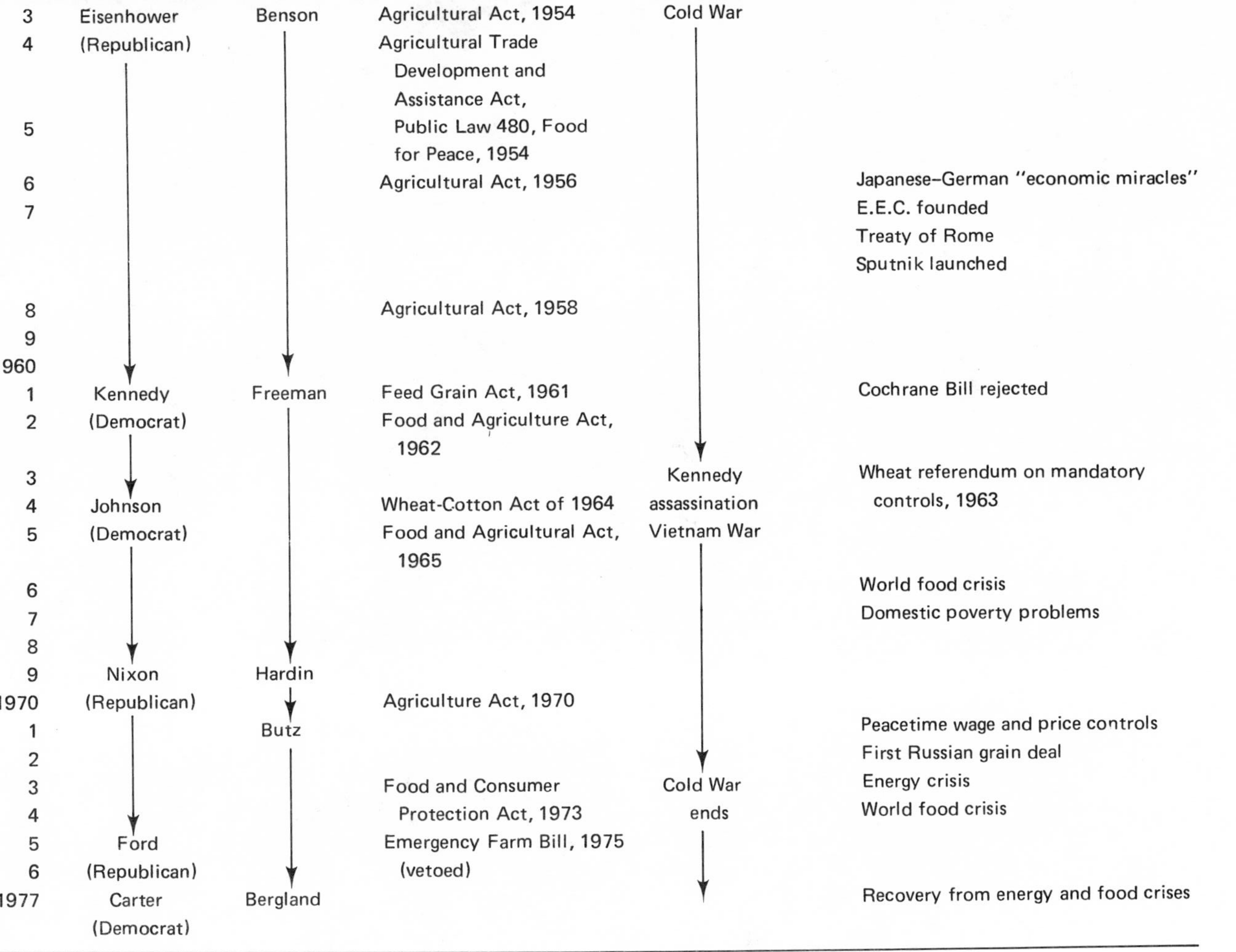

3	Eisenhower	Benson	Agricultural Act, 1954	Cold War	
4	(Republican)		Agricultural Trade Development and Assistance Act,		
5			Public Law 480, Food for Peace, 1954		
6			Agricultural Act, 1956		Japanese–German "economic miracles"
7					E.E.C. founded Treaty of Rome Sputnik launched
8			Agricultural Act, 1958		
9					
1960					
1	Kennedy	Freeman	Feed Grain Act, 1961		Cochrane Bill rejected
2	(Democrat)		Food and Agriculture Act, 1962		
3				Kennedy	Wheat referendum on mandatory controls, 1963
4	Johnson		Wheat-Cotton Act of 1964	assassination	
5	(Democrat)		Food and Agricultural Act, 1965	Vietnam War	
6					World food crisis
7					Domestic poverty problems
8					
9	Nixon	Hardin			
1970	(Republican)		Agriculture Act, 1970		
1		Butz			Peacetime wage and price controls
2					First Russian grain deal
3			Food and Consumer Protection Act, 1973	Cold War ends	Energy crisis
4					World food crisis
5	Ford		Emergency Farm Bill, 1975 (vetoed)		
6	(Republican)				
1977	Carter (Democrat)	Bergland			Recovery from energy and food crises

Key Words	Central Concepts
Cold War	Hostile relations and attitudes between rival powers falling short of actual fighting. The Cold War between the Western allies and the USSR began shortly after World War II and gradually dissipated during the 1960s. The Cold War prevented normal trade relations between countries not actually at war.
Compensatory payments	Payments to compensate farmers for incomes below a target level.
Wheat referendum (1963)	Wheat growers voted on a proposal for restrictive regulation of wheat production. Vociferously opposed by the American Farm Bureau, the proposal was defeated in favor of a less restrictive alternative.
Centrally planned countries	Term applied to countries having communism as their official ideology. Economic affairs are usually state directed under five-year plans.
Economic miracle	A loosely defined term applied to periods of rapid economic growth, especially under unfavorable circumstances.

QUESTIONS

1. Does the party occupying the presidency or in control of Congress affect agricultural policy?
2. To what extent have secretaries of agriculture been able to alter agricultural policy?
3. Since 1933, how many years has U.S. agriculture been affected by ongoing wars?
4. Since 1933, which (if any) years could be characterized as normal for U.S. agriculture?
5. During the Eisenhower years, price support levels were gradually reduced but surpluses continued to build up. Illustrate for wheat, corn, or cotton.
6. Why would farmers vote in favor of voluntary controls if mandatory controls would give increased price supports?
7. In 1973, net farm income rose by more than one-third, yet Congress preferred to retain farm income support programs. Was Congress justified?
8. In what ways were the target price provisions of the 1973 Agriculture and Consumer Protection Act rendered inoperative? Give examples.

five

AGRICULTURE AT WORK

In my judgment, most writers on agricultural policy have focused too much on farmers and on commodities to the exclusion of many other participants and factors in the development of past policies. For that reason, Chapters Two and Three attempted to give a broader perspective on the environment in which agricultural policy is framed. However, the individual farmer's production of commodities still plays a central role in agricultural policy. New legislation is justified on the farmer's behalf. Without his cooperation, most policies will be ineffective, or at least less effective. Even though the goal of a policy is to help some other group (lower cost to taxpayers of surplus stocks in government warehouses or cheaper food for consumers), that goal must be achieved through the agency of the farmer producing (or not producing) commodities in response to market and nonmarket incentives. Accordingly, if the student is to understand or evaluate much of past agricultural policy or to formulate improved future policy, an understanding of agriculture at work is essential. We need to know why and how the individual farmer, or farmers in general, reacts to market conditions like, product price changes or nonmarket factors such as government acreage limitations. In addition, a clearer understanding of the farming enterprise, including supply, production and marketing aspects, will reveal the many points in the enterprise at which alternative policies might be applied.

Unfortunately, no simple model of the farming system is sufficient to give the student the flavor of the farming environment. Accordingly, in the next two sections, we will draw heavily on neo-classical price theory (consumption, production, and exchange) on input–output analysis, and on analysis of the structure of the food and fiber industries to highlight the farmer's decision problem. We will not be able to describe farming exactly. Neo-classical price theory is most highly developed for the ideal economic system of perfect competition, below which perfect standards competition in agriculture frequently falls. Input–output analysis is limited in application by its assumption of a fixed relationship between inputs and outputs. Structural analysis suffers from lack of much relevant data and a universal theory. In addition, the tremendous diversity and the rapid changes in U.S. agriculture make generalization very dangerous. However, we hope at least to give the reader a framework useful in pursuing more intensely any specific commodity or region.

Essentially, in any economic system, individuals have control over limited resources which they can use either to satisfy immediate wants (like a kid spending his entire allowance on candy), or hoard, or put to use in producing another product or service which can be subsequently exchanged for more of a preferred resource. The U.S. economic system has developed to a point where the main resource of most of its citizens is income derived from hiring out their labor. Most, therefore, do not devote any of their labor or other scarce resources to production of food or fiber but use their wage income to satisfy such wants. In turn, few farmers continue to produce solely their food and fiber needs but devote their resources of land, labor, and capital to production of a small number of commodities which can subsequently be exchanged for income to satisfy their wants. However, in order to produce effectively, farmers now buy much of the resources used in production from a further group of specialists, such as the producers of tractors, gasoline, fertilizer, hybrid seeds, etc. And to bring farm products from areas where land is plentiful and consumers are scarce to areas where consumers are plentiful and land is scarce, a vast network of specialists has been developed to provide marketing services.

Decisions taken by the farmer cannot be looked at in isolation from the decisions of U.S. consumers, marketing agencies, and supply firms. The outcome of such decisions can be influenced by the initial resource endowments of each party, the rules of exchange (whether laissez-faire, government-imposed, or privately regulated), the vagaries of weather (still a major and unpredictable factor), trade groupings and alliances, and many other factors which tend to keep the system interconnected but unstable. So as incomes rise throughout the world and more and more foreign consumers want to trade their wage or other income for U.S. agricultural products, the decisions of the U.S. farmers become subject to an almost infinite number of possible pressures. It was difficult enough to understand agriculture at work in the relatively closed economic system of the thirties, or in the fifties and sixties when chronic excess capacity was taken for granted. However, one must approach any examination of agriculture at work in the seventies with more than the usual dose of humility.

DEMAND FOR FARM PRODUCTS— THE DISCIPLINE OF THE MARKET

Theoretical Underpinnings of Demand

Neo-classical theory explains the individual consumer's demand for any product in terms of the relative utility of that product compared to other possible bundles of goods. The actual amount that will be bought at any time will depend on the price of the product, the price of other possible bundles of goods, and how much the consumer has to spend (called his "budget constraint"). Utility determines the set of choices the individual will be willing to consider: the budget constraint and relative prices, and which choice he will make on any occasion. The fact that utility is a rather vague and elusive concept need not concern us. It is sufficient to note that utility is highly individualistic, the result of each person's combination of appetites, tastes, preferences, diet, allergies, addictions, susceptibility to group pressure, and so on. It can vary with changes in age, social status, weather, and other factors, but is in general assumed to change fairly slowly over time. Accordingly, short-term changes in the individual's demand for a product are usually traced to changes in relative prices or the budget constraint, but longer-term changes may also reflect more fundamental shifts in the set of choices that the individual is willing to consider.

While it is not possible to add the utility functions (sets of choices) of a group of individuals (except in certain limited cases), it does appear that groups in turn have a fairly stable set of choices among products which they are willing to consider and that the actual amount a group will choose will depend largely on relative prices and the group's budget constraint. Over time, the group's set of choices will change, both as individual circumstances change and as groups are subject to common influences such as advertising, education, propaganda, and many more subtle forces of change.

We can use the same reasoning to support a theoretical explanation of national or even world demand for any farm product. Such demand will lie in a stable but slowly changing range, dependent on the combined preferences of all consumers. However, at any point in time, the quantity demanded will be sensitive to relative prices of this and other commodities. For example, U.S. demand for eggs has almost certainly over time been affected by adverse publicity about cholesterol, but in any one year demand is more immediately influenced by the availability of competing protein foods.

In theory, the demand for any one product will be influenced by its own price and the price of every other product. Therefore, in a grocery store carrying 10,000 items, the demand for large eggs would be affected by the price of large, medium, and small eggs, cheese, hamburgers, boot polish, window cleaner, cut flowers, and 9,992 other items. In practice, only a few products have any measurable effect on demand for the specific product we are interested in. Again, over the years, the set of relevant complements or substitutes will change, but in general analysts can fix fairly precisely the relevant set of *other* products at any point in time. One complicating factor is that many crops have residual uses which occur only when their prices are low and those of competing products high, i.e., use of wheat for feed, potatoes for starch, apples for wine. Such combinations of prices may occur only once or twice in a decade.

A strength of the theoretical approach to demand analysis is that it can be applied to products singly or in combination. We can look at demand for bagels in Baltimore, or for cereal products in the U.S., or for all food in world markets, as long as the relevant quantities and prices can be defined and measured. However, this very facility has often led policy analysts into defining their problem too narrowly, for example, in analyzing the demand for corn in isolation from the demand for hogs, although both are inextricably linked in many farm operations.

In looking at changes in national or international demand over a period of years, we need to adjust the raw data on quantities and prices in order to separate out the influence of three factors: population growth, per capita income growth, and rises in the general price level (generally called "inflation"). It stands to reason that more people with the same budgets will demand more in total of any product; so, in general, analysts prefer to look at per capita demand (quantity divided by the relevant population). Similarly, growth in per capita income loosens the budget constraint and, if not separately accounted for, obscures the true effect of relative prices on quantity. Finally, changes in the general price level also alter the real budget constraint and are usually accounted for by deflating all prices and incomes used in the analysis.

A final general comment concerns the relationship of the price received by the farmer to the price determined at the consumer level. Demand for farm products is said to be derived from consumer demand. That is, if the retail price for one pound of pears is 39 cents and marketing charges are 25 cents per pound, the effective demand price at the farm level is 14 cents per pound. In a similar manner, a farm level demand curve can be derived from the retail demand curve (Figure 5.1). Clearly, then, farm level demand depends both on the

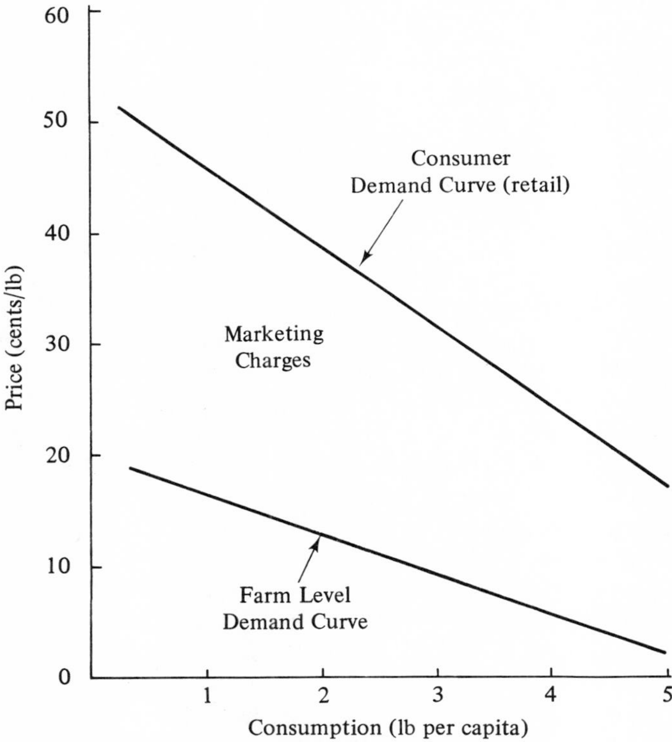

Fig. 5.1. Derived demand curve for fresh pears.

factors affecting consumer demand and on how the marketing charges vary. In a nation with highly varied consumption patterns, highly specialized production patterns, long distances to market, and sophisticated processing and distribution systems for bridging the gap in time, form, and space between producer and consumer, marketing charges tend to be high. This is not the appropriate point to discuss whether or not they are too high, but rather to emphasize what a major influence they are on farm level demand.

Domestic Demand for Food

While the demand for both food and nonfood (cotton or tobacco) farm products is influenced by common factors, it is practical to discuss them separately because of the different market channels involved. Per capita consumption of all foods in the U.S. declined dramatically between 1947 and 1962, during a period when per capita disposable income was rising more rapidly than retail price of all foods (Figure 5.2). Undoubtedly, this was related to the rapid population growth, mostly as a result of the postwar baby boom which lowered the average age of the population. The recovery in per capita food consumption from 1963 to 1972 was probably related to the movement of this large group of postwar babies into the higher consumption teenage and young adult age cohorts. The more rapidly rising retail price of food in that period did not inhibit consumption because per capita incomes rose even more rapidly. After 1972, per capita food consumption again dropped as food prices outstripped both income gains and increases in the general price level. For the 1976–86 decade, the growing proportion of teenagers and young adults is likely to exert an upward pressure on per capita food consumption. However, declines in birth rates may lead to a reversal of this upward pressure by 1990. Even under the most favorable income and price conditions, peacetime per capita consumption of all foods in the United States is unlikely to rise by more than 10 percent in the next decade. While some products will undoubtedly exceed this ceiling, the increasingly productive U.S. farmer will have to continue to maintain a growing export market to avoid a return to the chronic surplus conditions of the fifties and sixties.

Clearly, if there is an absolute limit to the volume of farm food products that can be sold, the trend of farm prices and returns becomes the key to changes in the farmer's income. The farmer's share of consumer expenditures on food has remained close to one-third for the last two decades, only rising above 37 percent in the shortage years, 1973 and 1974. This means that, in general, only one-third of any increase in consumer expenditures is likely to be passed back to

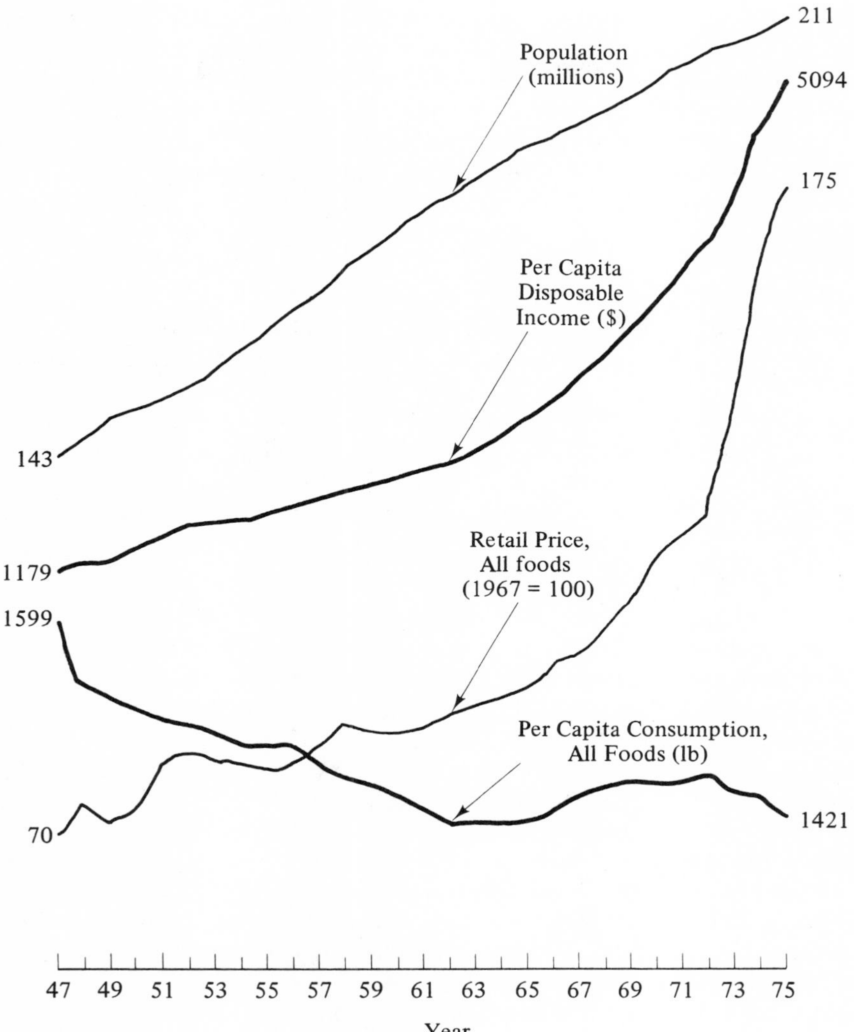

Fig. 5.2. Trends in U.S. population, per capita disposable income, per capita consumption of all foods, and retail price of all foods, 1947–75.

farmers. Looked at in current dollar terms, food demand rose by $78.3 billion at retail in the 1965–75 decade and by $29.9 billion at the farm level. However, only one dollar in six represented a real increase in the price of food, the remainder being accounted for by changes in the general price level. While farmers seem able to capture their share of inflationary price increases, real price increases due to shifts in consumer preferences for food versus other items appear small. The 1973 and 1974 "golden years" appear more likely to have been a temporary aberration in an otherwise minimal growth situation for farm prices and returns from domestic food sales.

This conforms to what one would expect on the basis of Engel's law, namely that as people's incomes increase, the proportion of their incomes spent on food decreases. Food expenditures in the U.S. as a percentage of disposable personal income fell steadily from 20.0 in 1965 to 15.4 in 1972 before rising (probably temporarily) in 1973 and 1974 when food prices outraced all other prices. In contrast, since per capita income in most countries of the world is lower than in the United States, more of each additional dollar of income abroad will tend to be spent on food. For this reason, too, export markets are more likely to offer greater growth potential for U.S. food sales. Besides the spectacular income gains of the oil-producing nations in the seventies, many other countries have had faster growth in incomes than the United States and have helped to boost U.S. export demand.

The Cost of Marketing Services

The fact that only one dollar in each six additional dollars of retail sales in the 1965–75 period represented a real increase in the price of food contrasts sharply with experience in the previous two decades when about three of every four additional dollars represented a real increase. The first two postwar decades covered the period of the great American leap into supermarketing, processing, and eating away from home—three of the vehicles by which more and more services per pound of food product were sold to American consumers. Marketing services cover such diverse items as improved storage (which benefits the consumer directly); computerized inventory systems (which aid in retail accounting); and grading, inspection, promotion, transportation, and other services where the real beneficiaries are a matter of much controversy.

The bill for all marketing services related to food products has grown steadily in dollar terms since statistics were first collected in the 1920s, but actually declined in real terms in some recent years (Figure 5.3). Despite the tremendous changes in technology, labor costs continue to account for about half of the marketing bill, reflecting the continuing need for people to handle many of the chores involved in nationwide marketing. In 1975 packaging accounted for 12 percent of all costs. Packaging has many functions, including product protection, hygiene, storage, merchandising, and consumer convenience. Transportation, both long-haul and intercity, accounted for a further 10 percent of costs. A further 25 percent went to such firm

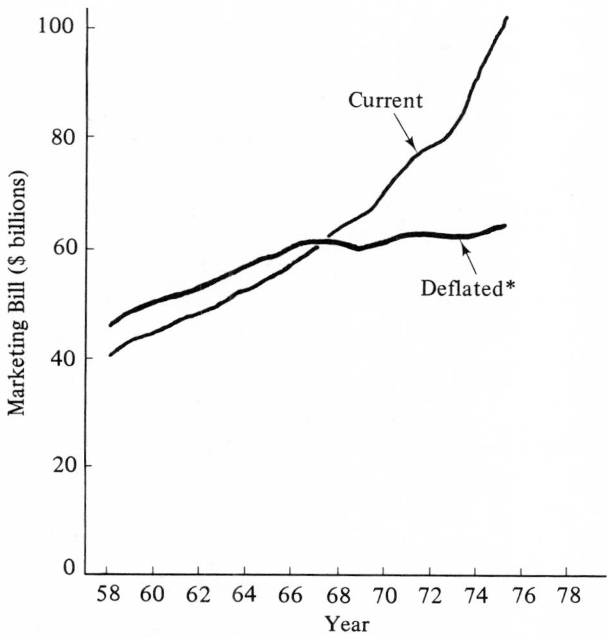

Fig. 5.3. Marketing bill for U.S. domestic food, current and deflated, 1958–75.

overhead costs as interest, rent, profits, taxes, utilities and fuel, repairs, and advertising. However, such a recitation gives the reader little of the flavor of the U.S. marketing system.

Food Processors

A much more instructive approach is to examine the operations of the leading marketing agencies: processors, retailers, wholesalers, and restaurants, each of which comprise some of the largest forms of industrial enterprise in the world. Food processing is (in terms of value of shipments) the largest manufacturing industry in the U.S. However, it is very diverse, ranging from single product, single plant firms to highly diversified, multiproduct (including nonfood) and multiplant concerns. Charles R. Handy and Daniel I. Padberg classified processing firms into an oligopolistic core and a more numerous fringe of small processors. W. Smith Greig proposed a second useful dichotomy, that between "commodity"-processing and "packaged goods"-processing. He describes commodity processing as "nearly a direct extension of farm production," in that the raw product is subjected to a simple process and emerges as a standardized product (for example, raw sugar), indistinguishable among firms. "Packaged goods" processors compete by exploiting differences in form, promotion, packaging, market appeal, or other elements of product differentiation which have been shown to provide at least temporary influence over customer loyalty. For the former group, the key is access to raw product and technical efficiency in production. For the latter, large financial resources are essential to pay the high information, development, and technology costs of survival. At the same time, their raw product prices and technical efficiency must be sufficient to keep them competitive with commodity-processing firms.

While the total number of processing firms has shown a decline at each postwar census, there were still 22,172 companies operating 28,180 establishments in 1972. While 56.2 percent of all establishments had less than 20 employees, these accounted for only 5.2 percent of the value of products shipped. Traditional measures of concentration suggest that food processing is less concentrated than many other manufacturing industries. A. A. Araji and J. Roetheli examined the eight major categories of food processors in the 1954–67 period and found little change in concentration over the period. Because of the nature of food processing—most raw products must be processed near to the production point—one or a small number of processing firms may be the only relevant outlet for a grower's output. Industrywide measures of concentration may not be as relevant to farmers as the actual or potential local monopolies that may exist. Farmers are further handicapped in bargaining with multiplant firms which can play off one producing area against another. There has been a rapid growth in the number, sophistication, and mutual cooperation of grower bargaining associations to offset this processor advantage.

For most processed foods, the greatest point at issue between growers and processors is the price which will be paid for the raw product. Some products, such as peas, must be processed at the moment of harvest, so a contract price must be negotiated well in advance. Other products, such as asparagus, are harvested over a period of months and have an alternative fresh market, so growers can at times choose to bypass the processor and the processor can at times discontinue buying the raw product in hopes of getting a more favorable price later on. Other products, such as potatoes or apples, can be held in storage by either growers or processors for long periods within a season, so both groups often aim to secure the price of part of their annual output or needs by preseason contracts, and at the same time are prepared to buy or sell in the open market. For a product like wheat, where storage is possible over a number of seasons, the well-financed grower can select the year in which he will sell any season's output, with the result that contracting generally has had little appeal.

In his dealings with the processor, the grower is concerned about the price required to cover production, labor, interest, and management costs (which will be discussed in the next section). The processor, in contrast, tends to look forward to the price he can expect for his final product, and, taking account of processing costs and profit goals, arrives at an offering price to growers. The price the processor can expect for the volume he sells is dependent on demand in the outlets he serves—wholesalers, retailers, and restaurants—to which we now turn.

Food Wholesalers

Food wholesalers once dominated the national food distribution system. They concentrated around the major ports and railroad terminal markets and were an almost essential link in every exchange between geographically separated producers and consumers. The growth of large food processors with national distribution capacity and large grocery retailers with the ability to obtain supplies nationwide and the development of a national highway system and long-distance truck fleets threatened much of the wholesalers' bulk business. As retail chains began to dominate the grocery trade in the 1930s, some wholesalers fought back by joining forces with the beseiged independent retail stores to form voluntary group or cooperative buying organizations. By the early 1960s, one-third of all grocery stores were in such groups. Like the retail chains, they espoused the concept of supermarket retailing, and thus maintained their share of the total retail food trade. However, because there continues to be such a tremendous diversity and number of small-volume suppliers, processors, retailers, and restaurants, handling both fresh and processed products, in every market wholesalers continue to be an essential link in transforming the amazing variety of U.S. agricultural products into the rich selection that U.S. consumers enjoy.

Wholesalers remain vulnerable to any increases in concentration among suppliers or customers. The most serious erosion in the past decade has occurred as fast food chains with central commissaries, displaced many of the single-unit "mom and pop-type" restaurants. Incidentally, these fast food chains, capitalizing on the increasing younger population and the number of working wives, have become a serious competitor to retail grocery stores for much of the family's food menu. In contrast to food bought for use at home, the proportion of income spent on food away from home has tended to defy Engel's law by remaining at about 4 percent of disposable personal income for almost two decades. Thus, eating away from home has grown at approximately the same rate as growth in income. Slightly more than 20 percent is served in schools, hospitals, and similar institutions. The remainder of the market (76 percent) is divided between very large enterprises (restaurant chains, government or industry in-plant cafeterias, etc.) and many small, locally owned restaurants. Johnston suggests that fast food operations and the large restaurant chains have contributed most to market growth. The demand for prepared, precooked quality- and portion-controlled food for rapid feeding of large numbers has generated a very large commercial food service industry, often closely combined either with processors or food centers. For example, many industrial plant cafeterias are served under contract by centralized kitchens, so that cafeteria employees need only reheat and serve. The 1966 USDA survey of the food service industry showed that the larger eating places were more likely to procure supplies from parent organizations. The implications for consumers and farmers are wide reaching. Consumers increasingly trade extra service charges for the savings in time involved in meal preparation. Farmers see more of their product marketed through channels which impose a much higher percentage of marketing charges than the traditional retail grocery channel. In 1975, of each dollar spent on food for use at home the farmer got 40.8 cents; on food away from home, 22.9 cents.

Food Retailers

Trends in the retail grocery trade, however, are no more reassuring for the vitality of farm level demand. *The Progressive Grocer* survey of the grocery industry reported that in 1975 the concentration of the U.S. grocery trade was continuing a 50-year-old trend. The number of food stores fell to a new low of 191,810, approximately half the number in business twenty years previously. The average size, whether measured in floor space, number of items handled, or dollar sales, continued to increase reflecting the continued dominance of the supermarket form of grocery retailing. Supermarkets represented over 72.4 percent of all grocery store sales, mostly controlled by retail chains with 11 or more stores or by affiliates of voluntary or cooperative buying groups. While speciality stores selling meat, seafood, produce, and other items continued to account for 5.7 percent of total food store sales, multiproduct supermarkets were the single most important outlet for almost all food products as well as for many nonfood items. The patron of the supermarket expected generous parking, air conditioning, unit pricing of items, product dating, even carpets, piped music, and many other services, the cost of which was inevitably included in the retail price charged. The Cornell University annual study of Operating Results of Food Chains reported that gross margins of sample chains in 1974–75 continued to lie in the range of 20 to 22 percent of retail sales. *The Progressive Grocer* reported gross margins for independent supermarkets at about 2 percentage points lower. In neither case was there evidence that the continuation of trends in concentration were leading to lower marketing charges for the benefit of either farmers or consumers.

Meanwhile, the supermarket itself was facing a whittling away of its supremacy in the food trade from convenience stores (the small, neighborhood self-service stores usually operated by chain franchises) and from the newer forms of restaurants, notably fast food chains which in the 1960s rapidly increased their sales of convenience, snack, lunch, and dinner foods and in the mid-1970s were making a determined assault on the breakfast food market. In addition, independent supermarkets, through greater flexibility in adapting to changing retail conditions were outperforming the chains, and the largest chains were being outperformed by the medium-sized chains. Higher costs of private transportation were threatening to alter the size of local retail markets and the optimal density of stores. The revival of population growth both in rural areas and small towns and in large city centers was forcing reconsideration of the optimal location of stores.

Farmer Marketing Efforts

Farmers have not tended to be pacesetters in food marketing, given the size and financial strength of the processors, wholesalers, and retailers who must handle their products. However, as farms become fewer, larger, and better capitalized, the farmers tend to become more willing to support merger, consolidation, and greater size in their own marketing organizations. They have made great strides in avoiding harvest-time gluts by orderly marketing, market promotion, use of futures and forward contracts, and securing greater bargaining power through concerted action. They still have not solved the problems of highly variable production and inelastic demand for many products. Efforts to achieve control of volume under marketing orders and agreements or through farmer cooperatives have been harassed by recent administrations more worried about consumer concerns with rising retail food prices. However, in an economy increasingly dominated by large power blocs, the farmer must eventually form such a group, if only in self-defense.

Integration in Marketing

For expository purposes we have discussed each of the marketing agencies separately. However, one of the biggest concerns of farmers, consumers, and other students of the U.S. food marketing system is the links that have grown up both between firms in the same line of business (horizontal integration) and firms at different levels of the marketing channels (vertical integration). Multiunit operations now dominate sales of processing, retailing, and restaurant firms. Amfac is a large processor and farmer; A&P is a large retailer and processor; Tenneco, primarily a vertically integrated oil company, is a large farmer and producer of packaging equipment. The Southern Pacific Railroad also has vast holdings of agricultural land, and Heublein, a large distiller, owns one of the largest food chains, Kentucky Fried Chicken. Studies of the benefits or evils of such integration tend to be inconclusive because no two analysts give equal weight to the desirability of such goals as efficiency and equity. Owners of capital may desire, while providers of labor may fear, further integration. To date, the owners of capital have tended to overcome this fear; whether this will continue appears to depend on the continued prosperity of the providers of labor.

Demand for Nonfoods

While the output of nonfoods by U.S. farms is smaller than food output, nonfood markets provide up to one-third of U.S. farm income. The big four are corn for feed, cotton, hay, and tobacco. However, production of food frequently involves joint nonfood products, such as hides from cattle or wool from sheep. In addition, many products used primarily for food may be diverted to nonfood uses as market conditions dictate. Nonfoods are the basis for large, specialized transportation, processing, wholesaling, and retailing industries, although some, for example tobacco products, may be processed in specialized plants but retailed alongside foods in grocery stores and restaurants. Nonfoods, notably feed grains, cotton, and tobacco, are also crucial in exports. Feed grains and hay are examples of nonfoods which are used in the production of food products through that marvellous but humble processor, the cow. Many other nonfood farm products undergo extensive changes in form and many processes before being sold to final consumers. Wool and cotton may be spun into thread; combined with other textiles; woven into cloth; cut into garments, clothing accessories, household goods, etc., before being sold to the final consumer. Because of these many changes of form and the many levels at which inventory of raw or semi-processed product may be held, it is difficult both to predict the derived demand for nonfood products and to measure farm–retail price spreads. The addictive properties of tobacco are likely to maintain its demand. Cotton and wool are likely to benefit from the consumer loyalty to natural (as opposed to man-made) fibers. Hay and feed grain demand may face wide fluctuations, dependent as they are on the volatile livestock and export markets.

Future Direction of Demand

Many analysts rely heavily on measured elasticities of demand to predict the future demand for farm products. However, in making their studies they must use published data relating to a past period. For example, in their major study, P. S. George and G. A. King used the 1965 Food Consumption survey. The structure of demand may have changed since then. In addition, elasticities are usually reported at the mean levels for price and quantity. Price and quantity in the 1970s may be outside the range of values previously studied, so, measured elasticities should be used in conjunction with other market information to develop hypotheses about the future direction of demand.

An example of the use and limitations of demand projections based on measured elasticities is drawn from the work of George and King who built on the pioneering work of George Brandow a decade earlier. Table 5.1 presents some of the income and price elasticities at retail levels, generated by George and King from the 1965 Household Budget Survey and from time series analyses. George and King used these measured elasticities to project per capita consumption of each item in 1980 and compared this with average annual consumption in the 1962–66 period. Note that in such projections the effect of relative price changes cannot be taken into account. We have added comparable consumption data for the 1971–75 period, roughly midway to their projected year. First, note that all income elasticities are positive, but only beef, butter, cheese, and chicken are above the average for all food, which is only one-seventh of that for all nonfood. The price elasticity for nonfood is about unity, but for all the food items it is inelastic, that is, a 1 percent increase in price will be associated with a less than 1 percent decrease in quantity demanded and vice versa. In eight of the thirteen items reported here, George and King projected per capita consumption to rise above the 1962–66 level in 1980, in three to fall, and in two to remain about the same.

Table 5.1. Quantity and Income Elasticities and Actual and Projected Consumption of Selected Foods

Item	*Estimated Elasticities (Retail)*		*Per Capita Consumption (Pounds Retail Weight)*			
	Income	*Price*	*1962–66 Actual*	*1971–75 Actual*	*1980 Projected*	*Expected Direction of Change*
Beef	0.290	–0.644	72.1	85.2	80.8	Increase
Pork	0.133	–0.413	57.8	60.1	60.8	Increase
Chicken	0.178	–0.777	32.2	41.3	39.2	Increase
Fish	0.004	–0.230	10.7	12.2	10.7	None
Eggs	0.055	–0.318	40.3	37.6	41.3	Increase
Cheese	0.249	–0.460	14.0	13.6	21.5	Increase
Butter	0.318	–0.652	6.6	4.8	4.9	Decrease
Margarine	0.000	–0.847	9.8	11.2	9.8	None
Apples, fresh	0.140	–0.720	17.0	15.9	18.0	Increase
Potatoes	0.117	–0.309	106.2	114.2	104.5	Decrease
Wheat flour	0.083	–0.300	108.2	108.2	93.4	Decrease
Rice, milled	0.055	–0.320	7.2	7.3	7.4	Increase
Sugar, refined	0.032	–0.242	96.8	98.6	98.1	Increase
All food	0.176	–0.237	1419.0	1438.0	n.a.	
Nonfood	1.243	–1.018	n.a.	n.a.	n.a.	

Sources: P. S. George and G. A. King. ***Consumer Demand for Food Commodities in the United States with Projections to 1980.*** Berkeley, Cal: Giannini Foundation Monograph No. 26, March 1971. U.S. Department of Agriculture. ***Food Consumption, Prices, Expenditures.*** Washington, D.C.: Economic Research Service, AER-138, 1969. U.S. Department of Agriculture. ***National Food Situation.*** Washington, D. C.: Economic Research Service (quarterly).

The actual 1971–75 consumption was on the correct path of change in six cases and was close to expectations considering the intervening factors that have affected demand, including very sharp fluctuations in supplies, price swings, health scares, dietary fads, etc. In the case of eight items, the 1971–75 level of consumption was higher than one would expect if consumption changed uniformly each year from the 1962–66 base level to the projected 1980 level. That is, in the case of such staple items as beef, chicken, potatoes, wheat flour, and sugar, consumption was higher than measured elasticities would lead us to expect. However, recent work by Corinne Le Bovit suggests that much of this was due to changes in household size and in age and sex of the population in the decade after 1965, and that these changes will tend to have offsetting effects in the next decade or two.

Government in Marketing

While most agricultural policy has been aimed at altering farm level conditions, government has considerable impact on market conditions. Marketing orders and agreements operate under the aegis of government. Laws governing fair trade, antitrust, safety and health, packaging, grades and standards, etc., affect the type of marketing organizations that have emerged and their costs and efficiency. For example, the Interstate Commerce Commission can limit entry into the transportation industry and regulate commodities carried and rates charged. Agricultural products are exempt, but agricultural inputs are not. While the Ford administration promised to re-examine the economic impact of the ICC and other regulatory agencies, it had not made any significant changes when it was voted out of office in 1976.

Government also has an important impact on the demand side. The Food Stamp program provided a $5 billion stimulus to demand (in the form of bonus stamps) in 1975. Other government domestic and foreign food programs, defense department demand, Commodity Credit Corporation activities, etc., roughly matched this expenditure. On the other hand, export embargoes had the effect of reducing demand. While government influence on demand is small relative to total demand, its marginal effects can be important in certain years.

Key Words	Central Concepts
Nonmarket conditions	Includes such factors as government regulation, weather, and political and social changes which affect supply, demand, and price.
Input-output	The output of every industry is used as an input by another industry or for consumption. Input-output tables show these relations for one sector or for the whole economy. An input-output model can be used to trace through the likely effects of a change in final demand or output or both.
Interconnected	U.S. agriculture is now linked with events in every part of the world and with its own supply and marketing system.
Utility	A term describing the satisfactions a consumer derives from consumption. Utility cannot be measured cardinally.
Budget constraint	When the cost of goods desired exceeds the consumer's budget, the consumer's choice is said to be subject to a budget constraint.

Derived demand	Final demand refers to the wants of consumers. This demand is transmitted back to farmers through the marketing system. Hence farm level demand is said to be derived from consumer demand.
Per capita consumption	Total demand is affected by the number of consumers (population) and by the average consumption per consumer.
Real price increase	An increase in price greater than the increase in the general price level.
Marketing bill for farm products	Cost of marketing equals retail value less farm value of farm products.
Local monopoly	The position of a single firm as sole buyer or seller in a local market. The technically correct term for the case of the sole buyer is "monopsony".
Concentration	Ownership or control of a large share of an industry by a few firms.
Horizontal integration	Merger of firms at the same level in the marketing system, for instance, retail food chains.
Vertical integration	Merger of firms at successive levels in the marketing system, such as, processing and retailing.
Demand projections	Estimates of future levels of demand derived from past experience.

QUESTIONS

1. In what ways is actual farm production central to all agricultural policy measures?
2. How are producers, consumers, and holders of resources linked in the modern economy?
3. Review the theory of consumer demand in a basic economic textbook.
4. Illustrate how concern about adverse effects on health could, over time, affect the price of a food product.
5. How can two products be competitive with each other in one season and not in the next?
6. The average U.S. household spends less than 20 percent of its income on food, but some households spend more. Who are these households? Why do they spend a higher proportion of their income on food?
7. What is "derived" demand?
8. Review Engel's law.
9. How has inflation affected marketing charges for food?
10. Food processors vary in size and mode of operation. Discuss.
11. Discuss the nature of competition between giant retail, wholesale, and restaurant chains. How is the farmer affected?
12. How do the viewpoints of farmers and processors diverge in establishing a contract price?

13. What would be the effect on agriculture of increases in (a) horizontal integration and (b) vertical integration in marketing?
14. How do population shifts affect food marketing costs?
15. Describe the similarities and differences between the marketing systems for cotton and tobacco.
16. How reliable are measured elasticities in forecasting future levels of demand for food?
17. How does the Food Stamp program affect demand for food?

PRODUCT SUPPLY—IN NEED OF A GURU

Resources in the hands of consumers and the marketing system set the range of demand possibilities faced by the farmer. The range of supply possibilities is determined by the farmer in light of the resources he owns or can acquire or borrow. Economic theory provides a neat if oversimplified description of the farmer's decision process.

Theoretical Underpinnings of Supply

The farmer has a physical limit to the resources available for production. He may use some or all of the available labor, land, etc. He may leave some land fallow, or use his labor part-time off the farm. And within the limits of his total resources, he can choose any combination of land, labor, and other inputs for use in any season. The quality of the resources is also important; soils vary in richness, laborers in skill, machines in power and efficiency, and so on. However, for given levels of skill and technology one can relate the output a farmer will get to the amount of inputs used. This relationship is the production function of economic theory.

A naive farmer with only one crop possibility might seek to produce at that point on his production function where his output would be greatest. Most farmers, however, have more than one crop possibility. They are aware that if all decide to increase production of a product simultaneously, market price will tend to fall. So, expected behavior of other farmers and expected price temper their decisions.

Since they can produce two or more products it is necessary to decide how much of farm resources to devote to each product. Our theory assumes that the farmer resolves the decision of what and how much to produce by finding the level of production which will maximize profits. Profits are simply the total revenue from product sales less the cost of all inputs used in production. Since price is fixed at the point of maximum profit, the combination of inputs chosen to produce the needed output will be the minimum cost combination for that level of output. The demand for inputs will, therefore, be derived from the demand for products. So, if two workers and one tractor can produce the same output more cheaply than one worker and two tractors, the former combination will be used. If the price of corn rises, the demand for fertilizer to produce corn will tend to rise. If the price of labor rises (thus increasing the cost of any input combination using labor) the farmer will tend to substitute machines or other inputs for labor.

Economic theory, then, neatly links the farmer's production decisions to both the product market and the market for inputs. Of course, in the real world, farmers can only guess at the general direction in which maximum profit lies. They can rarely predict how other farmers will react or the impact of weather, disease, or pests on yield. Actual output may differ greatly from targeted output, and eventual market price may be far from that expected. In a similar way, input prices may deviate from those expected. The cobweb model of farmer decision making, which was an attempt to explain real world behavior in certain products, assumes that farmers' expectations will always be wrong.

However, we need not be quite so sanguine about farmers' supply decisions. Government or private information services, forward contracts, and hedging in futures markets are just some of the devices which have been used to lessen price uncertainty under free market conditions, while in the field, irrigation can be used to reduce the reliance on capricious rainfall, chemicals to reduce pest damage, and treated seed to ensure plant germination. In addition, it may be of more practical value to be able to move toward higher profits than to agonize over where the maximum point might be. For example, as energy costs rise, the farmer knows that if he uses the same amount of energy to produce the same output his costs will rise and his profits fall. To avoid this, each unit of energy used must become more productive (produce greater output per unit of input) or other inputs must increasingly be substituted for energy. The economic health of the agricultural industry depends on the ability of farmers to make such adjustments as markets, production relations, and supply systems changes. In turn, the most effective policies for agriculture will be those which promote rather than retard farm level adjustments.

Just as in demand theory, the concepts originally derived for the decision making processes of the individual farmer or enterprise can be applied, under limiting assumptions, to groups of farmers, regions, or to the whole of U.S. agriculture. Decades of economists have generated such aggregate production functions, cost curves, profit functions, and derived demand for inputs. They have attempted to answer such questions as if and what a group should produce, how they might maximize revenue or profits or reduce cost, and what might be the optimal mix of inputs to use. Of course, the bigger the group involved, the harder it is to assume enough factors fixed, for example, product prices or input prices, to permit answers that have much practical value to farmers. For example, if studies suggest that to produce the same output at lower cost, the U.S. wheat industry should use less land and more fertilizers, the increased quantity of fertilizer required would be enough to cause a price increase and alter the marginal rate of substitution between land and fertilizer. In addition, a large increase in the quantity of fertilizer, for example, nitrogen, will put the wheat industry in competition with consumers and industrial users of natural gas, the major source of nitrogen. Aggregate adjustments, therefore, become even more complex than those of individual farms or farmers.

Input–Output Table of Interindustry Transactions, 1967

The U.S. Department of Commerce periodically publishes input–output tables for the whole economy. Table 5.2 shows some of the main interindustry transactions affecting agriculture in 1967. Reading across, we can see that the livestock industry sold \$19,777 million of its output to the Food and Kindred Products industry; only \$55 million went for net exports. In contrast, the Other Agricultural Products industry sold more to itself than to the Food and Kindred Products industry and had net exports of over \$3 billion. Reading down, we can see that other agricultural products were the major input to the livestock sector, but not vice versa. Paperboard, containers, and boxes were not a major input to livestock or other agriculture but were important to the Food and Kindred products (processing) industry. Value added as a percentage of total output was less for livestock and for food processing than for other sectors presented. Table 5.2 can also be used as a first step in estimating the direct and total requirements per dollar of gross output in any industry. For example, for each dollar of added output of livestock products, 27 cents worth of other agricultural products would be required directly. However, since some livestock products will also be used to produce livestock, it will require \$1.31 of livestock products in total to permit delivery by the livestock industry of a further \$1.00 of livestock products to other industries. Other relationships within the agricultural sector can be examined in the same manner.

Table 5.2. Principal Interindustry Transactions in the U.S. Economy Involving Agriculture, at Producer Prices, 1967 (millions of dollars)

	1. Livestock and livestock products	*2. Other agricultural products*	*4. Agricultural, forestry, and fishery services*	*14. Food and kindred products*	*25. Paperboard, containers and boxes*	*65. Transportation and warehousing*	*69. Wholesale and retail trade*
1. Livestock and livestock products	5,610	1,448	169	19,777	—	—	—
2. Other agricultural products	8,379	905	507	6,882	—	41	10
4. Agricultural, forestry and fishery services	603	1,335	—	—	—	—	139
14. Food and kindred products	3,694	—	44	14,828	1	166	892
25. Paperboard, containers, and boxes	2	3	123	1,704	109	26	571
65. Transportation and warehousing	690	452	27	2,592	227	5,228	1,235
69. Wholesale and retail trade	1,333	1,527	28	3,286	151	1,627	3,382
71. Real estate and rentals	475	2,062	79	744	96	1,360	8,608
Intermediate inputs, total	22,552	14,587	1,146	65,459	3,813	21,829	45,101
Value added	8,086	13,953	1,524	23,993	2,218	30,996	118,265
Total	30,638	28,540	2,670	89,451	6,031	52,825	163,365
Transfers	228	408	500	2,898	152	2,774	5,717

Table 5.2. (*cont.*)

	71. Real estate and rentals	Intermediate outputs, total	Personal consumption expenditures	Net inventory change	Net exports	Total final demand	Total
1. Livestock and livestock products	1,127	28,620	1,811	129	55	2,018	30,638
2. Other agricultural products	1,200	21,691	3,756	1,031	3,184	6,849	28,540
4. Agricultural, forestry and fishery services	159	2,486	136	–	14	185	2,670
14. Food and kindred products	138	24,540	60,974	899	1,906	64,911	89,451
25. Paperboard, containers, and boxes	4	5,841	73	39	24	191	6,031
65. Transportation and warehousing	1,096	32,172	11,396	228	3,891	20,653	52,823
69. Wholesale and retail trade	1,612	42,551	109,367	508	2,615	120,815	163,365
71. Real estate and rentals	3,654	38,798	70,868	–	577	74,456	113,253
Intermediate inputs, total	29,181	–	–	–	–	–	–
Value added	84,073	–	–	–	–	–	795,388
Total	113,253	–	490,660	10,034	5,132	795,388	–
Transfers	11,996	–	–	–	–	–	–

For the distribution of output of an industry, read the row for that industry. For the composition of inputs to an industry read the column for that industry.

Table 5.3. Comparative Income Statement of U.S. Agriculture, Selected Years, 1940–74

Item	1940		1950		1960		1970		1974	
	($ million)	*(%)*	*($ million)*	*(%)*	*($ million)*	*(%)*	*($ million)*	*(%)*	*($ million)*	*(%)*
Total realized gross farm income of farm operators	11,059	100.0	32,291	100.0	38,497	100.0	58,604	100.0	101,112	100.0
Production costs:										
Feed bought	998	9.0	3,283	10.2	4,552	11.8	7,976	13.6	14,996	14.8
Livestock bought (except horses and mules)	517	4.7	2,004	6.2	2,506	6.5	4,324	7.4	5,154	5.1
Fertilizer and lime bought	306	2.8	975	3.0	1,347	3.5	2,390	4.1	5,606	5.5
Repairs and operation of capital items	1,038	9.4	2,975	9.2	3,982	10.3	4,539	7.7	6,462	6.4
Depreciation and other consumption of farm capital	797	7.2	2,665	8.3	4,337	11.3	6,760	11.5	10,640	10.5
Taxes on farm real estate and personal property	451	4.1	919	2.8	1,530	4.0	2,928	5.0	2,980	2.9
Seed bought	197	1.8	518	1.6	519	1.3	927	1.6	2,032	2.0
Wages to hired labor (cash and perquisites)	1,029	9.3	2,811	8.7	3,062	8.0	4,349	7.4	6,031	6.0

Table 5.3. *(cont.)*

Item	*1940*		*1950*		*1960*		*1970*		*1974*	
	($ million)	*(%)*	*($ million)*	*(%)*	*($ million)*	*(%)*	*($ million)*	*(%)*	*($ million)*	*(%)*
Net rent and government payments to nonoperator landlords	448	4.1	1,233	3.8	1,108	2.9	1,577	2.7	5,907	5.8
Interest on farm mortgage debt	293	2.6	264	0.8	628	1.6	1,717	2.9	2,986	3.0
Miscellaneous	784	7.1	1,808	5.6	3,847	10.0	7,085	12.1	10,611	10.5
Total production costs	6,858	62.0	19,455	60.2	27,418	71.2	44,572	76.1	73,405	72.6
Realized net farm income of farm operators	4,201	38.0	12,836	39.8	11,079	28.8	14,032	23.9	27,707	27.4
Realized net farm income per farm (dollars)	662	–	2,273	–	2,796	–	4,750	–	9,789	–

Source: U.S. Department of Agriculture. *Balance Sheet of the Farming Sector, 1975.* Washington, D.C.: Economic Research Service, Agriculture Information Bulletin No. 389, September 1975.

The summary income statement of U.S. agriculture provides a broad view of the relative importance of various inputs to production (Table 5.3). Because of changing money values, the percentage of each item in total income is shown for each year. Despite record prices in the early 1970s, production costs in total took a much larger share of gross farm income than in 1940, 1950, or 1960. They grew by more than tenfold in the 34-year period, while gross farm income grew less than tenfold. Above average growth was experienced in purchased feed, fertilizer and lime, depreciation, net rent, and miscellaneous items. Wages to hired labor grew least in the 34-year period and was the only item to show a consistent decline in share of total production costs. These data reflect the trend toward use of greater capital and purchased inputs in U.S. agriculture and lower use of hired labor. The items, repairs, and operation of capital items and miscellaneous include many of the costs incurred to maintain a capital-, technology-, and knowledge-intensive agriculture (gasoline, irrigation, pesticides, veterinary services, consulting services, and telephone and utility costs). Taxes are a further cost related directly to the services provided by various levels of government. Many of these services are valuable aids to the productivity of farm inputs, for example, erection and maintenance of irrigation systems or weather information services.

A further guide to the role of various inputs in modern U.S. agriculture can be gained from examining the Balance Sheet of the Farming Sector over the years (Table 5.4). Claims show where U.S. agriculture got its funds; assets show the uses made of such funds. The largest single source of funds continued to be proprietors' equities, with farmers in each of the selected years providing over 80 percent of funds from their own sources. The fastest growing source of funds was credit extended for nonreal estate loans by banks, production credit associations, and others. Real estate debt continued to be about as large as nonreal estate debt. The greatest growth in use of funds occurred in machinery and motor vehicles, reflecting the "power" revolution in agriculture since 1940. Apart from investments in cooperatives, the financial assets farmers could set aside as a reserve had shrunk to less than 4 percent of assets. In general, during the war and in the decade thereafter, the farming sector built up proprietors' equities and reduced its debt to equity ratio, but by 1970 it had fallen back to a position similar to that of 1940 when agriculture was still struggling to escape the Great Depression. However, even in 1974, when minimal government programs were in operation, capital gains from land were almost double the net realized income from productive activities.

Table 5.4. Balance Sheet of the Farming Sector, January 1, Selected Years, 1940–75

Item	*1940*		*1960*		*1970*		*1975*		*Ratio 1975/ 1940*
	($ billion)	*(%)*	*($ billion)*	*(%)*	*($ billion)*	*(%)*	*($ billion)*	*(%)*	
Assets									
Physical assets:									
Real estate	33.6	63.5	130.2	64.0	206.9	67.6	371.4	71.4	11.1
Nonreal estate:									
Livestock and poultry	5.1	9.6	15.2	7.5	23.4	7.6	24.6	4.7	4.8
Machinery and motor vehicles	3.1	5.9	22.7	11.2	32.3	10.6	55.8	10.7	18.0
Crops stored on and off farms	2.7	5.1	7.7	3.8	10.9	3.6	23.2	4.5	8.6
Household equipment and furnishings	4.2	7.9	9.6	4.7	9.7	3.2	15.4	3.0	3.7
Financial assets:									
Deposits and currency	3.2	6.0	9.2	4.5	11.9	3.9	15.0	2.9	4.7
U.S. savings bonds	0.2	0.4	4.7	2.3	3.7	1.2	4.3	0.8	21.5
Investment in cooperatives	0.8	1.5	4.2	2.1	7.2	2.4	10.5	2.0	13.1
Total assets	52.9	100.0	203.5	100.0	306.0	100.0	520.2	100.0	9.8
Claims									
Liabilities:									
Real estate debt	6.6	12.5	12.1	5.9	29.2	9.5	47.4	9.1	7.2
Nonreal estate debt:									
Excluding CCC loans	3.0	5.7	11.6	5.7	27.0	8.8	45.9	8.8	15.3
CCC loans	0.4	0.8	1.1	0.5	2.7	0.9	0.3	0.1	0.8
Total liabilities	10.0	18.9	24.8	12.2	58.9	19.2	93.6	18.0	9.4
Proprietors' equities	42.9	81.1	178.7	87.8	247.1	80.8	426.6	82.0	9.9
Total claims	52.9	100.0	203.5	100.0	306.0	100.0	520.2	100.0	9.8
Debt to asset ratio	18.9		12.2		19.2		18.0		0.95

Source: U.S. Department of Agriculture. *Balance Sheet of the Farming Sector.* Washington, D.C.: Economic Research Service (annual) miscellaneous issues.

The changes in expenditures on farm inputs illustrated by the income statement and balance sheet of the U.S. farming sector reflect changes in both volume and price of inputs. While the weighted index of total inputs has varied little since the 1920s there has been a 9 percent decline in farm real estate inputs and a 74 percent decrease in use of farm labor between 1920 and 1974. Use of mechanical power and machinery; fertilizers and liming materials; and purchased feed, seed, and livestock grew from a relatively small base in 1920 by 228, 1625, and 288 percents, respectively. Taxes and interest and miscellaneous expenses grew by less than 100 percent in the same period. Prices have tended to rise and fall with the fluctuations brought about by depression, war, and inflation in the intervening years.

In the decade of the 1960s there was a small decline in farm real estate use and a slowing decline in use of farm labor. Use of mechanical power and machinery fell during the years of chronic surplus in the early sixties but recovered after 1965. Use of all these items was inhibited by escalating price increases in the late sixties and early seventies (Table 5.5). Fertilizer consistently had greatest volume increases in each period, aided by fairly stable prices until the energy crisis of 1973 precipitated a doubling of prices in a subsequent 12-month period.

Table 5.5 Changes in Use and Prices of Selected Farm Inputs, by Five-Year Intervals, 1960–75

	1960–65 % Change		*1965–70 % Change*		*1970–75 % Change*	
	Use	*Price*	*Use*	*Price*	*Use*	*Price*
Farm real estate	+ 1	+26	− 2	+37	− 3	+ 83
Farm labor	−25	+16	−13	+50	− 6	+ 47
Fertilizer	+48	+ 0	+41	− 3	+22[a]	+146
Mechanical power and machinery	− 3	+12	+ 5	+26	+ 5	+ 65
Interest		+67		+81		+ 93
Taxes		+26		+48		+ 21
Total production outputs	+ 1	+ 4	+ 4	+15	+ 0	+ 68

[a]1970–74.
Source: USDA, ERS, *1975 Handbook of Agricultural Charts*, Economic Tables—ERS 559.

Price and Productivity of Inputs

Because of equal or greater increases in prices received by farmers, the rise in input prices had slowed but not decreased input use by 1975. However, past experience makes it clear that a major drop in farm product prices could lead to an actual decline in input use in the next decade. In general, during the 1960s prices paid by farmers rose more rapidly than prices received (Fig. 5.4). Farmers compensated for this to some extent by increased productivity of the inputs used. Between 1971 and 1973, prices received raced ahead of prices paid, and productivity also increased. By 1975, prices paid had caught up with prices received, and productivity had faltered due to drought, reduced demand, and shortages of some key inputs, notably fertilizers. It would appear that 1975 is near the peak of a farm boom similar to those triggered in the past by major wars. Farm prosperity

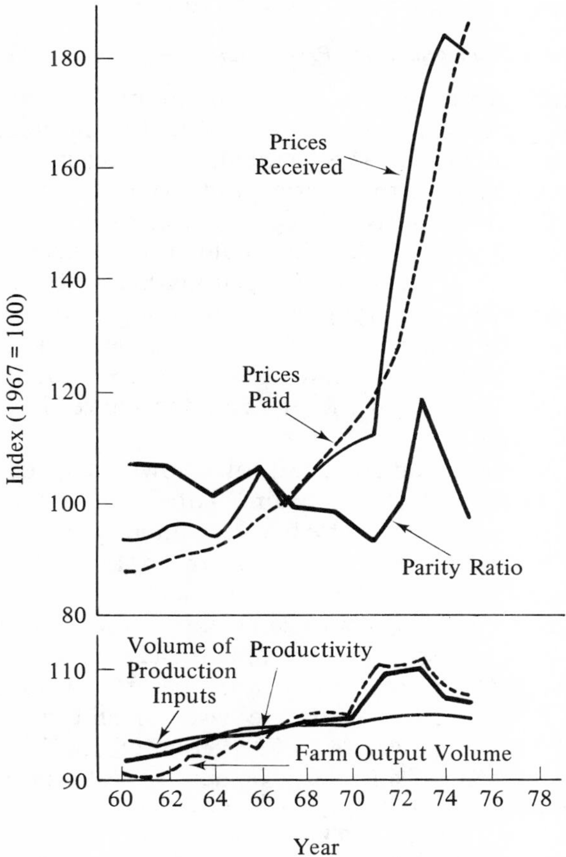

Fig. 5.4. Indexes of farm output, production inputs, productivity, prices received, prices paid, and parity ratio for U.S. agriculture, 1960–75.

in the next decade may hinge heavily on the ability of farmers to offset price declines by increasing the productivity of inputs.

Some of the greatest increases in productivity in the past have occurred where certified or hybrid seed, machine technology, application of fertilizer and farm chemicals, and improved management have been combined with irrigation to produce dramatic improvements in yields. With a crop like potatoes, the difference between yields in new irrigated acreage and in traditional growing areas lacking this combination has been so great that production has moved steadily to the better endowed regions. However, the high cost of and limited acreage available for new irrigation, and problems of increased price, pollution, and government regulation of the other key inputs may prevent a new leap forward in yields.

Who Will Control Agricultural Production?

The price, quantity, and quality of inputs, and who will have access to such inputs, will be the crucial factors in determining the future product supply of U.S. agriculture. Already the battle has begun over who shall share in farm production and how much control they will have. The North Central Regional Study under the umbrella description of "Who shall control agriculture?" discussed five possible systems; a dispersed, open market system; a corporate system; a cooperative system; government control; or a combination of the previous four. If we consider the dispersed, open market system as close to the general state of agriculture prior to 1900, it is clear that some elements of the other systems have already made inroads on agriculture.

As the previous tables have shown, ownership of land is the primary key to control of agriculture. Total land in farms has been falling by about a half percent each year under pressure of demand for housing, highways, recreation, etc. In contrast, the number of farms has fallen by about 2 percent annually and the average size of the farm has increased by about 2 percent. At the same time, the percentage of farm operators who are tenants has dropped at each census, so that in 1969, 87 percent of farm operators were either full or part owners. However, these data are based on all farms. Farms with sales of $100,000 and over in 1974 accounted for 4 percent of all farms and 47 percent of all sales. The next largest group, farms with sales of $40,000 to $99,999, accounted for 12 percent of all farms and 24 percent of all sales. The remaining 84 percent of all farms accounted for less than 30 percent of all sales. Farms with sales of $20,000 to $39,999 earned 30 percent of all income from off-farm sources. Smaller farms earned from 0.5 percent to 94 percent (in the smallest category) of all income from off farms. Clearly, farms engaged primarily in agriculture generally had sales above $20,000 and numbered about one million in 1974. Of the remaining 1.8 million farms, many were being used as hobbies, tax shelters, supplementary sources of income, retirement homes, rural homes, or for motives other than that of generating income from farm sales.

While there is some concern about the concentration of landholdings and farm sales among fewer farmers, even more public concern revolves around the increased share held by corporations, especially those primarily engaged in nonfarm activities. Most corporations engaged in farming are small (less than 10 shareholders), and have been used for limiting liability as farms grow and for inheritance or tax purposes with no change in the internal operations or external relations of the farm. In 1969, such farms accounted for 1.1 percent of all farms with sales over $2,500 and 11.3 percent of all marketings in the 48 contiguous states. Larger corporations were only 0.1 percent of all farms but accounted for 2.9 percent of all sales. However, larger corporations accounted for 55 percent of all sales in Hawaii, over 10 percent in Florida and Connecticut, and over 5 percent in Massachusetts, Delaware, and a belt of arid and semi-arid states from Texas, west to California and north to Washington. News reports of corporate land purchase or development indicate that the corporate share of farm sales is still growing.

The intrusion of multiunit and multiproduct firms into farming parallels the developments in horizontal and vertical integration noted in food marketing. A study of such firms by Donn A. Reimund using 1969 and 1970 data found that slightly more than one-third were primarily engaged in farming, about one-fifth in activities unrelated to agriculture, and the remainder divided fairly equally between agricultural input, agricultural processing, and agricultural distribution firms. Farm production accounted for about 5.5 percent of total sales of the sample firms. In most cases, corporate participation involved some form of vertical integration or extension of their business activities, with input firms tending to integrate forward into livestock and poultry and processing and distribution firms integrating backward into fruits, nuts, and vegetables. Reimund estimated that the type of corporation studied accounted for about 7 percent of 1969 U.S. farm sales, considerably higher than that indicated by the *1969 Census of Agriculture.*

Clearly, the importance of large corporations in agriculture cannot be separated from the trends in concentration in food marketing and the trend toward contracting by many of the same firms. While farm land continues to be predominantly under the control of family-type farms, the continued growth of large corporate farming would pose many difficult questions about the control of U.S. food sources. If the family farm could continue to have equal opportunity in competing with large corporate farms, such growth could arise only through increased efficiency. However, through their marketing ties, financial resources, and market power, corporate farms gain advantages not available to the family farm. For example, a processing firm may continue to farm land to provide a controlled source of raw materials and to provide comparative data on costs, returns, and yields, both of which give the processor leverage in contract negotiations with other farm suppliers. Such a farming operation may survive even though it yields a lower return on investment than other farms or than other parts of the corporation's business. Furthermore, for reasons other than superior efficiency, such corporations may be able to outbid family farms for the available land. Whether large corporations will continue to expand in agriculture may depend on such private corporate policies and on the relative return on investment in agriculture and in other enterprises.

Farm Labor Changes

The decline of the labor input in agriculture reflected just such a differential between what farmers and farm workers could earn in agriculture and the much higher potential earnings elsewhere. While the ratio of hired farm workers to family workers has remained about 1 to 3 for the last 45 years, total farm employment dropped by over 8 million. However, the number of hired workers is reported to have risen in each of the years 1973 through 1976, while the number of family workers continued to fall by an average of 2 percent per year, until it too turned up in 1976. These diverging trends undoubtedly reflect in part the continued demise of small farms and the increase in size (and need for hired labor) of the survivors. In addition, due to the push of threatened unionization and the pull of higher farm product prices, increases in farm wages have exceeded the rate of inflation, while the rest of the economy has been hit by recessions in 1970 and 1974.

There have also been changes in the quality of farm labor which will have an important bearing on future labor supply. On the family farm, all labor was a generalist, with one person often being both boss and worker and responsible for many different kinds of work. On the larger farms, work can be more specialized. A large corporate farm may employ college graduates in agronomy, entomology, and business administration and its own highly skilled mechanic, irrigation supervisor, storage operator, etc. Unskilled or semi-skilled farm jobs such as hoeing, weeding, or harvesting are increasingly being handled by machine as the traditional labor sources dry up; for example, migrant workers are being encouraged to settle, illegal aliens mainly from Mexico are being harassed and deported if caught, rural depopulation is reducing the pool of local part-time housewife and student labor, and welfare regulations often make farm work relatively unrewarding. The demand for farm labor will continue to favor workers with specialized skills, while at the same time the shortage of unskilled labor will sustain efforts to replace such labor with machines.

Capital Requirements

The size and cost of operating the large modern farm means that both maintenance and growth require large infusions of capital. This is particularly true for new entrants who must acquire land in which past program values have been capitalized. For over a century, farm groups have been concerned about their inability to borrow either long-term or operating capital. As a result, the Federal Farm Credit system, the Farmers' Home Administration, and the Commodity Credit Corporation have over the years come to supplement and compete with private credit institutions such as banks, insurance companies, and other sources of credit such as suppliers or marketing agencies. The publicly financed share of farm real estate debt tends to fluctuate with general economic conditions but was about one-third in 1974, mainly from federal land banks. The Production Credit Associations (PCAs) and other public agencies provided only one-fifth of nonreal estate loans. Banks were the leading private lenders, slightly ahead of nonfinancial institutions such as merchants. Commodity Credit Corporation (CCC) loans were used mostly for financing of storage and delayed marketing of crops under government support programs.

The essential problem of farm financing over the years has been the farmer's inability to generate cash flows. Capital gains on land cannot be realized without reducing farm size, and realized net income in most years is not sufficient to permit retention of earnings for future financing. The individual farmer who is vulnerable to the vagaries of weather on the supply side and market uncertainty on the demand side is a poor credit risk relative to other businesses. However, agriculture in the aggregate is a very large and, in the long run, very profitable industry. The Farm Credit System borrows by selling bonds in central capital markets on the strength of agriculture's average solvency and is able to lend these funds to individual farmers so that the high individual risks are diffused throughout the system.

So successful has this approach been that the system's bonds are among the safest in U.S. financial markets. Accordingly, the Farm Land Banks and Production Credit Associations can provide farmers with funds at competitive or lower rates than private financial institutions.

The Federal Farm Credit System consists of three farmer-owned banks, each catering to different credit needs.

1. Federal Land Banks–which make 5 to 40-year real estate loans,

2. Federal Intermediate Credit Banks–which fund 440 local Production Credit Associations which make short- and medium-term (up to seven years) loans to farmers, and

3. Banks for Cooperatives–which make both capital and operating loans to farmer cooperatives.

The Farmers' Home Administration tends to provide loans for emergency situations or for farmers denied other sources of credit. Loans by the above agencies are made on the basis of the farmer's managerial ability, soundness of the proposed use of funds, and collateral, as in the case of commercial lenders. However, nonfarm borrowers are not competing for the available funds. Entitlement to receive a Commodity Credit Corporation loan is granted automatically according to the rules laid down for the commodity in question under a government program.

The rapid growth of the system's share of both real estate and nonreal estate debt in the 1960s caused private lenders much concern. They wanted more farm business but lacked the government guarantees supporting the system. The Farm Credit Act of 1971 increased the lending power of the system and allowed PCAs for the first time to participate in loans with nonpublic lenders such as commerical banks. However, it made more restrictive the privilege the Federal Intermediate Credit Bank had of discounting commercial bank loans. Under further pressure, Congress, in the Rural Development Act of 1972, permitted private bank loans to be covered by an FHA-administered government guarantee. Not surprisingly, in the early 1970s commercial bank loans to farmers increased more rapidly than all other sources except PCAs. Insurance companies, which have been major sources of real estate debt showed very little growth in the same period.

As the larger corporate farms have sought farm financing, smaller rural banks have turned to more joint bank and correspondent banking arrangements to meet these needs. However, farm loans are still a small part of the business of the leading national banks. There is real concern that corporate farms, with their integrated or conglomerate activities will absorb funds which would previously have been channeled into family farms, at the same time that family farms' financing needs are growing. The banking system still has no proven method for selecting qualified new entrants for financing. Accordingly, farmers will be forced more and more into relatively new financing arrangements such as leasing of land and equipment, forward contracting, or increased financing through dealers and merchants. There still remain many doubts about the availability of the total credit needs of agriculture in the future.

The cost of borrowed funds may also remain a problem for farmers as long as inflation continues at the rates experienced in the early 1970s. A lender will charge an interest rate which will cover both compensation for the use of his funds and any possible loss in value due to inflation during the period of loan. If a lender requires a real return of 3 percent and the rate of inflation is 6 percent, he will charge a borrower 9 percent. Average PCA loan rates exceeded 9 percent in 1974. This means that a farmer must earn 9 percent on borrowed funds just to make his interest payments, in an industry which rarely earns more than 1 percent on all capital employed. The high cost of debt may cause the demise of many of the weaker farm firms.

Farmer Bargaining Power

Of course, continued borrowing is necessary to purchase the inputs which are the key to the productivity of modern agriculture—fortified feeds, tested seeds, fertilizer, agricultural chemicals, irrigation, electric power, machinery and equipment, information and consulting services, dues to farm and bargaining organizations, research and promotional checkoffs, and many others. The bargaining power of farmers in acquiring these inputs is weakened by the oligopolistic, multinational, and conglomerate nature of the leading suppliers. In addition, in the short run, the farmer cannot easily find alternative sources of seeds in the spring, fertilizer in the growing season, or fuel for combines at harvest. Farmers have to some extent reduced the pressure by joining buying groups or supply cooperatives. However, as technology encourages larger scales of operations, only a few can compete with the corporate conglomerates as primary sources of supply.

The livestock feed economy continues to show the most diverse mix of relationships with input suppliers. At one extreme is the system of small cow–calf operations, serving range-feeding operations and fattening cattle on grass. The animals are sold at open markets at each level and feed is either produced on the farm or bought on the open market. At the other extreme, according to Philip M. Raup, are the chicken broiler producers, "who typically do not own the chickens they feed and are usually obligated by their contracts to buy feed supplies from designated suppliers, and to sell the broilers only to specified processors." Many variations in between also exist. However, prepared feeds have become an indispensable part of many livestock enterprises. Feed manufacturers have a major influence both on the demand for corn, soybeans, and other crops and on the supply price of feeds to livestock producers. The squeeze on livestock feeders between 1973 and 1975 illustrated how critical this relationship is. While price of meat animals fell 12 percent and feed prices rose 13 percent, the price of feeder cattle fell by 32 percent. Interestingly enough, many of the operators squeezed were the very corporate or tax-shelter farms which so concern the family farmer. Agriculture, in its many facets, is just too diverse to be neatly pigeonholed.

Changing Technology

Fertilizers, motor vehicles, and farm machinery are also provided to farmers by conglomerate industries with high concentration in individual markets. For example, most farmers buy their tractors from a few firms and their plows, balers, etc., from a few (frequently different) firms. Fertilizers have gone through the full cycle of overcapacity–falling prices through shortages–high prices and back to surplus again in the last decade. Total revenue continued to rise as volume increases compensated for any price declines. However, in the machinery and equipment industries, the decline in the number of farms has decreased the potential number of sales. Manufacturers have responded by producing larger, more complex, and more refined units. Sales of four-wheel drive units accounted for 2 percent of tractor sales in 1971, close to 7 percent in 1975. Average horsepower increased in the same period by an estimated 24 percent. Average farm machinery prices between 1971 and 1975 increased by 55 percent. In the fashion typical of similar oligopolistic industries, the farm machinery, tractor, and equipment manufacturers will, with reduced demand in the future, cut back production rather than reduce price. Thus this oligopolistic practice will be one of the forces which prevents the index of prices paid by farmers from falling, as theory tells us it eventually should, in response to decreases in the index of prices paid. One must wonder too about the farming industry's emphasis on more energy-intensive machines in view of the sharp increases in fuel prices and the oligopolistic structure of the petroleum industry which will impede any decline in those prices.

The sharp upswing in U.S. agricultural product prices, triggered above all by weather-induced increases in foreign demand, has been rapidly offset by comparable increases in major inputs. In other, less favorable market situations, much of agriculture's adjustment to increases in the price of petroleum-based products would already have taken place. This adjustment will, however, have to take place if the prices of oil, gasoline, fertilizers, and agricultural chemicals do not fall. U.S. agriculture was able to meet the challenge of expanding production during past food crises by drawing on its reserve of research and technology. It remains to be seen whether it can develop a new knowledge-based technology (substituting rotation or other cultural practices for fertilizer, using minimum-tillage planting, replacing pesticides with biological control, etc.) if its present energy-intensive system becomes unsustainable.

Key Words	Central Concepts
Production function	Specifies the relationship between production and quantity of inputs used.
Maximize profits	The rational producer is assumed to produce at the level of output and mix of inputs which brings greatest profit.
Cobweb model	Explains supply response when farmers base expected price on the previous year's price.
Aggregation	Combining the effects of the actions of all individuals in an industry.
Marginal rate of substitution	The rate at which the last (or marginal) unit of one input would exchange for another input at a given level of output.
Interindustry transactions	Sales or purchases between one industry and another.
Balance sheet	The sources and disposition of funds of a firm, industry, or sector at one point in time.
Proprietor's equity	The part of the assets of a firm belonging to the owner. In agriculture, this consists mainly of land.
Labor quality	The level of health, skill, education, etc., of a worker which affects potential productivity.
Farm Credit System	Includes the Federal Land Banks, Federal Intermediate Credit Banks, Production Credit Associations, and Banks for Cooperatives.
Livestock feed economy	Includes inputs of grains, hay, and grass and outputs of cattle, hogs, sheep, and animal byproducts.

QUESTIONS

1. Explain the theoretical process by which a farmer decides what and how much to produce and what mix of inputs to use.

2. Can farmers actually maximize profits?
3. How might farmers get more productive use from their energy inputs? What policies could government employ to stimulate such actions?
4. Why is percentage of value added so much higher in wholesaling and retailing than in livestock and livestock products?
5. Discuss the relative importance of intermediate and final demand for agricultural products and services.
6. Do the production costs for U.S. agriculture in the years 1945, 1955, and 1965 confirm the trends shown in Table 5.3?
7. Why have capital and purchased inputs been substituted for labor and farm-produced inputs in U.S. agriculture?
8. Are farm debts becoming dangerously large relative to liquid assets in U.S. agriculture?
9. Should taxes on farm land be made to vary with net farm income?
10. Explain the relationship between productivity and net farm income? Will increased productivity put U.S. agriculture back in Professor Cochrane's agricultural treadmill?
11. The structure of modern agriculture has been heavily influenced by the relatively low prices of power, fertilizer, and chemicals from petroleum and cheap water. What will be the long-run effect of a doubling or tripling of energy and water prices?
12. What have been the reported advantages and disadvantages of conglomerate-owned farm operations?
13. Capital gains to land have been experienced in most years since World War II. What factors could cause a decline in the value of land?
14. Why has corporate farming been so prominent in Hawaii? Will the same factors arise in the future in mainland states?
15. List reasons why nonfarm firms would wish to own farm operations.
16. How can the quality of farm labor be improved?
17. Can small, independent farms secure sufficient capital to remain competitive with large corporate farms?

six

CATAPULTED INTO THE 1970s

INTRODUCTION

We have seen that agricultural programs in the United States in the past have frequently been caught off guard by sudden changes in the tide of events. Agriculture had limped through the late sixties on the arm of increasing government payments which reached almost 30 percent of realized net income in 1969. The Kennedy–Johnson boom, the longest period of economic expansion in U.S. history, had crested in 1968, and unemployment, prices, and interest rates began to rise simultaneously. Agricultural exports fell by over 6 percent in 1969, while domestic demand slackened. Economic experts, who had hoped that the application of Keynesian policies to economic management in the 1960s would end forever the cycle of boom and recession, scurried around trying to explain what had gone wrong. One convenient scapegoat was the Vietnam War, which had absorbed so much of the national resources and emotional reserves in fighting an uncertain enemy overseas and in fratricidal clashes at home. In a similar way, it was reasoned that a national recession would inevitably hurt agriculture.

Before the seventies were half over, both these assumptions were shown to be wrong. A further, more severe recession hit in 1974, even though the Vietnam War was over and agriculture, despite that recession, was enjoying one of its greatest peacetime booms. However, agricultural policy makers had little idea of what lay in store as they haggled over how the welfare of their farm constituents might be improved. Farm organizations were, as usual, divided in their recommendations. The Nixon administration, which came to power in January 1969, was committed to reducing government involvement in agriculture, while many economists warned of the dangers of dropping existing farm programs, and vested interests resisted change in any provisions which would hurt their pocketbooks. There was almost unanimous agreement, however, that U.S. agriculture still had an excess capacity problem and the problem of inadequate farm incomes.

Events outside agriculture were to be the main causes of the amazing change of fortune which overtook agriculture in the 1970s. Under President Nixon, bold political and economic initiatives were taken in the early seventies which changed the world economic picture dramatically. The dollar was devalued, its convertibility into gold withdrawn, and the price of gold freed from the level at which it had been arbitrarily pegged by F.D.R., almost 40 years previously. The Mainland (Red) China regime was formally recognized and relations with the Soviet Union altered from subdued belligerence to cautious but earnest efforts at working together to solve major problems. For U.S. agriculture, the practical effect was that it could now trade directly with two of the world's largest food importers whose markets had been closed to it. In 1973, the energy crisis hit with full fury and created the first huge question mark over the continued productivity of the U.S. agricultural machine.

THE 1970 AGRICULTURAL ACT

The Agricultural Act of 1965 had been framed in the years of chronic farm surpluses, depressed farm incomes, and a continuing belief in the ability of traditional government programs to solve the farm problem. With a Republican president in office, the latter belief was being challenged. However, the administration was not yet ready for a showdown with a democratically controlled Congress. Both acquiesced in the extension of the 1965 act for one year, 1969. For 1970, Congress faced the choice of framing a new act or of passing a further extension which would automatically trigger off some older provisions passed in 1958, mostly of a high support price nature. Experience during the 1960s had suggested that higher prices would be likely to lead to further increases in the productivity of U.S. agriculture. Fear of a return to a cycle of farm surpluses, depressed market prices, and large government expenditures was widespread. The Farm Bureau had a plan to break agriculture out of its chronic problems. They called for massive land retirements, a five-year phase-out of price support and diversion payments, and adjustment payments to encourage marginal farmers to leave farming. However, such a frontal attack on past farm programs had little chance of passage in a Congress where many of the advocates of past programs were still powerful.

The Nixon administration approached the issue more positively, calling for a more "market-oriented" policy with:

1. Pricing and price supports at or near the long-run equilibrium of supply and demand,
2. Production guided by market prices, and
3. Direct income payments in place of high price supports.

This would ostensibly allow a gradual reduction of government intervention and reassertion of market forces in U.S. agriculture.

New Goods or New Packaging?

The actual package which the administration presented to Congress in the fall of 1969 was a compromise between economic realities (what would help achieve greater market orientation) and political realities (what could be passed into law). One new piece of jargon, "set-aside," was added to the growing list of guide words around which policy would rotate. Farmers who set aside a specified part of their allotment of wheat, upland cotton, and feed grains, that is, kept land out of production, would qualify for price supports and would have greater freedom to grow whatever they wished on the remaining acreage. Permissible set-aside extended up to a maximum of 28 percent for upland cotton. Set-aside was a variation on the old theme of attempting to reduce supplies by paying farmers to keep land out of production. However, freeing production on the remaining land was intended to permit farmers to gain the benefits of economies of scale and specialization which had been blocked in previous programs. For example, a farmer with both a wheat and a feed grain allotment was free to grow only wheat on the acreage kept in production without losing his feed grain allotment.

The administration proposal contained much of the familiar to offset any serious resistance to the set-aside concept. In addition to price supports, loans were to be available to program participants. Parity was still used as a basis for determining certain support prices. Wheat producers could qualify for marketing certificates on a share of their domestic allotment. Smaller cotton producers got preferential payments. Milk price supports were continued, and a number of additional sweeteners were suggested for wool and mohair producers, beekeepers, and others.

The Key Issues

The haggling over the 1970 farm bill in both houses of Congress was long and often heated. A few key issues protracted the debate.

1. *Set-aside.* What was the desired level?

2. *Payment limitations.* A proposal in 1969 to limit payments from government funds to $20,000 on any one commodity had been narrowly defeated. A few sensational cases of payments to single farmers exceeding $1 million had caused a public outcry.

3. *The extent of the discretionary authority of the secretary of agriculture.* Could or should Congress write ever more complex laws to cover every possible foreseeable situation that might arise, or should they draft broad legislation to cover their intent and permit the secretary of agriculture wide discretion in interpreting the law as situations developed?

4. *Producer flexibility in decision making.* There was a real fear that allowing producers to decide on the crop they should grow could lead to surpluses in one item and shortages in another.

5. *Level of loan rates.* For most of the 1960s, the loan rate had been the effective floor below prices of major U.S. crops. Commodity representatives wanted higher loan rates to prop up farm incomes. However, loan rates above world market prices would run counter to efforts to make farm production more responsive to the market.

Terms of the 1970 Act

Passage of the bill was delayed by the approaching 1970 midterm elections. With all farm organizations more or less opposed to the bill, senators and congressmen from farm districts seeking reelection preferred to tread lightly on controversial issues. The House and Senate passed conflicting bills. A compromise bill was reached on October 7, 1970, but the Senate blocked a final vote until after the November election. When the president signed the bill on December 1, 1970, no members of Congress were present, an indication of their lack of pride in authorship.

The Agricultural Act of 1970 was to be in effect for the crop years 1971, 1972, and 1973. The set-aside and freedom-to-plant provisions survived. Loan and price support levels were almost identical to what they would have been under the 1965 act. A payment limitation of $55,000 per person per crop was approved, leaving the secretary of agriculture to define "person." The bureaucratic system to manage the programs was left intact.

The first crop year (1971) that the 1970 act was in operation did not gain support for the act from those who had opposed it. Realized net farm income fell below 1970 levels, partly because of a drop in government payments. Cropland withheld under set-aside and other programs was below 1970 levels. Acreage of all major crops planted rose despite the program. With higher yields, gross production also rose. Prices paid rose more rapidly than prices received, so that the relative position of farmers (as measured by the parity ratio) deteriorated. The administration's response was to try to increase participation in the set-aside programs and further restrict acreage by keeping loan rates unchanged despite a 7 percent increase in farm production costs and by offering generous payments on set-aside acreage (up to 40 percent of loan rate).

In its major provisions, then, the Agricultural Act of 1970 represented some breaks with the past but was still heavily dominated by the legacy of previous farm programs oriented to individual commodities and short-term remedies. Given a continuum of 1960s conditions, it is doubtful if it could have done much better in solving farm problems than its predecessors. However, it was not to be put to the test. Events in 1972 during the growing and harvesting period were to herald a sudden turnaround in the fortunes of U.S. farmers.

However, before moving on to discuss those events, we need to look briefly at some other developments which are likely to have a continuing influence on agricultural policy, on farmers, and on citizens and taxpayers. First, in the 1970 Agricultural Act a small program for beekeepers opened up a whole new area of government responsibility for private losses. If beekeepers could show that their colonies had been damaged or destroyed by contact with harmful agricultural chemicals, they could receive compensation (called an "indemnity") for their loss. No provision was made for establishing the liability of the person(s) who had used the offending chemicals or for recovering the costs of losses from them. Nor was account taken of the relative risks of beekeeping in different locations, but the precedent was established of indemnifying others for losses due to the side effects of farm production. A second provision of the original farm bill, the use of target prices against which actual prices could be compared in determining price supports, did not survive but was to become a key element in future farm legislation.

Forces of Change

Two other related forces were to have a major impact on agriculture after 1970. One was the wave of consumerism which expressed itself largely in attacks on the failures of the established government, regulatory agencies, and the food and fiber industries to protect the consumer from the unsafe, unscrupulous, or fraudulent activities of agriculture and agribusiness. Their activities led to passage of the Truth in Packaging Act, unit pricing in retail stores, dating of perishable products, and many other restrictions and limitations on how food marketing might be conducted. In the automobile industry consumerism was stimulated most by safety issues; in the food market, by rising prices.

Concern for what man was doing or might be doing to an ever more crowded planet was also behind popular movements to safeguard soil, air, and water; to control indiscriminate land use; and to protect natural environments, fish, and wildlife. Farmers were affected in varying degrees by the tighter federal controls on air and water introduced in the early seventies. Burning of stubble, an integral part of cropping programs for grass seed and other crops, and orchard heating by smudge pots were typical of the limited, but unacceptable, air pollution problems caused by agriculture. Water pollution problems were more serious, for example, nitrogen run-off which stimulated algae and choked waterways; chemical runoff which poisoned fish; and waste from large feedlots which caused offensive smells, discoloration, and problems in reuse of waterways. However, the most all-pervasive new controls were those imposed by the Occupational Safety and Health Agency (OSHA) of the Department of Labor and by the independent Environmental Protection Agency (EPA).

OSHA's mandate extended whereever workers were employed. Its goal was to eliminate hazards to health and safety within the work situation. In agriculture, it decreed the need for roll bars on tractors, for protective clothing when using dangerous tools or equipment, for fire alarms, safety instructions, sanitary facilities, and many other items not found on American farms. Its most controversial action was to set re-entry standards for agricultural chemicals, that is, after spraying certain materials on crops, workers could not re-enter the same field until the harmful effects of the material on man had been allowed to dissipate.

The EPA was even more all embracing in the scope of its regulatory ativities, with responsibilities for reducing automobile emissions and aircraft noise, eliminating the dumping of waste in waterways, and searching out other sources of environmental damage. In agriculture, its most controversial activity was also related to use of chemicals. Under the Federal Environmental Pesticide Control Act of 1972, the EPA had power to suspend temporarily, or ban permanently, use of any chemical substance because of its threat to the health and safety of man or the natural environment. The EPA was particularly concerned about cancer-causing (carcinogenic) substances. It established a registry of all chemicals, determined their permitted use, and tested and licensed applications.

By banning some important agricultural chemicals, EPA locked horns with the agricultural establishment, just as OSHA did with its pesticide re-entry standards. Before the dust of battle had settled, the American farmer was saddled with an array of additional costs, procedures, and restrictions which will squeeze some more marginal farmers out of business. All three agencies, USDA, EPA, and OSHA, now realize that the farmer's responsibility for the safety of his workers and the wholesomeness of his products requires him to use chemicals wisely and with caution. At the same time, the present level of productivity of U.S. agriculture is heavily dependent on continued use of chemicals. It will be decades before safer alternatives become available. In the meantime, society must continue to withstand some measure of risk in chemical use if it desires greater output and lower prices. As new knowledge becomes available and preferences change, society may continue to change the trade-off point between more chemicals and more food and fiber.

Key Words	Central Concepts
Vietnam War	In 1966, the U.S. began a massive buildup of fighting men and weaponry in South Vietnam to defend the pro-Western regime against internal rebellion and threat of invasion from North Vietnam. Despite staggering costs in men and materials the war was inconclusive. U.S. forces were gradually withdrawn after 1970.
Recession	Two consecutive quarters of declining gross national product.
Excess capacity	Too much of the nation's resources devoted to a particular sector.
Convertibility of gold	The right of a holder of gold to exchange it for its equivalent value in dollars.

Market orientation	Permitting free market price to guide production and consumption decisions.
Set-aside	A term to describe part of an allotment voluntarily taken out of production.
Payment limitations	Under pre-1970 farm acts, payments were made per acre or per unit of product. Larger farmers often got payments exceeding $1million. Public pressure forced inclusion of a $55,000 limitation in the 1970 act and a $20,000 limitation in 1973 legislation.
Discretionary authority	Authority to make specific interpretation of general legislation.
Loan rates	Rates at which the Commodity Credit Corporation lends money on stored crops.
Beekeeper indemnity program	Beekeepers were reimbursed for bee colonies damaged or destroyed by noxious farm chemicals.
Consumerism	Looking at economic affairs from the viewpoint of consumers' welfare.

QUESTIONS

1. Contrast the condition of U.S. agriculture in the five years before and after 1972.
2. Discuss the main forces which alter the environment for U.S. agriculture in the 1970s.
3. "The 1970 Agricultural Act was a victory for the administration point of view." Discuss.
4. What was new (and not new) about the 1970 Agricultural Act?
5. Do payment limitations reduce the incentive of larger farmers to increase their productivity?
6. Did disagreement among farmers and farm organizations about future agricultural policy prevent emergence of a strong congressional program?
7. To what other agricultural situations could a program similar to the Bee Indemnity Program be applied?
8. Was the influence of consumerism evident in the terms of the 1970 act?
9. In what ways did OSHA and EPA regulations bring benefits and costs to agriculture and to other sectors of the economy?

THE AGRICULTURE AND CONSUMER PROTECTION ACT OF 1973—EQUAL PARTNERS

The "Russian Grain Deal," publicly announced in early July 1972, has been seen by both consumers and agricultural interests as a critical turning point for agricultural prices. It was to alter decisively the environment in which agricultural policy would be discussed in future years. And indeed, the sales of 400 million bushels of grain (mostly wheat) to Russia from the 1972 crop was a major factor in the sharp recovery in farm incomes and in the domestic price of food. However, other, perhaps more permanent, factors were responsible for the turnaround. The world's output of food per capita was growing slightly faster than was population. So in most years, food supplies would be adequate, but in a year of below average production, severe regional or local shortages could arise. Such a deficit did emerge in 1973 and 1974 with acute shortages in the northern desert regions of Africa. Devaluation of the dollar and the upward valuation of other key currencies made U.S. grain exports a special bargain overseas. At the same time, booming economies in many parts of the world created an unprecedented demand for many commodities. Prophecies of doom, such as the Club of Rome's *Limits to Growth*, triggered off a speculative grab for the resources the world was supposedly running out of. As a result, many less developed countries found the value of their leading export soaring. As economic theory would have predicted, these increases in income led to increased demand for food and fiber, of which the U.S. was the major supplier.

World market growth boosted U.S. agricultural exports by almost 100 percent in the year beginning July 1, 1972, and a further 100 percent the following year. Total marketing receipts of the farming sector rose by over 40 percent and realized net income by over 70 percent in 1973. Unfortunately, much of the attention of the public was focused on the transient (but controversial) element of the situation, the Russian grain deal, with little attention paid to whether the underlying demand for U.S. agricultural exports had changed significantly. As policy makers struggled to develop a new agricultural act to replace the 1970 act in time for the 1974 crop year, they still tended to see the problems of U.S. agriculture as they had been in the 1960s. While price supports for all major crops were continued, the secretary of agriculture attempted to bring cropland back into production by reducing set-aside payments for the 1973 planting season. Once again, a policy designed for chronic surpluses was being thrown into reverse by the need to fill unexpected shortages. Farmers, putting aside memories of how many times in the past they had been bitten by the same sorts of sudden shifts, responded by increasing plantings in 1973 by almost 10 percent.

However, each time that prices dipped, pessimists saw the specter of farm depression ahead. Many feared that the administration's call for increased production was a trap to drive down prices and force the farmer back into the arms of government. Thus, the

Agricultural and Consumer Protection Act became law in August 1973 after over 12 months of difficult bargaining. The administration's arguments that U.S. agriculture was ready for the free market fell on deaf ears. Its stated goals of eliminating excess farm income supports and broadening production allotments from a per crop to a total cropland basis were not achieved. Instead, the act contained some incremental changes from the 1970 act and some new provisions that could increase government expenditure and involvement in agriculture at a later date.

Terms of the 1973 Act

The act was to be effective for the 1974 through 1977 crops. It had all the titles contained in the 1970 act, plus a tenth title on Rural Environmental Conservation. Much emphasis continued to be placed on individual commodities. The stated objectives of the act were to:

1. Assure ample supplies for home and export,
2. Provide price protection for farmers,
3. Give farmers full freedom to produce for the market, and
4. Assist farmers in conservation programs.

In view of the then prevailing high prices in agriculture, Congress did suspend many of the past restrictions on production and reduced the payment limitation to $20,000 per person (from $55,000 per crop per individual in 1970). Once again, the secretary of agriculture was authorized to define the term "person." The Wheat Certificate Program and the maximum set-aside on wheat were suspended for the duration of the act.

The common provisions affecting the wheat, feed grains, and upland cotton programs were as follows.

1. They would be effective for the years 1974–77 with no marketing quotas.
2. Loans and target prices (a new concept) would apply on production from allotment acres.
3. Allotments were intended to reflect domestic and world needs.
4. Set-aside provisions remained available if needed.
5. Additional substitute crops were authorized for allotment preservation.
6. The conserving base requirement was made discretionary.
7. A new crop insurance feature was added.

The payment rate per unit and the payment to an individual farmer would be determined as follows.

$$\text{Payment rate (\$/bu)} = \text{target price} - \text{average market price}$$

$$\text{Individual payment (\$)} = \text{payment rate (\$)} \times \text{allotment (acres)} \times \text{farm yield (units)}$$

Escalator clause governing 1976–77 target prices:

$$\text{Increase in target price} = \text{increase in cost of production} \pm \text{productivity change}$$

The "target price" concept had failed to make it into the 1970 act, but was central to the financial provisions of the 1973 act. In addition, spurred on by the rapid increases in production costs, an escalator clause stipulated how the target price would change as production costs changed during the life of the act. The average prices for all wheat and corn, on August 15, 1973, were $4.45 per bushel and $2.68 per bushel respectively, well above the target prices under the new act (Table 6.1). Shortly thereafter, cotton prices rose above target levels. Three years later, although target prices were 12 percent higher for wheat and 14 percent higher for corn and upland cotton, market prices were still above the target levels permissible under the 1973 act. However, as we shall see, Congress was not elated with its own foresight.

Table 6.1 Summary of Key Program Provisions, 1973 Act

	Wheat	*Feed Grains*	*Cotton*
Loan rate	$1.37/bu	$1.10/bu corn	90% of previous three-year average world price
Target price 1974–75	$2.05/bu	$1.38/bu corn	$0.38/lb
National allotment level	3 times 1970	70% of 1970	Same as 1970 11 million acres min.
Proclaimed by	April 15	January 1	–

Production restrictions were eased in the case of all set-aside by allowing the secretary to permit producers to plant or graze sweet sorghum and hay or produce guar, sesame, safflower, sunflower, castor beans, mustard seed, crambe, plantago ovato, flaxseed, triticale, oats, rye, or other commodities if he determined that such production was needed to provide an adequate supply, was not likely to increase the cost of price support programs and would not adversely affect farm income.

Provisions were also made for a number of studies: (1) an annual cost of production study of the wheat, feed grain, cotton, and dairy commodities needed to update target prices; (2) a dairy import study to appease those in the dairy industry who were calling for more restrictions on imports; (3) research to develop wheat and feed grain varieties more efficient in utilizing fertilizer, resistant to disease, and enhanced in their conservation and environmental varieties; (4) an agricultural census to be conducted by the secretary of commerce (the Nixon administration had opposed this); and (5) a livestock loss-in-transit study.

A new program was set up for cotton insect eradication, although most scientists and economists argued that eradication was infeasible. Prime targets were boll weevils and pink bollworm. The program would permit regionwide, concerted pest control approaches. As a result of allegations of wrongdoing in the Russian grain deal, and a fear of shortages on the home market, exporters were subjected to new reporting requirements for wheat, wheat flour, feed grains, oil seeds, cotton, etc., with provision for considerable flexibility on the part of the secretary of agriculture. As circumstances in the world market changed, the secretary, under this authorization, had recourse to prior approval, licensing, outright embargoes, and temporary suspensions of export sales. While usually U.S. farmers were protesting the import controls of other governments, they found themselves clamoring against the export controls of their own government.

For the first time disaster payments were granted on allotment acres in the case of abnormally low yields, crop failure, or other natural disasters. Payment rate would be one-third of target price. This was an extension of the principle of government responsibility for indemnifying producers against abnormal risks—first applied to beekeepers in the 1970 act.

Title X of the 1973 act contained a new program—the Rural Environmental Conservation Program. It permitted the secretary to make contracts for 3, 5, 10, or 25 years with, and at the option of, eligible owners and operators of land covering such matters as:

1. Purchase of perpetual easements.

2. Practices to protect wildlife, nearby populace, and communities from erosion, deterioration, pollution, etc.; to ensure an adequate supply of timber and wood products; to conserve surface waters and preserve and

improve habitat for migratory waterfowl; to further enhancement of the natural beauty of the landscape; and to bring about the promotion of comprehensive and total water management study. Advisory boards at state and national levels would be set up to assist the secretary in developing program provisions. However, despite the grandiose aims of Title X, the annual expenditure authorized for the whole country was only $25 million.

Public Law 480, as amended in 1966, was to continue unchanged. Commodities could continue to be sold for foreign currency or dollar credits, to be donated or to be bartered. The Food Stamp program provisions remained much the same, after an effort to deny food stamps to strikers failed. It was to be extended to Puerto Rico, Guam, and the Virgin Islands. At the bottom of the 1975 recession almost 20 million people were receiving food stamp benefits, two-thirds more than in June 1973. While increased exports and rising food prices reduced the need for PL480, it increased the need for and cost of domestic food programs.

Evaluation of the 1973 Act

As in the case of the 1970 act, there were few in or out of agriculture who saw the 1973 act as providing an approach to agricultural policy that could effectively forestall future problems. As free market prices soared above loan rates and target prices, the latter's role as stabilizers of prices was lost. Price uncertainty was severe. In the 1973–74 season, the average price of all wheat rose by $2 per bushel between July and August 1973, remained at a stable high level for six months, and then fell by $2 per bushel between February and May 1974. These sorts of price changes were outside the ranges normally found in program commodities. Neither government nor private forecasters could provide farmers with much guidance. U.S. agriculture had become open to economic upheaval anywhere in the world. The environment for wise decision making on the basis of reasonable expectations was shattered.

The consumer was equally upset by the violent price swings in agricultural commodities. Although the eventual form of the 1973 act bore little relation to consumer needs, consumer interests had succeeded in keeping target prices down and in reducing payment limits per person per crop further and had been thrown a sop by having "Consumer Protection" invoked in the title of the act. Consumers had also been disturbed by actual or threatened shortages of meat and other products, so that the goal of full production no longer meant high costs for government disposal of surpluses, but meant instead lower costs of farm products to them.

Conceptually, the 1973 Farm Act was a failure before it went into operation. Originally intended to take government out of agriculture, it ended up committing government to target prices higher than average prices in the preceding decade. The provision for target prices to vary as costs of production varied was dependent on the ability of researchers to measure average or representative costs of production. The results of this exercise were of varied quality and magnitude. What is a cost in any instance is a matter of both political and economic judgment. It is possible to justify many different levels of cost. Programs continued to be piecemeal and commodity-oriented, with no effort to treat producers of different commodities in a consistent manner. The freedom to plant other commodities on allotment acreage was extended, but mainly to minor and less profitable crops. Protectionism still prevailed in cotton, tobacco, and rice. In the tradition of congressional procedures, the existence of such exceptions was a useful precedent for other preferential exceptions in future years.

However, the basic problem with the 1973 act was that from where its sponsors started one could not hope to reach the goal of a national food and fiber policy. Such a policy could only be developed from a complete review of (1) the nation's agricultural resources and those of major trading partners or competitors throughout the world; (2) the nation's goals for food and fiber for home consumption, for commercial exports, and for aid or other diplomatic purposes; (3) the alternative ways in which resources could be used to achieve these goals; (4) the acceptable rules of the game under which goals might be achieved–government monopoly or free market; (5) the influence of developments in the supply and marketing systems on achievement of these goals; and (6) the procedures by which disagreements between parties (producers and consumers) could be resolved. In other words, a national policy for food and fiber must first determine *what* society's overall wants and needs are, and then determine *how* the food and fiber system can best meet them.

Key Words	Central Concepts
Russian Grain Deal	A secretly negotiated agreement for Russian purchases of U.S. grain in 1972. Critics charged that the price had been unrealistically low because of the secrecy and that grain trading companies had gained an unfair advantage over farmers.
Club of Rome	A privately financed study group which published pessimistic projections of future world society.

Escalator clause A clause establishing a formula for changing target prices when farm costs of production changed.

Target price The minimum price government wishes producers to receive. If market price falls below target price, the government may pay the difference to the producer.

Insect eradication It is an attractive illusion that by wiping out an entire insect population, expenditure on insect control can be avoided in the future. However, eradication of a species is impossible—the marginal cost of wiping out the last insect becomes infinite. (Can you explain why?)

Trade embargo A government prohibition on imports or exports.

Preferential exceptions Exceptions to a general law giving favorable treatment to one or more groups.

QUESTIONS

1. Did the 1973 Agriculture and Consumer Protection Act provide the U.S. with a comprehensive agricultural policy?
2. What impact on price of grains would one expect from an increase in demand of 400 million bushels?
3. Were there real shortages underlying the boom in raw material prices of 1972–74 or was the price rise due to speculation or hoarding?
4. Did the rise in net farm income in 1973 and 1974 convince Congress that the days of low incomes in U.S. agriculture were over?
5. How did farmers achieve increased production in 1973? By increased acreage, increased use of inputs, increased yields or some of each?
6. Did the provisions of the 1973 act ensure ample supplies for home and export?
7. Explain the operation of the target price system of maintaining farm incomes.
8. How free were farmers to plant what they wished?
9. Dairy farmers would be helped by limits on both grain exports and dairy product imports. Discuss.
10. What were the similarities and differences between beekeeper indemnity payments and crop disaster payments?
11. Should the Department of Agriculture be concerned with enhancement of the natural beauty of the landscape?
12. Trace the changes in PL480 shipments under various titles from 1954 to 1974.
13. Was price uncertainty more severe in the early 1970s than in the early 1960s? Than in the early 1950s? How would you suggest measuring uncertainty?
14. Did the U.S. consumer need protection?

THE EMERGENCY FARM ACT OF 1975—CRYING WOLF

Perhaps the fairest commentary on the 1973 Agriculture and Consumer Protection Act was that Congress began the process of replacing it while it was still in its first year of operation. Changes in the apparent direction of the economy had continued to come in rapid succession. In the summer of 1973 President Nixon, just about to sink in the morass of Watergate, began the process of abandoning wage and price controls originally instituted in August 1971. In October 1973, the outbreak of the Yom Kippur War between Egypt and Israel precipitated in rapid succession sharp price boosts on Arab oil, then an Arab oil embargo on nations deemed to be friends of Israel, and finally a solid cartel of petroleum exporting countries including some non-Arab countries committed to holding oil prices at triple pre-embargo levels. Other economies, notably Japan and Western Europe, who were heavily reliant on imported petroleum, were stunned. In the United States, the automobile, construction, trucking, and other energy-dependent industries plunged into a deep recession. Worldwide demand slackened, and the spiral of raw material price increases, which a few months before had been driving crazily upwards, collapsed as rapidly as it had risen.

The outlook for agriculture in 1974 was clouded both by weakened demand and by the prospect of rising prices of inputs. The ending of controls would mean "catch-up" price increases by many agricultural suppliers. The energy price boosts meant large increases in costs of fuel, fertilizers, tractors, and other powered equipment. The parity ratio (index of prices received divided by index of prices paid) which had been exactly 100 (that is, equal to the 1967 base) on July 15, 1972, peaked at 137 in August 1973, was still at 128 in February 1974, but fell to 99 in June 1974. U.S. agriculture had seen cycles like this before. Many observers wondered if a comparable decline in parity was just ahead. Prices of all major crops and livestock appeared to be falling simultaneously, while export demand was generally less buoyant.

Beginning with the first quarter of 1974, the general economy declined in five successive quarters. Gross National Product fell by 7.0, 1.6, 1.9, 9.0, and 11.4 percent. The popular indicators of the economic health of the nation—unemployment, real earnings, industrial production, and interest rates—all moved unfavorably. Recession combined with inflation and relaxed eligibility conditions swelled the rolls of welfare and Food Stamp recipients to record levels. Parallels with the Great Depression, which are dusted out during each economic downturn, were taken more seriously than at any time since World War II.

Tenure of the Emergency Farm Act of 1975

In such an environment, the leading Democrats in Congress, spurred on by freshmen congressmen with no ties to previous farm programs, pushed through the Emergency Farm Act of 1975. The main thrust of the act was major increases in target prices for wheat, feed grains, and cotton. Congress was indicating that the target prices agreed to under the 1973 act were out of line with the new cost situation. The Ford administration opposed the act as inflationary, as did many consumer groups. The American Farm Bureau Federation opposed the concept and the level of target prices as a restoration of government subsidy of U.S. agriculture.

However, Congress was not to be denied. The Emergency Farm Act of 1975 was approved by the House (259 to 162) on March 20 and in a Senate version on March 26 (57 to 25). The joint bill was approved on April 22 and vetoed by President Ford on May 1. The veto was upheld when the House vote to override (245 to 182) failed to reach the necessary two-thirds majority.

The target prices and loan rates finally contained in the bill were sharply higher than those specified in 1973 (Table 6.2). Secretary of Agriculture Butz estimated the bill would cost the government $1.8 billion in its first year and $4 billion to $5 billion in its second year. Congressional committees had estimated the cost at $210 million for the first year, excluding loans. Butz said he opposed the bill because it reversed the trend to get government out of agriculture, it was not necessary to encourage planting, and prices were rising anyway.

Table 6.2 Comparison of Target Prices and Loan Rates, 1973 Act and 1975 Bill

	Target Prices			*Loan Rates*		
	1973	*1975*	*% Change*	*1973*	*1975*	*% Change*
Wheat	2.05	3.10	+51.2	1.37	2.50	+82.5
Corn	1.38	2.25	+63.0	1.10	1.87	+70.0
Cotton	0.38	0.45	+18.4	0.34	0.38	–

After the demise of the Emergency Farm Act, agricultural prices seesawed around 1967 parity. The return of the USSR to the world wheat market and the conclusion of a five-year pact for large quantities of grain restored confidence in the market despite record world output. The economic recovery which got underway in the United States in spring 1975 appeared to have spread to other major industrial nations. However, costs of production continued to creep upwards. Congress remained impatient with the operation of the 1973 act, which provided no cushion against late season price declines. The secretary of agriculture continued to use his powers under the 1973 Act to encourage all-out production. Set-aside was not required for the 1975, 1976, or 1977 crop years. In addition, allotments on which payments would be made were increased and loan rates and target prices adjusted modestly upwards.

Protecting Farmers First

The Emergency Farm Act of 1975 dropped any pretense of concern for consumers that had been apparent in the framing of the 1973 act. Agriculture appeared to be heading for trouble, and in the scramble to its aid, the good intentions of getting government out of agriculture, of protecting the consumer, or of restoring efficiency were summarily set aside. The basic goal was to protect farmers from income losses, regardless of the cost to the taxpayer. Ironically, the freshmen congressmen, who had helped bring about the change of leadership, enlargement, and supposed democratization of the House Agriculture Committee, were even more enthusiastic than those they had ousted for high price supports. Opponents of the Emergency Farm Bill predicted that it would not pass the full House, but it did by a comfortable majority. Even after President Ford vetoed the bill, the house only fell short of the two-thirds majority needed to override the veto by 40 votes. Had farm prices continued to fall in 1975 it is probable that those 40 additional votes could have been won over.

The 1975 price recovery in agriculture was stimulated by a number of factors. During the worst of the recession and inflation of 1974–75, U.S. consumers cut back spending on automobiles, electrical appliances, and other durables but maintained or increased their spending on food. The USSR was predicting grain production of 185 million tons, 14 percent below the 1975 target, and was expected to make very large purchases in world markets. This helped to turn around the sagging grain market which had been depressed by expectation of large U.S. crops. Livestock prices also recovered as supplies fell and real incomes of consumers rose. The price of farm inputs, which had risen by 8 percent in the last half of 1974, rose by only 4 percent in the first half of 1975 as energy costs stabilized. The USDA was predicting net farm incomes close to the record 1974 levels. Foreign demand was also expected to stay strong as the oil-rich countries increased their purchases of U.S. farm products. In addition, the balance of world food supply and demand was still in doubt, as many countries attempted to build stocks to safer levels than had been experienced in the previous two years.

Bilateral Grain Deals

As 1975 ended, the farm boom, begun in 1972, was still alive. Prices received and prices paid by farmers had stabilized in a relationship close to parity. The marketing system looked as if it could comfortably digest the largest U.S. grain crop ever produced. Indeed, spurred on by labor union pressure, President Ford imposed a temporary moratorium on U.S. wheat exports, which was lifted only when the United States and Russia reached a five-year agreement on trade in grain. The USSR agreed to take a minimum of 6 million tons of corn and wheat each year, with a proviso for purchases of an additional 2 million tons if approved by the president of the United States. To protect the U.S. consumer from sharp price changes in years of small crops, only 6 million tons could be sold if the U.S. grain crop fell below 225 million tons. At the same time, the U.S. applied diplomatic pressure to other large grain buyers to moderate their purchases so as to prevent a speculative "free-for-all" as in 1972–73. Farmers objected to any form of export control either by presidential fiat or by informal arrangements, arguing that the United States was risking the loss of its customers to other more reliable suppliers.

CONTROL OF AGRICULTURAL POLICY MAKING, THE UNITED STATES AND THE WORLD

The year 1975 marked little progress on a number of fronts related to agricultural policy. Secretary Butz openly declared his wish to see the Food Stamp program, which was taking half his department's appropriations, placed under HEW or another welfare agency, so as to permit his department to concentrate on the business of agriculture. Congress refused to act on this request. At the same time, the Departments of State and Treasury and other executive agencies continued to seek influence over the direction of agricultural policy because of its increased importance in the domestic economy and in relation to other countries. For example, President Ford's decision to impose a moratorium on grain exports reflected a victory for these rival agencies over the view of the secretary of agriculture and almost all farm groups. However, in early 1976, President Ford set up a new

Agricultural Policy Committee at cabinet level to consolidate domestic and international policy making on agriculture. The secretary of agriculture was appointed to chair this committee, a move which was seen by some as a victory for the USDA, by others as a pre-election ploy which could be rapidly reversed at some future time.

However, if the events of the early 1970s had shown any one thing clearly, it was that worldwide agricultural productivity could not be taken for granted and that the business of agriculture was the business of everyone, not just farmers. For example, the World Food Council, convened in Rome in late 1974, was attempting to find a formula to ensure increasing world per capita food supplies and, in the event of regional or widespread crop failures, to ensure adequate reserves and an equitable distribution of supplies. However, the World Food Council represented a challenge to the independent control of agricultural policies which countries had jealously guarded for decades. As it became clear that world food production had recovered from the depressed 1974 levels and as the atmosphere of crisis waned, the will to find a solution also waned. Since many of the major producing countries did not have a comprehensive food policy for their own country, it had probably been premature to hope that they could coordinate their diverse, piecemeal programs in a coherent world food policy.

In early 1977, Congress was wrestling with a new agricultural act to replace the 1973 act. With prices again below parity, stocks building up, the cost of many inputs still rising, and a Democratic president in the White House, the preconditions for passage of legislation similar to the 1975 Emergency Farm Bill were all present. While Congress could decide to extend the 1973 act or allow agriculture to revert to basic legislation still on the statute books, the odds appeared to be weighted in favor of a resumption of government's involvement in price supports and stockholding.

Key Words	Central Concepts
Arab oil embargo	Arab oil producers refused to sell oil to countries allied with or deemed friendly toward Israel.
Oil cartel (OPEC)	Formed by the Organization of Petroleum Exporting Countries (OPEC), it dramatically boosted world oil prices in 1973.
Inflationary	Causing or likely to cause general price increases. Note: The increase in prices of one product or group of products may not be inflationary if offset by decreases in other product prices.
Real income	Income in terms of purchasing power corrected for changes in general price levels.

Bilateral deals Deals between two parties. A very common approach to international trade when multilateral arrangements are too restrictive or difficult to negotiate.

Moratorium A temporary suspension of an activity, e.g., exporting of wheat.

World Food Council One of the agencies set up by the 1974 World Food Conference to coordinate world food policies.

QUESTIONS

1. Why did Congress change its mind so rapidly about the 1973 act? Are such rapid changes common in agricultural policy making?
2. Have recent recessions hurt net farm income?
3. Could another Great Depression occur? What are the odds against it? Should agricultural policy be geared for such an eventuality?
4. The American Farm Bureau represents more farmers than any other farm organization? Why then did Congress override its wishes on target prices?
5. How would the Emergency Farm Act of 1975 have helped consumers?
6. Is the U.S. experience of rapid recessions followed by rapid recovery inevitable in an industrial economy?
7. Are sales of agricultural products under long-term contracts likely to make farm prices more stable?
8. Who now controls U.S. agricultural policy making?
9. Who now controls world agricultural policy making?
10. Can a weak international agency compete with strong national bureaucracies in framing a world agricultural policy?

seven

THE UNITED STATES AND THE WORLD

FOREIGN TRADE— BUILDING BLOCKS FOR GROWTH

In many ways, foreign trade is much like trade between businesses within a country. Trade depends on mutuality of interests between the traders, confidence in the quality of goods sold and the solvency of the purchaser, competitiveness, reliability, availability of transportation, communication, etc. The one essential difference is that foreign traders operate under the jurisdiction of different governments. Throughout history, governments have shown a propensity to tax, restrict, regulate or ban foreign trade. The reasons for such actions have ranged from religious (fighting heretics) to strategic (fighting enemies) to economic (mercantilist desire to curb gold outflows) to ideological (fighting fascism, communism, and other "isms"). Foreign trade has been stimulated where infighting between governments was minimized, by imperial domination (Britain and its colonies), by the dominance of one trader (the United States in the

1950s), or by mutual agreement (the EEC's common trade policies). Occasionally, too, in the past governments have given one organization a limited monopoly in foreign trading, as was the case with the Hudson's Bay Company in North America and the East Indies Company in southern Asia. Since World War II, governments of every political coloration have given state trading companies monopoly control over some or all aspects of foreign trade. In foreign trade, economics and politics are inseparable.

The benefits of free trade were widely accepted under classical laissez-faire economics. Under perfect competition, one can demonstrate by the theory of comparative advantage that trade can benefit both traders and lead to a "Pareto optimum" world. However, the emerging European economies in the nineteenth century and the lesser developed countries in the twentieth century have frequently been critical of the distribution of benefits from trade in the real imperfect world.

Taking into account such factors as population, income per capita, costs of production, and location, there is a theoretical optimum combination of production and trade which would maximize producers' income and minimize consumer costs worldwide at any point in time. In such an ideal regimen the U.S. would probably become a specialist in grains and import much of its fruit and vegetable needs. The United States might also have a comparative advantage in grain-based livestock production. The optimum would of course change from time to time as demand, technology, etc., changed.

The Political Economy of Trade

However, the political economy of trade puts many obstacles in the way of efforts to approach that optimum. For example, in its trade negotiations the U.S. seeks:

1. *Political gain* in the form of alliances with friendly countries, sanctions against unfriendly countries, strategic military advantage, reciprocal benefits, and so forth.

2. *Economic gain* which can be conveniently categorized into access for (a) U.S. raw products, mainly agricultural, such as grains, tobacco, and cotton; (b) U.S. finished goods, mostly industrial, such as, Boeing planes; (c) U.S. capital, mostly in the form of investment by U.S.-based multinational corporations, such as General Motors' holdings in Opel of Germany, Vauxhall of the United Kingdom, etc.

While U.S. farmers want access for their raw products and freedom to import needed inputs, U.S. trade negotiators often have different priorities. Other countries, in turn, have their trade priorities; acceptance of more U.S. agricultural products may not have high priority. Trade factors cannot be separated from domestic economic policies. For example, for four decades the U.S. Sugar Act, which allocated imports to many developing countries, had great impact on the total economy of producing countries (especially Cuba and the Philippines) and on the sugar beet economy in the United States.

Historical Developments

Despite the opposition of its farmers, the U.S. imposition of the Hawley–Smoot tariffs in 1930 led to retaliatory measures from other countries. A notable reaction was the Commonwealth preferences of 1932 which governed access to the United Kingdom market. Australia, New Zealand, Canada, and Ireland, all major exporters and Commonwealth countries, gained a trade advantage over the United States in the United Kingdom market. World trade was greatly depressed during the thirties. The outbreak of World War II brought a surge in demand for farm exports from the United States, whose productive capacity was not affected by war. After the war, while both victors and vanquished were rebuilding their agriculture, U.S. exports continued to be strong. However, by the mid-fifties, many countries sought new strategies for their total economies and for their agriculture. Undoubtedly, the U.S. model of a large, protected domestic market with high price supports and government-aided exports, influenced their thinking. The United Kingdom, a major importer, encouraged extensive imports, allowed market price to find its own level, and provided high payments to domestic producers to increase their share of the market. Their consumers got plentiful supplies at low prices, their farmers an enlarged market. The main countries of Western Europe, the original EEC of France, West Germany, Italy, Netherlands, Belgium, and Luxembourg, set up the Common Market in 1958. The Common Agricultural Policy which emerged provided for a high price support, protected community agricultural sector. In addition, a common fund could be used to subsidize exports of commodities in surplus. Japan, in contrast, made the decision to build economic growth on imports of strategic raw materials, especially from countries such as the U.S. which would provide markets for its industrial goods. The Soviet bloc in general sought to mesh its economy more closely with those of Eastern Europe by *encouraging* reciprocal trade and *resisting* trade with other countries.

Rapid economic growth throughout the world permitted a steady rise in U.S. agricultural exports throughout the sixties, but not rapidly enough to alleviate the problem of surplus farm production. While the General Agreement on Tariffs and Trade (GATT), first initiated in 1947, negotiated many significant steps toward freer world trade, the benefits tended to go mostly to industrial goods, in particular, industrial goods produced by the highly developed nations. Again, this is what our knowledge of income elasticities would lead us to expect. In high income countries, as incomes continue to rise the demand for an increasing number, variety, and choice of nonessential items tends to rise even more rapidly than the demand for food. Advanced countries either cannot meet many of these new demands from their existing resources or can more efficiently produce other items with those resources. In either case, they will attempt to gain the new items by trade.

Trade and the Balance of Payments

Each individual will seek to buy from any part of the world those items which maximize his utility, and importers in his own country and exporters elsewhere will push to satisfy his demands. However, if all individuals in a country are buying more abroad than they are selling, a country will find an increasing amount of its currency in the hands of foreigners. As long as foreigners can use this currency to purchase other goods or to hold it as savings, no problems arise.

Unfortunately, currencies behave just like farm commodities. When the supply is plentiful, the value in exchange falls. Fear of further falls causes speculative selling and further falls, so countries are wary of letting their balance of payments in any period get far into deficit. They like their payments to the rest of the world for goods and services to match closely what they earn from sales of goods and services to the rest of the world. Trade in goods is generally the most important source of international transactions. However, other items, such as transportation services, tourism, remittances from emigrants, flows of investment funds, and flows of interest or dividends on investments, also affect whether or not the balance of payments actually balances. The number of American tourists spending dollars in Europe may thus have an important bearing on how much U.S. wheat the Europeans will be willing to buy. Accordingly, government efforts to stimulate or discourage free trade among nations may often reflect concern about the broader issues of international payments rather than the direct effects of increased competition on domestic producers.

Prior to World War II, the pound sterling was the major reserve currency, that is, the currency in which nations held their net balances as a store of value either to meet future foreign purchases or to back their own currencies. However, to finance the war effort, the sterling area spent more than it earned abroad, so the value of sterling began to fall. Eventually, in 1951, the British government was forced to devalue the pound by 30 percent. That is, over night holders of sterling lost 30 percent of the value of their holdings in terms of other currencies. As a result, many countries began to use the U.S. dollar as the main reserve currency. However, in the late 1960s, the United States overspent abroad to finance the Vietnam War. As a result, in 1971, after allowing the dollar to float (move freely with respect to other currencies), the dollar value in other currencies was pegged at about 10 percent below pre-1971 levels. The Smithsonian Agreement between the major advanced countries later in 1971 patched together an international payments system which has survived a number of crises but still seems grossly inadequate for the enormous scale of world trade flows. For example, between 1972 and 1976 the exchange rate for German marks in terms of sterling doubled, thus dramatically cheapening U.K. exports to Germany and increasing the cost of German imports into the U.K. Such drastic currency realignments put enormous pressure on governments to take countermeasures which were often trade restricting.

World trade continued to grow during the sixties and early seventies, spurred on by economic growth in both developed and lesser developed countries, by the advantages of freer trade in a period of growth, and by the willingness of centrally planned countries to participate more fully in external trade. The worldwide recession which followed the energy crisis of 1973 temporarily halted economic growth, aroused a new wave of protectionist sentiment, and slowed down the demand of the centrally planned countries. In a bid to avoid a repeat of the retaliatory spiral of trade barriers, OECD member countries agreed not to take such action for a full year beginning in early 1975. This helped to avert rash action until the recession was beginning to fade and protectionist sentiment lessened. Indeed, as unemployment persisted at high levels in 1976 and 1977, many countries were turning to a new protectionism of seeking voluntary curbs by low-cost suppliers on the quantities they would ship, presumably to avoid the importing country being pressured politically to limit imports more forcibly.

U.S. Agricultural Exports

U.S. agricultural exports have been influenced by the general considerations discussed so far and by other factors relevant to specific commodities. The value of U.S. agricultural exports gained little during the sixties. The real growth came between 1971 and 1974 when agricultural exports tripled (Table 7.1). In 1962, 30 percent of all agricultural exports were under specified government financed programs, e.g., PL480. In 1974, this proportion fell to less than 4 percent. The share of total U.S. exports represented by agricultural products was the same in 1974 as in 1962, indicating a broad-based growth in demand for all U.S. exports over the period. However, since the agricultural share of U.S. imports fell from 24 to 10 percent between 1962 and 1974, the agricultural sector's contribution to the U.S. balance of payments increased over the period. Essentially the United States is in favor of free trade in grains and protectionist in

Table 7.1 Value of U.S. Agricultural Exports to Selected Countries, Selected Calendar Years, 1962–75 ($ million)

Country	*1962*	*1967*	*1972*	*1973*	*1974*	*1975*
Japan	481	865	1,427	2,998	3,479	3,082
Canada	512	556	843	1,034	1,282	1,333
Netherlands	366	492	702	1,241	1,604	1,722
West Germany	391	436	682	1,181	1,588	1,565
Italy	176	226	338	674	763	798
Belgium–Luxembourg	132	156	138	223	259	347
France	86	148	245	390	492	412
United Kingdom	408	424	480	616	655	589
Spain	99	167	300	462	711	766
Denmark	64	87	101	163	112	111
People's Republic of China	—	—	193	406	653	80
USSR	6	19	430	920	300	1,136
Africa	375	257	297	583	1,138	1,156
Middle East	n.a.	n.a.	n.a.	n.a.	1,262	1,160
World	5,031	6,383	9,401	17,680	21,999	21,894
Agricultural percentage of all U.S. exports	23	20	17	23	23	21
Agricultural percentage of all U.S. imports	24	17	12	12	10	10
Agricultural exports under government financed programs	1,513	1,269	1,153	867	859	1,383

Source: U.S. Foreign Agricultural Trade, *Statistical Report*, annual.

livestock products. The conditions of world demand and supply made such a stance both lucrative and acceptable to its trading partners in the early 1970s. However, world surpluses in livestock or dairy products would make the ambiguous U.S. stance the source of much discontent among its trading partners.

The growth of U.S. agricultural exports has been geographically broad based. Leading customers in 1962 such as Japan, Canada, and West Germany continue to be important. Japan, the Netherlands, Italy, France, and Spain have grown even faster than the average. The USSR and the People's Republic of China (Mainland China) have become important but erratic customers. Many lesser markets have grown even more rapidly than average. In turn, certain traditional markets such as the United Kingdom and Canada have become relatively less important.

Part of the reason for this can be explained by changes in the mix of U.S. agricultural exports (Table 7.2). The really spectacular increases have been in food grains (wheat and rice), feed grains, soybeans, and oilseeds. The reasons for these increases have been the growing demand and reduced supply of food grains, notably in developing countries where cereals are an important part of the total diet, and the demand for more livestock products as income levels rise, triggering off a demand for animal feed. The United States has proven to be the only source from which rapid increases in supply of food grains or feed grains might come. However, in the longer run, continued high prices of grains would tend to stimulate production of these and other substitutes in other countries. Continued high prices of animal feed would tend to discourage livestock production. Accordingly, no one can predict how buoyant these export-inducing

Table 7.2 Value of Leading U.S. Agricultural Exports, Selected Calendar Years, 1962–75 ($ million)

Item	*1962*	*1967*	*1972*	*1973*	*1974*	*1975*
Animals and animal products	588	712	1,115	1,584	1,776	1,693
Wheat	942	1,120	1,366	4,046	4,437	5,162
Rice	153	314	388	539	852	858
Feed grains	787	1,052	1,522	3,539	4,646	5,239
Fruits and preparations	285	309	429	535	596	699
Vegetables and preparations	159	211	257	373	473	504
Oilseeds	432	827	1,658	2,967	3,828	3,145
Soybeans	407	772	1,508	2,762	3,537	2,865
Tobacco, unmanufactured	373	514	672	714	886	877
Cotton, ex linters	528	464	503	929	1,335	991

Source: U.S. Foreign Agricultural Trade, *Statistical Report*, annual.

factors will continue to be. While there has been much attention paid to the emergence of communist nations as major importers of U.S. agricultural products, centrally planned economies accounted for less than 10 percent of all U.S. farm exports in 1975. Developed countries led by the EEC-6 continued to purchase more than half of U.S. farm exports, with the less developed countries accounting for about one-third of all purchases in 1975. So, while there have been some spectacular changes in demand for U.S. agricultural products, three key factors—rising incomes, domestic shortages of food and feed, and favorable government attitudes toward trade—remain crucial.

Trade Act of 1974

The Trade Act of 1974 attempted to alter U.S. trade policy in line with new international realities. The president was authorized to give "Most Favored Nation" treatment to Communist countries, and to extend adjustment relief (retraining, relocation, etc.) of firms injured by import competition. The act also increased preferences for some items (mostly manufactures) from developing countries and permitted the U.S. to retaliate against export controls of its suppliers by putting on its own export controls. However, Wilbur F. Monroe maintains that while U.S. international trade through the 1974 act has made major adjustments, it will remain for some time in a transitional period where further adjustments must be made. The act was timely in that it gave the U.S. a more modern bargaining weapon in the trade negotiations (both bilateral and multilateral) of the mid-1970s. How effective it will be seen to have been in retrospect may depend on the sorts of new trade relations that emerge between already developed countries and with newly developing countries.

Future Directions

What can we say about the likely direction of U.S. agricultural exports in the future? So far we have looked only at trends in the value of U.S. agricultural exports, since it is difficult otherwise to add units of grain and units of cotton or beef. However, the USDA does publish quantity indexes of U.S. exports which to some extent remove the effects of price changes and allow us to compare changes in the volume of agricultural exports and imports (Table 7.3). These indicate that the volume of U.S. agricultural exports peaked in 1973, even though value continued to rise for a further year. The volume of imports, after falling off in 1974, continued to rise in 1975, so the real balance of trade began to worsen after 1973. While the volume of exports of grains and oilseed products had grown most between

1967 and 1975 and the volume of cotton and unmanufactured tobacco least, all four categories had shown year-to-year volume changes of over 30 percent. Rather surprisingly, exports of animals and animal products showed the most modest but most consistent growth. Clearly, for its major export products, the U.S. is sensitive to world supply and demand conditions.

Table 7.3 Quantity Indexes of U.S. Agricultural Exports and Imports, 1967–75 (Base 1967 = 100)

Item	*1967*	*1970*	*1971*	*1972*	*1973*	*1974*	*1975*
All agricultural imports	100	110	113	118	121	115	125
All agricultural exports	100	111	111	129	166	155	156
Exports of:							
Animals and animal products	100	108	129	126	128	130	133
Cotton	100	78	110	81	146	138	103
Tobacco, unmanufactured	100	90	83	110	109	119	103
Grains and preparations	100	105	96	129	191	153	175
Oilseeds and products	100	159	159	163	172	195	163

Source: U.S. Foreign Agricultural Trade, *Statistical Report*, annual.

Agricultural exports are also likely to be affected by the factors which affect overall U.S. foreign trade relations. The EEC has consistently absorbed over 20 percent of U.S. agricultural exports. Given the level of its income and structure of its agriculture, it could continue to be a major market for U.S. wheat, corn, and soybeans (if protectionist fervor is kept in check). The EEC's desire for agricultural self-sufficiency and U.S. protection for dairy and beef products has been a constant source of friction. Yet without agreement between these major powers, further freeing of world agricultural trade is unlikely. The USSR needs U.S. technology to improve its industrial productivity and U.S. grains to improve the diets of its people. Both of these should encourage closer trade ties. However, the variability of Russian output may bring very wide year-to-year swings in demand for U.S. agricultural exports. Japan and other Southeast Asian countries have been prepared to buy U.S. agricultural products in exchange for improved access to the U.S. industrial and consumer markets. However, the higher bill for imported energy will also have to be considered in the trade-off. Mainland China appears eager to acquire U.S. technology and so may be willing to fill its intermittent agricultural shortages from U.S. sources. The OPEC nations, under the impetus of dramatic increases in income, will become markets for U.S. agricultural products comparable to the markets of Europe and Japan. Even the less developed nations, out of choice or necessity, will have to turn to the U.S. for most essential supplies. Demand there may partly depend on the stimulant of U.S. government financing. However, over all, the outlook is for an erratic but growing volume of U.S. agricultural exports.

In turn, this growth is likely to have a destabilizing effect on U.S. farm prices. By 1975, three out of every ten acres of cropland was being devoted to serving export markets. The export dependence of leading crops in the fiscal year 1975 was 58 percent for wheat, 56 percent for rice, 48 percent for soybeans, and 34 percent for tobacco. Clearly, the government stabilization programs of the past would be less effective, more costly, and more subject to error in an agricultural economy so open to external influences. In summary, the opportunities for agricultural trade are likely to expand in the next decade, but so are the risks.

Key Words	Central Concepts
Foreign trade	Trade between persons or firms living under separate government jurisdictions.
State trading	All trading by a country in one or more commodities is conducted by a government-owned or -appointed monopoly.
Theory of comparative advantage	Even though one party has an absolute advantage over another party in production of all items, it will profit both parties to trade if one has a comparative advantage over the other in the production of any item.
Common Agricultural Policy	One of the provisions of the original European Economic Community was that members should adopt a Common Agricultural Policy. Such a policy has gradually added common market, pricing, trade, and structural provisions.
General Agreement on Tariffs and Trade (GATT)	Almost one hundred countries are signatories of GATT, committing themselves to negotiated multilateral reductions in trade barriers. GATT began on a modest scale in 1947.
Reserve currency	A currency in which countries prefer to hold the reserves needed for foreign trade settlements or to back their own currency.
Smithsonian Agreement	Emergency agreement on the international payments system worked out by the advanced countries in 1971.
Protectionist	Seeking or adopting policies to protect the domestic market for domestic producers.
Trade Act of 1974	Began the process of adjusting U.S. trade policies to changed international conditions.

QUESTIONS

1. Discuss the varying roles of exports in U.S. agriculture since the 1930s?
2. How important is agriculture to the U.S. balance of payments?
3. Why do governments routinely interfere in international trade?
4. Suggest some possible alternative goals of U.S. trade negotiations? How important is free trade in agricultural products?
5. Contrast the trade policies of the United Kingdom and the EEC in the 1960s. How have these changed now that the United Kingdom is an EEC member?
6. Review the achievements of GATT since 1947.
7. Why do rising incomes increase international trade?
8. Who is affected (and how) when the dollar is devalued?
9. Which countries and commodities have been most important in growth of U.S. agricultural trade?
10. What has been the trend in volume of U.S. exports and imports since 1970?
11. What factors are a prerequisite for continued growth in U.S. agricultural exports?
12. What impact will increased agricultural exports have on the stability of U.S. farm prices?
13. Why does Monroe argue that U.S. international trade policy is in transition?

AID AND TECHNICAL ASSISTANCE— "UNCLE SAM" OR "BIG BROTHER"

While the theory of foreign trade has been explained in elaborate economic models, the functions of aid and technical assistance have been left largely in a humanitarian limbo. The conventional wisdom is that the wealthier countries should give *short-term aid* to the poorer nations to meet temporary needs (usually food deficits) but in the long term should provide *technical assistance* to promote self-help economic development. The extent of aid or technical assistance given by any country is an arbitrary government decision. The spigot tends to open when an international disaster such as famine strikes, when public opinion becomes concerned about risks to developed countries (world unrest due to the population explosion), or when there are large food surpluses in advanced countries depressing domestic prices. The spigot closes abruptly when political alignments change (Egypt's flirtation with the USSR), when domestic budgets are tight, or farm surpluses disappear. From the viewpoint of the donor nation, control of the spigot is used to stabilize its economy. The receiving nation, already weak, is not helped by the destabilizing effect of off-again, on-again aid and technical assistance.

U.S. FOREIGN AID PROGRAMS

The U.S. foreign aid program is generally traced back to the 1942 creation of the Institute for Inter-American Affairs, a government agency responsible for providing U.S. technical assistance to Latin American countries in face of Japanese and German war threats. The first massive aid program was the Marshall Plan which aimed to help rebuild the Western European economies after World War II and to make them safe from communism. Europe recovered remarkably—it still had an advanced infrastructure and a highly literate and skilled populace. However, U.S. planners made a grave error in thinking that a similar game plan would work in building the economies of the developing world. The Mutual Security Act of 1951 attempted to apply the same principles worldwide. However, in its application, military assistance dominated all other goals, as the Korean War precipitated new international tensions.

Food Aid Programs

The Agricultural Trade and Development Act of 1954, popularly known as Public Law 480, or PL480, compensated for the Mutual Security Act by emphasizing surplus food disposal. Food was an important weapon in international diplomacy, and as long as the United States had a large surplus, until about 1966, PL480 was extended and expanded. Most early sales were made for foreign currency. The foreign currency was lodged to the U.S. account in the recipient country and could be used for U.S. needs such as embassy expenses or loaned or granted to the recipient country. As the U.S. balance of payments worsened in the late 1950s, a 1959 amendment to PL480 permitted sales for dollars on credit terms. The amendment of 1966, known as the Food for Peace Act, directed that a transition be made from local currency sales to dollar credit sales by the end of 1971. It allowed for an alternative of sales by convertible local currency credit. Loans were to be for a maximum period of 40 years at a minimum interest of 3 percent, extremely generous terms compared to most commercial loans; sales might also be made by private trade agreements between the U.S. government and private trade entities. The remaining shipments would be direct donations or barter, although most barter is now handled under the authority of the CCC Charter Act.

The following table shows the trend of exports under PL480 (Table 7.4). Total PL480 exports, which had been on the decline since 1964, reversed direction sharply and reached almost $1,300 million in fiscal years 1975 and 1976. Since 1966, there has been a very successful switch to greater use of dollar credits. One other major change in the 1966 act which has not as yet had such an impact is the incorporation of "self-help" principles designed to speed economic development in the recipient country. Each PL480 agreement must contain a description of self-help measures which the recipient country is taking in land use, infrastructure, research, education, public investment, and other areas. Since 1968, these *must* include voluntary programs to control population growth.

U.S. Technical Assistance

U.S. technical assistance to developing countries, as distinct from food aid, has had a sketchy existence over the years. Much emphasis has been given to "crash programs" and much effort expended in finding "model programs." During the 1950s, the form of technical assistance was strongly colored by the prevailing view that industrialization was the key to economic development. Much more emphasis in the 1960s was given to agriculture, although some critics assert that the present mistaken goal is industrialization of agriculture on the U.S. model. The Agency for International Development (AID) was established in 1961 to carry out nonmilitary foreign assistance programs. AID's apparent lack of success, especially in making inroads on the food–population crunch, has disillusioned many supporters.

Lesser developed countries (LDCs) have, in fact, made great progress despite great odds. An FAO study in 1971 (Agricultural Commodity Projections 1970–80) claimed that all continents had made slight gains in per capita agricultural production in the 1960s and that Africa and Asia would do even better in the 1970s. An AID study of 82 countries showed 72 with declining birth rates. However, hunger and poverty are still endemic to many countries, regions within countries, and social groups.

Persisting Problems in LDCs

Many reasons have been offered for these persisting problems. Schultz talks about three leading scapegoats, the adversity of nature, the perversity of farmers (in LDCs), and the fecundity of man. Others blame misguided economic plans, corruption of governments, inadequate bureaucracies, or lack of infrastructure. Still others see agriculture's plight in LDCs as a lack of credit, fertilizer, insecticide, or

Table 7.4 Exports under PL480, by Type of Agreement, Selected Years Ending June 30, 1955–74

Fiscal Year	Local Currency ($million)	Local Currency (%)	Dollar Credit ($million)	Dollar Credit (%)	Government Donations ($million)	Government Donations (%)	Other Donations ($million)	Other Donations (%)	Barter ($million)	Barter (%)	Total ($million)
1955	73	19	—	—	52	14	135	35	125	32	385
1960	824	74	—	—	38	3	105	9	149	13	1,116
1966	866	64	181	13	87	7	180	13	32	2	1,346
1971	204	20	539	53	138	13	142	14	—	—	1,023
1972	143	14	535	51	228	22	152	14	—	—	1,058
1973	6	1	653	69	159	17	128	14	—	—	946
1974[p]	[a]	[a]	573	66	146	17	144	17	—	—	863

[a] Included in government donations.

[p] Preliminary.

hybrid seeds. However, much careful research suggests that progress has taken place in agriculture where the reward for effort was available with reasonable certainty. It can be done.

However, William and Elizabeth Paddock, in a book appropriately called *We Don't Know How*, asserted that development assistance from the United States had been largely unproductive, because we were using the wrong models. They argued, "let us learn how to help the North American Indians to prosper before we try to help South American Indians in a strange environment. Let us clear slums in New York before we try to teach Bombay how to clear its slums." The Paddocks were critical of the $100 billion spent by the U.S. government on aid in the 1946–73 period. However, they found that other countries' efforts at development, land reform, agricultural extension, etc., had been equally futile.

Tweeten, analyzing a period of chronic farm surpluses, found considerable benefits from PL480 aid. He argued that the marginal value of cash aid would have been higher than that actually given under PL480. The net value of U.S. food aid was only 34 percent of the gross value in the 1964–66 period. However, since food aid was cheaper than cash aid (farmers would have to be paid to produce less) these two alternatives appeared about equal in cost. Tweeten argued that food aid should be sold at a discount per dollar equal to the USDA's cost of inducing farmers *not* to produce that dollar's worth of food. This argument would, of course, not apply if the nation was already producing at full capacity, as appeared to be the case in the first half of the 1970s.

INTERNATIONAL AID PROGRAMS

The success of the Marshall Plan, the effectiveness of the United States in buttressing many weak political regimes, and the absence of any other wealthy donor, led the U.S. into going it alone for many years in providing aid and technical assistance to lesser developed countries. However, populations of LDCs began to grow so rapidly that despite U.S. aid, per capita food production, income, savings, investments, and foreign exchange, reserves frequently deteriorated. As the real extent of the problem became more apparent, it became clear that no one country alone, no matter how rich, could provide the necessary aid and technical assistance. In the early 1960s, the United Nations instituted the First Development Decade, with the avowed goal of doubling GNP in the LDCs during the 1960s. To finance this growth, the United Nations called on each developed country to contribute 1 percent of its GNP to foreign aid each year. The average response was only one-third of this goal. In addition, much aid was given under restrictions such as requirements that it be used to purchase needed goods from the donor country. Despite these limitations, many LDCs experienced real economic growth in the 1960s, and the United Nations initiated a Second Development Decade for the 1970s.

A significant change in the attitudes of both donor and recipient countries began to emerge in the early seventies. An OECD Report on development assistance showed that the total flow of financial resources from its members to developing countries had increased steadily since the mid-sixties. However, in 1974, of the nearly $27 billion total flows, almost half came from private investment, private export credits, or as grants from voluntary agencies. Of the $11.3 billion in official development assistance, almost three-fourths was still grants or loans from one country to another. Only about one-fourth was in the nature of technical assistance. Not surprisingly, there was widespread sentiment among developing countries that development assistance in such a form and at such a level could not help them to overcome their mounting problems.

The Altered Environment for Aid

Many of the problems were the same ones that had stimulated earlier aid efforts. However, a number of new wrinkles had appeared. One was the concern about world food supplies, which was particularly pressing the LDCs. A second was the impact of increased energy prices on the ability of poorer countries to buy fertilizers for their agriculture and power for their industries, and on their solvency in international exchange. A third was the more assertive approach of the developing countries themselves to development assistance. Their basic argument was that their lack of development was due to past discrimination against them by the rich countries. This discrimination was evident in (1) credit—the financial agencies set up by the rich countries, IMF, World Bank, etc., primarily served the interests and needs of the rich countries; (2) trade—despite the dependence of most developing countries on exports of one or two key raw products, the rich countries put many obstacles in the way of access for those products; (3) the control of the rich nations over transportation, processing, and distribution; as a result, the LDCs captured only a small percentage of the price consumers paid for the final product; (4) labor mobility—immigration controls by the rich countries prevented the flow of excess labor from LDCs.

A further factor altering the nature of development assistance was the emergence of the OPEC nations (only recently LDCs themselves) as major sources of grants and loans. They had shown themselves willing to politicize trade by using oil prices as a weapon against Israel. The major existing power blocs—the United States, the Soviet axis, and Western Europe—were not willing to allow the OPEC nations to gain unchallenged influence in the LDCs. During the first shock of increased oil prices, estimates of the potential surplus funds which OPEC countries could build up in a few years reached astronomical heights. When their aid to LDCs jumped fivefold in 1974 to $2.5 billion, it was used as justification for some of the more outlandish projections. However, it has now become clear that OPEC oil revenues available for aid have been greatly reduced by massive domestic spending programs and that further oil price increases have been hindered by the slump in international demand, the emergence of new oil supply sources (the North Sea, Alaska), greater conservation efforts among consumers, and the possibility of finding alternative energy sources. Among OPEC countries the increases in domestic spending programs have been greatest among the producers, such as Iran and Saudi Arabia, with large populations.

The Response of Donor Countries

Perhaps the most rapid response to the changed position of the developing countries has come from the enlarged European Economic Community. The Lomé Convention, signed in February 1975, between the EEC and 46 developing countries in Africa, the Caribbean, and the Pacific, gave these countries improved access to EEC markets, a scheme (known as STABEX) to compensate LDCs for declines in the price of their products, and greatly increased aid commitments. In its first year of operation $86 million were paid to LDCs under STABEX. However, the developing countries continue to press for more international efforts to guarantee world food supplies and to fix raw material prices either by a producer cartel or by a combination of producing and consuming countries.

The World Food Conferences of 1974 and 1975 have spawned a World Food Council to develop an international program for food. The International Monetary Fund, the United Nations, OPEC, and many individual countries have stepped up their financial aid for the most seriously troubled LDCs. However, most of the initiatives taken in the 1970s are relatively untested and many changes and surprises lie ahead.

The United States has not committed itself firmly to any single initiative taken in the 1970s. The process of improving relations with Russia and China has lessened the "fear" motive for aid and technical assistance to LDCs. In addition, Russia, China, the OPEC countries, and many other countries not considered as LDCs have become major users of U.S. technical assistance–both agricultural and nonagricultural. Such assistance can be tied to relatively assured reciprocal benefits, unlike the experience with many LDCs, where assistance has often been resisted and unfruitful. Also many LDCs have antagonized the U.S. Congress by their attacks on the United States in the United Nations and other forums. As a result, while there is widespread acceptance of the U.S. role in solving world food problems, the missionary zeal of the 1950s for economic growth in LDCs is no longer there.

While the FAO projections for the 1974 World Food Conference estimated that the LDCs would have a grain deficit of 85 million tons by 1985, the official USDA view is that world food supplies for the next quarter century will be approximately in balance. The National Research Council Study of World Food and Nutrition estimated that LDCs could not afford to import their food deficit and would need to increase average yields by 2.5 percent per year to meet their food needs in 1985. It suggested that this could only be accomplished by greatly increased research in which U.S. technological expertise would play a major role. However, research, knowledge accumulation, and knowledge dissemination are slow processes. In addition, at some point knowledge must be combined with capital and labor for the output of LDCs to be increased. Just as in the U.S., the greatest advances in agricultural output in LDCs have occurred when there was an advance in the productivity of a combination of factors (hybrid seed, fertilizer, and irrigation) and in the profitability of the output. Pioneering research supported by liberal credit, adequate extension services, buoyant markets, or other compensating benefits may be essential if the LDCs are to meet their food needs.

Key Words	Central Concepts
Aid	May take the form of financial, food, or raw material help for other countries.
Technical assistance	Help in applying or adapting technology.
Donor nation	Nation providing aid or technical assistance.
Donations	Outright gifts of food or other aid.
Barter	Exchanging goods for other goods. The oldest form of trade.
"Self-help" principles	Requirements on recipients of aid that they adopt domestic policies to improve their economic or social structure.

Crash programs Programs designed to achieve economic goals in a shortened time span.

Model programs Programs designed to be used as an example for others to follow.

Agency for International Development (AID) The agency responsible for U.S. foreign assistance programs.

Development Decade Declared by the United Nations to focus world attention on economic growth in LDCs.

Immigration controls Controls on entry of foreign citizens into a country.

Lomé Convention (1975) Trade and aid agreement between the EEC and 46 countries in Africa, the Caribbean, and the Pacific.

QUESTIONS

1. Is there an underlying theory of aid and technical assistance?
2. Why has the flow of aid been so erratic over the years?
3. Describe the major U.S. foreign aid and technical assistance programs.
4. Does military aid conflict with economic aid?
5. Has PL480 successfully shifted from sales for local currency to sales under dollar credits?
6. How has the role of agriculture in economic development altered since World War II?
7. How do multinational agencies complement and compete with U.S. agencies in providing foreign aid?
8. What were the main criticisms which LDCs made of aid programs by the developed countries?
9. How did advanced countries respond to the changed environment for aid?
10. Review conflicting projections of the world food outlook. Is mass starvation a possibility?
11. What policies are needed to increase the productivity of agriculture in LDCs?

eight

POVERTY AND AGRICULTURE

POLICIES FOR SOCIAL ILLS

The biblical exhortation "The poor you have always with you" was accepted for centuries by fatalistic societies. Other social ills, such as illness, disability, mental retardation, old age, unemployment, etc., were accepted as fatalistically. Social ills were occasionally tackled on a limited scale by counties or townships (workhouses, orphanages, prisons); by organized groups (guilds, churches); by the mutual assistance of neighbors, relatives, and friends; or by the private philanthropy of noblemen or men of wealth.

The Industrial Revolution exposed the social aspect of individual misfortunes in a number of ways. It broke up many traditional family, neighborhood, and religious alliances. As populations became more concentrated in cities, the extent of poverty, disease, and unemployment, became more visible. For example, Dickens' novels helped to expose the more appalling aspects of nineteenth century industrial, urban living conditions. However, the prevailing laissez-faire concepts and the Protestant work ethic suggested that solutions lay within the power of the suffering individual. The first tentative steps at social policies emerged in the more advanced European industrial nations. One can perhaps cite two major reasons for these first attempts. Industrial capital had been accumulated in the form of machines, factories, vehicles, offices, etc., which were more vulnerable to the attacks of an angry mob than agricultural capital—primarily land. It was thus important to prevent any social ills which might cause popular unrest. In addition, widespread literacy and greater public awareness of the possibilities of social improvement brought increased demand for national social policies.

Table 8.1 Dates of Passage of Basic Social Laws, Selected Countries

	Germany	*U.K.*	*France*	*Sweden*	*Canada*	*U.S.*
Old age, invalidism, death	1889	1908	1910	1913	1927	1935
Sickness and maternity	1883	1911	1928	1891	1957	1965
Work injury	1884	1897	1898	1901	1911	1908
Unemployment	1927	1911	1905	1934	1935*	1935
Family allowances	1954	1945	1932	1947	1944	—

*Declared unconstitutional. *Source*: U.S. HEW Social Security Administration. *Social Security Programs Throughout the World*, 1973.

It is notable that in all countries, work injury benefits were among the first social assistance laws. Germany's lead in many social policies was related to the need to cement the union of many small (long rival) states. The United States was a notable latecomer to national social assistance policies (Table 8.1). Despite its strong ties to the United Kingdom, Canada imitated more closely the behavior of its North American neighbor. The earliness of the start a country had in policies for social ills is not an indication of its present policies. Political regimes in the intervening years have frequently altered direction. For example, many but not all countries under a Communist regime have no unemployment programs, presumably since unemployment is not officially recognized.

NATIONAL POVERTY: STAMPING IT OUT

U.S. Social Welfare Programs

Data for selected years since the late twenties give one indication of the growth and economic importance of social welfare programs in the United States (Table 8.2).

Table 8.2 United States GNP and Social Welfare Expenditures, Selected Fiscal Years, 1929–75

Item	*1929*	*1940*	*1950*	*1960*	*1970*	*1975*
Gross National Product ($ billion)	101	95	263	496	955	1,424
Social welfare expenditure ($ billion)	4	9	24	52	146	287
(% of GNP)	3.9	9.2	8.9	10.6	15.3	20.1
Social insurance (% of GNP)	0.3	1.3	1.9	3.9	5.7	8.7
Public aid (% of GNP)	0.1	3.8	0.9	0.8	1.7	2.8
Health and medical (% of GNP)	0.3	0.6	0.8	0.9	1.0	1.2
Veterans (% of GNP)	0.7	0.7	2.6	1.1	0.9	1.2
Education (% of GNP)	2.4	2.7	2.5	3.6	5.3	5.5
Other social welfare (% of GNP)	0.1	0.1	0.2	0.2	0.5	0.6

Source: *Social Security Bulletin*, miscellaneous issues.

Prior to the 1930s, U.S. social welfare expenditures were primarily for education. However, following the Great Depression and the enactment of the Social Security Act of 1935, the proportion of GNP devoted to social welfare programs grew dramatically. Full employment during World War II and economic growth thereafter meant that social welfare expenditures as a proportion of GNP remained stable for two decades.

A new spurt of growth in social welfare expenditures under the Great Society programs of the Johnson administration in the late sixties has continued on into the seventies. Public aid and veterans' benefits programs have tended to ebb and flow with war and depression. Education, on the other hand, has shown strong if not consistent growth and still accounts for 30 percent of all social welfare expenditures. Health care programs, which are still primarily directed at those over 65 (notably the Medicare program), have grown slowly and have actually accounted for a *smaller* proportion of all social welfare expenditures in 1975 than they did in 1929. A national health program for *all age groups* might reverse this trend.

Social insurance remains the chief vehicle for federal welfare payments. Basically, each employed worker in the U.S. is required to enroll in the program. A fixed percentage of his earnings is deducted by his employer in each pay period. The employer makes an equal contribution. These payments are deposited in special trust funds. When the need arises due to retirement, death, or disablement, the worker or his family is entitled to payments from these trust funds commensurate with their contributions. In 1971, social insurance payments were paid to 11.1 million retired workers, 3.8 million survivor families, and 1.4 million disabled-worker families; 6.5 million persons also received unemployment benefits in 1971. Some indication of the solvency of the social insurance system is that there were 93.7 million workers with taxable earnings (of which 63.4 million worked in all four quarters) in 1971, contributing 11 percent of earnings to old age, survivor, disability, and health trust funds. That is, it would take the contributions of nine employed persons to provide one person on welfare with the same income. Clearly, in 1971, the ratio of employed persons to welfare recipients was below this level. The growing number of eligible recipients as the U.S. population grows older and the need for increased benefits to offset the effects of inflation have forced Congress to steadily increase the tax rate and the income ceiling on which tax must be paid in order to keep the system financially sound. Many question how long the system could handle depression levels of unemployment; in addition, there has been criticism that money left in the social insurance fund could be profitably reinvested in the economy.

Public Assistance programs are financed by matching federal grants to state aid. They include money payments, medical care, and social services for the aged, blind, totally disabled, and needy families with dependent children. In 1971, 2 million persons received old-age assistance; and 80,000 blind, 1 million disabled, and 3 million families with dependent children received assistance. However, the programs are plagued by differences in eligibility, limitations, and level of payments between states and by the costly bureaucratic machine needed to administer them.

The U.S. Department of Agriculture has had primary responsibility for two major welfare programs not included in the above social welfare expenditures—the Commodity Distribution program (authorized in 1949 in its present form) and the Food Stamp plan, revived in modern form in 1961. The Food Stamp approach has gradually replaced direct commodity distribution. By 1975, near the low point of the 1974–75 recession, over 19 million recipients qualified for food stamps. The principle behind the program is that food stamps with a face value of $100 can be used as the equivalent of $100 cash in purchasing food and grocery items. The poor pay part of the cost of purchasing the stamps, the government the remainder. The lower a recipient's income level, the smaller his share of the purchase price. Only low income households have been eligible for food stamps. However, in response to recession and inflation, the qualifying income floor has been periodically raised. By 1975, the cost to the government of bonus food stamps exceeded $5 billion, roughly five times the level in 1970. Administration efforts to trim the program were resisted by Congress, as long as unemployment remained high.

THE MEANING OF POVERTY IN THE UNITED STATES

As should be clear from the previous discussion, the social ills, and the social policies designed to meet them, have frequently been concerned in only a limited way with correcting either temporary or permanent poverty. However, many social ills lead to or are the result of poverty. Poverty is frequently used as a synonym for other social ills. For example, in 1964 President Johnson characterized his broad social programs as a "War on Poverty." Then too, the persistence of poverty is a disturbing reminder of failure of a society which has produced many great modern industrial, agricultural, technological, and military achievements. Surely, the popular argument goes, if we can conquer space we can conquer poverty.

What is poverty? For administrative purposes, the U.S. government has defined poverty in terms of a minimum needed income for a given family size. For example, the average poverty threshold for a two-person household was $1,894 per year in 1959, $2,633 in 1971. For a seven-person household it was $4,849 and $6,751, respectively. By this income definition there were 39.5 million poor persons in 1959, 25.6 million in 1971. That is, after seven years of the War on Poverty, one out of every eight persons in the U.S. was poor. A few obvious problems with this approach can be seen. First, these "poverty" income levels exceed the high income levels in most countries in the world. Second, they must constantly be adjusted as prices change. Third, the same income level may represent quite different utilities to families in different circumstances. For example, many students have low incomes for some years while they are acquiring the training which will assure them of above average incomes in later life. The income test of poverty also ignores the tremendous waste of national resources that the poor represent.

Others see poverty as arising from maldistribution of wealth. Tax away surplus wealth, redistribute it to the poor, and all will be well. However, both the income and wealth approaches are inadequate. A personal inventory approach to poverty offers a more comprehensive basis for policies to overcome poverty (Table 8.3). It shows that there are personal, local, and national factors involved in each individual's personal situation. Poverty needs to be defined in terms of that situation. For example, where a person gets most of his/her income from dividends, employment factors are of lesser importance. Correctives to poverty need to be framed in the same way. There is little point in training engineers when no jobs are available and no federal program is geared to provide them. Seen in this light, the current social welfare programs are not likely to reduce the incidence of poverty. Conversely, any serious war on poverty must

Table 8.3 Personal Inventory Approach to Assessment of Appropriate Poverty Policies

Personal Factors	
Demographic	Age, race, sex, dependency.
Wealth	Land, real estate, stocks, bonds, savings, access to credit.
Income	Wages, rent, profits, dividends, interest.
Employability	Presently employed, alternative skills, capacity for retraining.
Community Factors	
Demographic	Population, in- or out-migration, natural increase.
Social assets	Schools, health services, utilities, transportation facilities, credit, etc.
Business vitality	Economic growth, replacement of declining industries, enterprise spirit.
Employment situation	Variety of jobs for changing range of skills.
Family situation	Relations within family, neighbors, church, and other social groups.
National Factors	
Economic	Growth of population, employment, GNP.
Government	Expansionary or restrictive policies, taxing and redistribution policies.
International	Competition, cooperation, war, etc.

mobilize efforts simultaneously at the individual, community, and national levels if it is to be successful.

By present income definitions of poverty, certain segments of society are most vulnerable. Most numerous are the aged, subsisting on inadequate pensions. Their main asset is their home. The average financial assets of the best-off group among the aged, married couples was only $1,480 in a 1962 study by Edna Wentworth and Dena Motley. Even among the aged, welfare programs discriminated against certain groups. Widows, blacks, the very old, and those in southern states got lower benefits while having fewer assets. Similar discrepancies occurred in unemployment benefits and public assistance payments.

Many unskilled workers in current employment may be only marginally or temporarily above the poverty level. In 1971, only 3.6 percent of those who worked year round and full time could be considered poor, but 20.1 percent of those who worked part time were regarded as poor. Slightly over 40 percent of those who did not work at all were poor. Of women under 65 who were family heads, 7.2 percent of full-time workers were poor, as were 40.2 percent of part-time workers and 64.5 percent of those who did not work at all. Over half of all black families with female heads were below the poverty level. Of all men employed for less than four quarters in 1971, 85 percent earned less than $3,000 in taxable wages.

The myth of the affluent society contrasts with the fact that most American families are asset-poor, so they have little defense against a temporary interruption of earnings. A study by Dorothy S. Projector and Gerturde S. Weiss covering 1962 data showed one in five households with zero liquid assets. Only one in eight households had liquid assets above $5,000. Scarcely any of these were low-income families. Only 1 percent of households with a head aged 35 or less had liquid assets above $5,000. Inflation and recession during the first half of the 1970s is likely to have increased financial distress among most poor people.

The inventory approach to poverty also makes it clear that rural poverty has the same causes as does urban poverty and the same resistance to easy remedies as do other brands of poverty. Many previous writers have tended to see rural poverty as a special problem. The USDA has promoted this viewpoint because it strengthens its claim to administer poverty programs in rural areas. However, the remedies for rural poverty are equally dependent on the coordination of programs at the individual, community, and national levels.

Key Words	Central Concepts
Industrial Revolution	The transformation from handcraft to factory production of goods, and the accompanying technological and social changes.
Social laws	Laws to alleviate social ills such as poverty and sickness.
Social Welfare Programs	Programs authorized by social laws.
Social Insurance	A system by which all citizens prepay so each can withdraw benefits if and when needed.
Social Assistance	No prepayment involved. Specified needs are met from general tax funds.
Poverty threshold	The income level below which a person or family is deemed poor.
Personal inventory approach	The view of poverty as involving both personal, community, and national factors.
Rural poverty	Poverty of individuals or families living in rural areas.

QUESTIONS

1. How has society treated the problem of poverty in different eras?
2. Why was the United States a relative latecomer in passing social welfare laws?
3. Is there a link between the timing of the Social Security Act of 1935 and programs to assist U.S. agriculture?
4. Is the Social Insurance program solvent?
5. How long can government meet the cost of continued, widespread unemployment?
6. How can and should poverty be defined?
7. Distinguish between assets, income, and affluence.
8. What are the factors most commonly associated with poverty?

POVERTY IN RURAL AREAS

Characteristics of Rural Poverty

The personal inventory approach makes it easy to itemize the chief characteristics of rural poverty. Age and race are the most important demographic factors. Although the majority of rural poor are white, the incidence of poverty among blacks, chicanos, American Indians, and other minorities is higher. Poor farmers suffer from having inadequate land, working capital, and financial reserves. Poor nonfarmers frequently have little or no tangible assets. In most cases, poor farmers are unable to supplement farm profits by off-farm wages. Poor nonfarm workers suffer from low and intermittent earnings, and most rural poor suffer from lack of alternative skills. In addition, underemployment, that is, the employment of manpower below its full potential in skills, productivity, and earnings is widespread.

Community factors are just as important in rural poverty as in ghetto poverty. Rural areas have relatively higher birthrates than the national average, higher dependency ratios, and a generally unfavorable population flow. The young have tended to flee rural areas while returnees or immigration have not usually compensated for the loss of the young. (There is some evidence that this pattern is being reversed as rural living becomes more attractive to many.) Areas with high concentrations of rural poor lack the economic vitality which derives from expanding business, industry, and commerce, and the spirit of enterprise associated with expansion. Their tax base suffers, reducing the quality and flow of public services (schools, hospitals, utilities, highways); and the weakness of final demand reduces the quality and flow of private goods and services (banks, retailers, professional services). The demand for public and private goods and services determines the demand for workers with varied skills, experience, and seniority. Family situation relative to the extended family, neighbors, religious, and other social groups can be both a buffer against the worst problems of poverty and a constraint on the socially acceptable remedies. Once again, the impact on any one person can be quite individual.

As explanations of rural poverty, national and international factors have gradually diminished, as the agricultural sector itself has diminished. In the thirties, the depth of the agricultural depression was interpreted to mean that agriculture dragged the rest of the economy down; hence the urgency of policy measures to stimulate agriculture. In the late forties and fifties, as the national economy grew, average earnings rose, and evidence of affluence (spending on consumer goods) became more widespread, it was recognized that the process was reversed. The hope was that as the national economy prospered, the agricultural sector would be stimulated, and benefits would trickle down to the poorer in every sector. The urban riots of the early and mid-sixties demonstrated that benefits were not trickling down fast enough to dampen explosive discontent. The War on Poverty was remarkable, not in the programs it espoused but in its recognition of poverty as endemic, requiring specific national policies outside the normal monetary and fiscal instruments. One offshoot was a Presidential Advisory Commission on Rural Poverty set up in 1966. Its reports, "Rural Poverty in the United States," and a briefer, more popular summary of recommendations, "The People Left Behind," became the Bible for USDA and land grant research and programs for rural poverty.

Policies for Rural Poverty

Professor Cochrane aptly characterized efforts directed at rural poverty prior to the 1960s as "Too little, too late." The Resettlement Administration of 1935 made loans and grants of nearly $300 million in two years to consolidate farms, resettle and rehabilitate farmers, and encourage the formation of debt adjustment committees. A report prepared by a special committee on farm tenancy appointed by President Roosevelt underlined the gravity of rural poverty at that time. In 1937, the Farm Security Administration (FSA) was created as a permanent agency of the USDA to take over the functions of the Resettlement Administration. At its peak, in 1943, the FSA made loans to 232,000 farm families. It was greatly curtailed in its activities when it became absorbed into the Farmers' Home Administration in 1946.

Professor Cochrane comments, "Three generalizations may be made about the programs of the Resettlement and Farm Security administrations. First, for the first time in the history of the United States, programs were designed and put in operation to deal specifically with low-production farms and farm families living in poverty. Second, although in absolute terms a large number of farmers were assisted, the programs of these agencies were inadequate to the task confronting them. Third, the programs of these agencies were farm-production oriented; they sought to eliminate poverty by turning each low-production farm they touched into a productive, adequate-sized unit."

World War II offered many poor rural dwellers the chance to escape farm poverty by providing more nonfarm jobs and information. However, underemployment (and resultant undercompensation) persisted as the modern technology of agriculture advanced. Studies demonstrated the many facets of the problem, but little in the way of effective policies emerged. The Rural Development Program of the Eisenhower administration had as its goals to provide "equal opportunity" to the poor. Local development committees would coordinate the efforts of existing agencies in rural areas in increasing farm productivity, opportunities for employment, opportunities for vocational training, and fuller utilization of farm resources in defense production. Professor Cochrane summarizes six years of the Rural

Development Program by saying "In my judgment the Rural Development Program never really moved out of the pilot stage."

President Kennedy, in 1960, inherited problems of mounting unemployment and extensive poverty. His Rural Areas Development Program (basically the same as Eisenhower's RPD) was supplemented by two other programs. The Area Redevelopment Administration provided loans, technical assistance, and retraining for commercial and industrial enterprises. The Accelerated Public Works Program could provide immediate public employment in poor areas and improve public facilities as an attraction to business and industry. During this period, the USDA began to recognize officially the distinction between commercial farmers and those nonviable farmers with a poverty problem. Since that time, aid for commercial farmers has been justified on criteria other than that of poverty.

Johnson's War on Rural Poverty

After the assassination of President Kennedy in late 1963, President Lyndon Johnson used his influence on Congress to push through the Economic Opportunity Act of 1964. It set up an Office of Economic Opportunity (OEO) to coordinate an extensive assault on poverty. The full power of government publicity and the appointment of the late president's brother-in-law, Sargent Shriver, as first OEO director, led to public expectations of rapid success that were unrealistic. The main thrust of the OEO programs were: (1) youth programs, such as the Job Corps, work–study programs, etc.; (2) community action programs, which sought to give the disadvantaged a leading role in formulating and administering poverty remedies in their locality; (3) work assistance programs—to give unskilled unemployed an opportunity to get work experience. Of the almost $1 billion appropriated by Congress for the first year, less than 4 percent was budgeted for rural assistance, although much of this was intended for small loans to improve farm production.

OEO was already in trouble from many sources before the Nixon administration began to dismantle it in 1969. The Departments of Agriculture, Housing and Urban Development, Labor, and Health, Education, and Welfare coveted control of its programs. The programs themselves emerged with the same deficiencies (underfunded, uncoordinated, often unsuccessful) as the proponents of the War on Poverty had ascribed to previous programs. Republicans suspected that President Johnson had used the community action features of the program to increase Democratic influence among the poor and black populations. By 1975, OEO had been broken up and the remnants distributed to various government departments.

Under the Nixon administration, there was continued expansion of social insurance expenditures, public assistance (especially Aid to Families with Dependent Children), health care, and the Food Stamp program. Stimulus for the latter in the late sixties came from the impact of the campaign of Senators Robert Kennedy and Joseph Clark, the Poor Peoples' March on Washington, and the publication of "Hunger U.S.A.," all drawing attention to the extent of existing poverty and hunger in the United States. Many southern congressmen fought a rearguard action to minimize the problems (particularly in their own rural constituencies) and prevent or limit the extent of proposed programs. By 1974, when President Ford took office, public sentiment began to turn against continued growth in welfare expenditures and toward reducing participation and easing the tax burden.

Probably the most notable achievement of social welfare programs since 1959 was to reduce the number of households still in poverty and headed by males. The major hard-core poverty group has become households headed by females. Persistence of high unemployment at predicted 1975 levels of 8 percent could undo much of the gains of the last 15 years. However, outside administration circles, there is almost no optimism that the War on Poverty is progressing. The number of poor in the U.S. exceeds the total population of Canada. Income distribution is still relatively lopsided. The lowest fifth and the highest fifth of the population retain approximately the shares they held a quarter of a century ago (Table 8.4).

Table 8.4 Share of U.S. Income Before Taxes, Selected Years, 1947–72

	1947 (%)	*1969 (%)*	*1972 (%)*
Lowest fifth	5.1	4.8	5.4
Highest fifth	43.3	41.3	41.4
All others	51.6	53.9	53.2
Total	100.0	100.0	100.0

Maldistribution of wealth is more severe. In 1962, the highest fifth held over 70 percent of all wealth. Such a maldistribution in favor of returns to capital rather than labor is a major cause of poverty. Finally, many studies show that government remedies tend to help those who are least poor and do little for those in deepest poverty.

Priorities for Rural Poverty Programs

Tweeten has suggested that cost effectiveness should be the criterion used to set priorities among prospective programs to combat rural poverty. Before setting priorities we need to distinguish between the (1) employable and (2) unsalvageable. For the employable he suggests that priority should go to:

1. Fiscal and monetary policies to achieve full employment
2. Improving factor markets
3. Education
4. Subsidies to rural industries
5. Guaranteed employment
6. Guaranteed annual income

For the unsalvageable he suggests that a guaranteed annual income would be most efficient.

Cochrane, writing some years earlier while the OEO was still a dashing knight on a white charger, thought that the main programs still needed were (1) education and training and (2) job creation.

The personal inventory approach to assessment of appropriate poverty policies suggests that due to its complex nature (its personal, community, and national dimensions) poverty can only be successfully reduced by coordinated programs at each level. Rural poverty has the same sort of dimensions. Piecemeal policies to improve factor markets or guarantee employment attack the symptoms, not the disease, and may often be contradictory. Until poverty is seen in its entirety, the policies designed to alleviate it will limp along with partial success but a continuing general record of failure. Unfortunately, too, as long as the poor are regarded as a burden on society and not as a tremendous untapped human resource, little effort is likely to be expended on a more creative approach to poverty.

Key Words	Central Concepts
Underemployment	The employment of labor below its potential marginal value product.
Trickle down theory	The theory that benefits in one sector of the economy will be passed on to other sectors. For example, if profits of employers increase, they will seek to hire more workers, so employee incomes will benefit.
Commercial farmers	Farmers earning incomes comparable to nonfarm incomes from their farm business.

Office of Economic Opportunity (OEO) A new executive agency set up to carry out the programs of the Economic Opportunity Act of 1964.

Community action programs Programs which sought to encourage the participation of the poor in programs for their benefit.

Unsalvageable The term for those who cannot be helped out of poverty by any known means.

QUESTIONS

1. In what ways is rural poverty different from and similar to urban poverty?
2. How does the loss of the young workers hurt rural communities?
3. Can rural poverty be helped or solved by national economic policies?
4. Why have programs for rural development been consistently underfunded and unsuccessful?
5. Will higher net farm incomes reduce rural poverty?
6. Why did the OEO programs fail?
7. Is poverty a political football?
8. Are malnutrition and hunger widespread in U.S. rural areas?
9. How does distribution of income and wealth differ between the U.S. and (a) underdeveloped and (b) developing countries?
10. Can education, training, and job creation solve poverty problems?

nine

THE ROOTS OF FUTURE POLICY

BELIEFS, VALUES, AND GOALS—PAST AND PRESENT

Ultimately, the worth of any policy must be judged by what is good for society. In simple situations, what is good may be easy to choose. For example, higher incomes for farmers would appear to be good if no one else were affected. However, in the real world, higher incomes for farmers may mean higher prices for farm products, and higher costs and less purchases for consumers. Even though only foreign consumers may pay the higher costs, one must still weigh the benefits to society of conflicting gains and losses. In making its choices, society moves from the relatively safe ground of goods and dollars to the elusive units of happiness and satisfaction.

Philosophical Roots of Policy

Modern economic theory and practice have generally refrained from making interpersonal comparisons of utility. However, in a discussion of the role of beliefs, values, and goals in policy making we get into just such comparisons. Much of the discussion would not be acceptable as scientific in the sense that, say, demand theory is scientific. First, it is extremely difficult to look into men's minds. Surveying beliefs or values is fairly imprecise. They are often not explicit or rational or consistent. Much of the discussion is framed in a historical context, tracing back present beliefs to Hamilton, Jefferson, and other writers and philosophers. However, the initial acceptance of those philosophies, their diffusion, and their handing down through the generations are not documented. Nor is it possible to work backwards from actual policies to the beliefs underlying those policies, since actual policies involve tradeoffs and choices.

Table 9.1 gives a summary of the way in which beliefs are

Table 9.1 The Role of Beliefs–Values–Goals in a Democratic Society

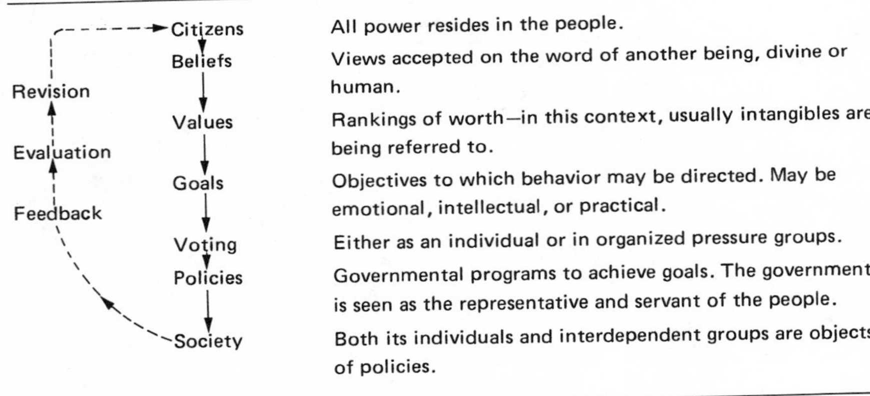

Citizens	All power resides in the people.
Beliefs	Views accepted on the word of another being, divine or human.
Values	Rankings of worth—in this context, usually intangibles are being referred to.
Goals	Objectives to which behavior may be directed. May be emotional, intellectual, or practical.
Voting	Either as an individual or in organized pressure groups.
Policies	Governmental programs to achieve goals. The government is seen as the representative and servant of the people.
Society	Both its individuals and interdependent groups are objects of policies.

Note: Dashed line indicates processes applicable at each stage of democratic control of society.

generally considered to be woven into policy making. A nation may choose to have its power derive from any source. For many countries, the divine right of kings is recognized. That is, all power and authority comes from God—and kings are God's representatives on earth. Aristotle suggested that power should lie ideally with a philosopher–king. Many countries vest power in the hands of a few enfranchised men chosen by wealth, caste, or party. The United States is a republic in which political power theoretically lies with the people. Through the democratic system, the people have control over their own destiny. For this reason, the people's beliefs and values are both a stimulus to desirable policies and a block to undesirable policies.

This democratic ideal has to be modified in actual practice. The people are subject to direct efforts to influence their views. Many groups—discussed earlier in this book—have powerful persuasive programs for swaying public opinion. Politicians and programs can be sold like prepackaged cosmetics. The people do have the ultimate power not to buy. However, as in the case of politics, they may be offered only a limited choice.

Beliefs, Values, and Goals

Beliefs are fundamental to modes of thought and action. As such they are often in the nature of permanent underlying assumptions. I believe the earth is flat. Ergo, if I go too near the edge, I may fall off. Beliefs come from various sources, such as the written word of the Bible, the spoken word of a parent, the unspoken word of community acceptance. Since beliefs cannot be scientifically verified, the distinction between belief and myth becomes difficult (a myth being an erroneous belief). Beliefs held by people lie on a continuum from sacred to condemned (Figure 9.1). What is sacred to me may be controversial to someone else and condemned by another. The beliefs said to underlie farm policy will be differently understood and ranked on the continuum by different farmers and farm groups.

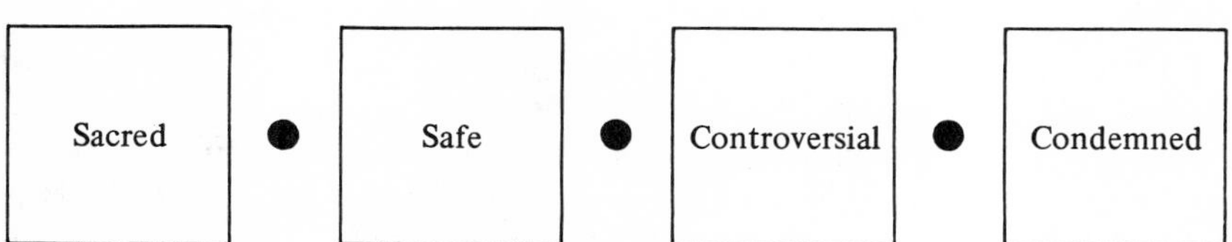

Fig. 9.1. Continuum of beliefs.

Values derive from beliefs. Now we are getting close to the concept of utility, which is value measured in terms of consumer satisfaction. Normally, values cannot be measured cardinally (as in dollar terms), but we can visualize a ranking of values. We can also describe values in terms of something being good or not good. Equality of opportunity may be good; any lapse from equality, not good. Justice may be good, injustice not good, and so on.

Goals derive from values. A person may choose death rather than a life which has lost the values he/she treasures. However, even goals are rarely single minded or independent in human affairs. A farmer may have an indifference system relating a goal of freedom of competition and a goal of monetary income. If freedom is low, a higher income would compensate (point A in Figure 9.2) for the greater freedom and lower income (at point B). In combining individual goals, one runs into exactly the same problems as in combining individual utility functions. One cannot say definitively what are society's goals.

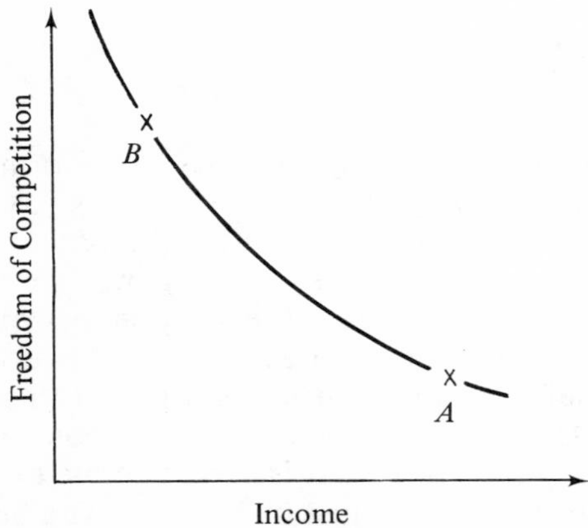

Fig. 9.2. Tradeoff between goals.

Translating Goals into Policy

Achievement of goals must be exercised in a democratic society through the people's elected representatives. In theory, the people choose a president, senators, congressmen, county commissioners, mayors, etc., who will act in office as they, the people, would. There are many hitches to this process. The people have difficulty in getting to know their candidate. He may conceal his true views or change them when elected; he is then subjected to lobbying effort (often of a forceful nature) and few issues are clear cut. A senator may object to higher spending but may see it as an absolute necessity for national defense. Or he may vote for a defense bill to get support for a pet agricultural bill. His own policy choices will have an indifference relationship. If this fails to reflect the views of those who voted for him, he may still get re-elected because he appears better than alternative candidates or because he has a glamorous wife or an effective electioneering machine.

The right to vote, accordingly, is only a minor part of what the citizen needs to do if his beliefs, values, and goals are to be translated into policy. He needs to write, speak, travel, and lobby on behalf of his views. Since this is impossible for most citizens, influencing policy is achieved by the grouping together of citizens with like-minded views. In this way, interested persons can more effectively exercise their full power as citizens. However, fairly rapidly even in these groups, responsibility must be delegated to elected leaders or paid organizers. The question arises as to whether the group is representing the views of members or of the group leaders. The same issue of control arises as in the case of the senator or congressman elected by all the citizens.

In actual policy development, a further conflict arises between the duty of an elected official to represent the partisan views of his supporters and his duty to serve all citizens. He who rises above partisan politics is considered a statesman, but to remain a statesman, he must get re-elected. Both considerations will enter into policy choices. In addition, as we have seen, the political process allows various levels of support in financing, administering, and implementing policies. A representative may vote in favor of a program and vote against adequate financing of it.

Even when "The People" succeed in having their goals translated into policies which are satisfactorily financed, administered, and implemented, the policies may still not be effective in changing society in the right direction. Society may change in ways which defeat the policy, as society adapted its ways to the strictures of prohibition. Or a very few individuals may be an unpredictable cause of failure, for instance, continued isolated hijacking attempts, despite nationwide preventive measures.

As laws have proliferated, it becomes very difficult for the people to evaluate "their" laws. Indeed, no set of criteria has ever been universally accepted for evaluating or revising laws. The citizen needs to know whether PL480 has (1) promoted economic development, (2) averted starvation and malnutrition, (3) subsequently led to opening of commercial markets, (4) aided the U.S. farmer, (5) penalized the U.S. consumer and taxpayer, or (6) led to other costs or benefits. Without that sort of knowledge, the citizen is in a weak position to suggest desirable policy changes. As the issues become more complex or technical, the citizen either delegates his responsibility to others or judges future policy by some naive criterion, such as humanitarian instinct, ideological preference, punitive feelings, etc. In either case, true political power passes into fewer hands.

Media Influence on Beliefs

Media-induced slogans, stereotypes, and myths today may have more influence on popular support or opposition to a measure than fundamental beliefs or values. The rediscovery and subsequent rapid forgetting of urban decay, rural poverty, environmental decay, energy shortages, etc., are symptomatic of how society flits from issue to issue at the prompting of the media. Or the general public may become the confused target of a media battle between those who fear an energy crisis and those who fear a nuclear holocaust, or between those who want a war on poverty and those who want a war on public spending on poverty programs.

The media, perhaps, realize more fully than the intellectuals that the mass of citizens have fundamentally bad as well as good or idealistic motivations. Humans are essentially egocentric—"I'm concerned first and foremost about what affects me." Humans are subject to greed, covetousness, envy, hatred, laziness, apathy, and fear, as well as to the more noble responses enshrined in Jeffersonian prose. While most people as individuals will prefer peace to war, a people can be persuaded to give overwhelming support to a particular act of war.

The farmer is possessed of the same human traits as all other citizens and can be swayed as easily as others. However, we must look at the *reality* of farmer beliefs and values—not the idealized picture—if we are to predict their impact on farm policies.

Key Words	Central Concepts
Divine right of kings	The belief that earthly power derives from divine power.
Democratic ideal	Rule by the will of the people.
Sacred	Anything revered by society as of divine origin.
Condemned	Totally disapproved of by society.
Delegating	Assigning one's obligations to another party.
Partisan politics	Choosing sides in political conflict on the basis of the parties rather than the issues involved.
Humanitarian instinct	Instinct for what will be good for one's fellow man.

QUESTIONS

1. How might you measure the existence, strength, and impact of farmers' belief in democracy? How accurate would you expect your results to be?
2. Explain the differences and relationships between beliefs, values, and goals.
3. What do you mean by trade-offs between goals?
4. Can policies run counter to society's goals? Explain.
5. Can desirable policies fail to meet their goals?
6. How might one evaluate the operation of a policy in terms of the underlying objectives?
7. Modern beliefs are more powerfully influenced by the mass media than by tradition. Discuss.

BELIEFS, VALUES, GOALS, AND AGRICULTURAL POLICY

The beliefs, values, and goals of farmers have been "politicized" in the process of developing and extending the farm programs of the 1930s. The "politicization" of an issue results from the deliberate actions of those involved in developing legislation on that issue. For example, all laws represent a curtailment of individual freedom. Freedom can become an issue–be politicized–only if some of the parties reacting to a proposed policy feel that it will significantly affect their freedom. All taxes have either a different absolute or a different relative impact on different income groups. The equity of tax incidence becomes an issue only if some groups are more concerned about the maldistribution of the tax burden than about the potential loss of the program for which the tax would be raised.

The Agrarian Philosophy

Don Paarlberg summarized the pre-1930s set of beliefs of farmers as follows.

> 1. Farmers are good citizens and a high percentage of the population should be on farms.
>
> 2. Farming is a way of life.
>
> 3. Farming should be a family enterprise.
>
> 4. The land should be owned by the man who tills it.
>
> 5. It is good to make two blades of grass grow where only one grew before.
>
> 6. Anyone who wants to farm should be free to do so.
>
> 7. A farmer should be his own boss.

Paarlberg's list is fairly typical of the sets of beliefs now known as agricultural fundamentalism or agrarianism or the agricultural creed.

It is difficult to say how extensively even this creed was believed by farmers prior to the 1930s. Much of the evidence is obscure. The fact that many presidents traced their roots back to log cabins may have owed as much to the favorable implications of pulling oneself up from poverty as to any aura of good citizenship attaching to a farm background. In many, many instances, too, farmers recognized the dangers of overproduction. Ranchers frequently opposed the freedom of homesteaders to enter farming in their area. Belief that farming was a way of life, that farmers should be their own boss, that farmers should own their own land, or that farming should be a family enterprise reflected actual farming conditions prior to the 1930s, rather than any soundly based philosophical view of the optimal farming system. Probably small retailers, fishermen, and other operators not yet absorbed by big business, commerce, and government shared their own similar sets of beliefs derived from their actual business operations. For example, the family grocery store fought a bitter rear guard action against the inroads of the chain stores in the 1930s. In their case, too, the creed was as much a plausible argument for economic survival as a deep-seated belief. Certainly, in the case of farm programs, many of the tenets of the agrarian creed have either been compromised or have fallen into disrepute.

John M. Brewster suggested that four more basic beliefs, the work ethic, democracy, enterprise, and self-integrity, underlie both rural and urban values in the nineteenth century. James L. Gulley traces the development of agrarian thought back through western culture and suggests the importance of other complementary beliefs:

1. Medieval belief in ownership of property as a mark of personal and social worth.
2. Reformation belief that all proficient work has ethical significance.
3. Enlightenment belief in the natural right of private ownership.
4. Belief in the inevitability of progress.
5. Belief in freedom symbolized by the New World.

Clearly, the issues raised by Paarlberg, Brewster, Gulley, and other writers have differing levels of validity in modern society after 40 years of government programs and dramatic changes in the structure of the agricultural sector. There is much merit in Tweeten's suggestion of the need for a new creed in terms of what society might expect from agriculture and what agriculture might expect from society.

Farm Group Beliefs and Platforms

Major farm groups, however, have been unwilling to drop the moralistic elements of their platforms. These they claim to be the deep seated views of their members. However, as Talbot and Hadwiger point out, "One should be realistic about this matter of grass-roots democracy. The leadership is at a tremendous advantage in 'leading' toward the adoption of policies which it desires. The propagandistic tools of the organization are in the leaders' hands and are used constantly, especially by the Farm Bureau, NFU, and NFO. While generally more pragmatic, the USDA has been willing to use slogans to shore up its programs and maintain its influence."

The Farm Bureau's annual policy statement is a lengthy document with an amazingly broad sweep. Under Farm Bureau Beliefs the 1973 policy stated,

> We, as Farm Bureau members, believe:
>
> In our Constitutional form of government and its division of powers,
>
> In freedom of speech, press and peaceful assembly. . . .
>
> In the American competitive enterprise system, in which property is privately owned, privately managed, and operated for profit and individual satisfaction, and in which supply and demand are the ultimate determinants of market price. . . .
>
> That such "planned economy" concepts as socialism, fascism, communism and other forms of totalitarianism should be opposed wherever and in whatever form they may be found. . . .
>
> That individual freedom and opportunity must not be sacrificed in a quest for guaranteed "security."

It continued with specific policy recommendations supporting a loyalty oath for federal posts in defense or teaching, stronger penalties for burners of draft cards, restoration of capital punishment, electoral college reform, curtailment of the powers of the Supreme Court, and other nonfarm national and international issues. It is clearly the intent of the AFB to link its beliefs to its policy prescriptions. Other farm groups and politicians play the same game of rhetoric, drawing on shared values as a rationale for policy proposals. The game can entrap necessary flexibility when an organization or politician becomes too strongly identified with a belief which stands in the way of a policy change it urgently needs. This may indeed be one reason for the weakened political clout of the individual farm organizations.

Summary

To summarize, in an ideal democracy with rational, responsible citizens, beliefs, values, and goals would lead directly to specific policies. The reality has shown that it is possible for some citizens' values to be translated into policies, but that in many cases the views of special interest groups and opinion leaders prevail over genuine grassroots goals. A further problem relevant to agricultural policy is the dynamic nature of the world in which policy must be made. Beliefs, values, and the goals deriving therefrom tend to develop slowly over time. The more stable a society, the more stable and consistent will be the beliefs, values, and goals of its citizens. New goals can emerge slowly over time and policy can be gradually adapted. However, modern U.S. agriculture has had to face a continuing series of turbulent events which require an immediate pragmatic response. There is no time to test these responses against existing goals and often no clear goal against which to test the response. For example, should the American Farm Bureau's belief in freedom of speech, press, and peaceful assembly make its members unwilling to sell grain to countries where such freedoms are lacking? Or are these beliefs only ideals for Americans, irrelevant to citizens of other countries? Even if AFB members were unwilling to make such trades, could or should they prevent others from so trading? Faced with these sorts of dilemmas, the response of U.S. agriculture has been to shove beliefs, values, and goals under the table and do what is expedient. Where past generations of farmers were too often shackled by the outmoded views of dead philosophers, our generation may suffer from not having a coherent enough philosophy to provide some moral guidance against which future generations can judge our actions.

Key Words	Central Concepts
Politicization	Deliberately posing an issue so that it can be resolved only by political action.
Agricultural fundamentalism	Belief in the basic superiority of the agricultural way of life.
Work ethic	Belief in the innate value of work.

QUESTIONS

1. Why would agricultural policy be politicized?
2. What beliefs would you expect modern U.S. farmers to have? How would they differ from those of the pre-1930s?
3. Cite examples of farmer behavior inconsistent with the agrarian creed described by Paarlberg.
4. Develop a new creed in terms of what society might expect from agriculture and what agriculture might expect from society.
5. How much of the position statement of a farm group can be considered rhetoric, how much a guide to their policy goals? Give examples.
6. Is the modern farmer guided more by expediency than by philosophy?

GOALS FOR THE FUTURE— WHICH WAY IS UP?

What Type of Policies?

The most valuable lesson a reader can hope to gain from the previous chapters in this book is new awareness and insights into the sort of policy he or she would like to see for U.S. agriculture in the future. It is relatively easy to point out the inconsistencies of the past. It is a wholly different matter to develop a blueprint for the future that will stand the test of time. Indeed, many would argue that one should not even seek such a blueprint. If, they say, in terms of measuring social welfare, we still cannot say for sure which way is up, why waste time trying to develop a comprehensive agricultural policy? Let us, instead, try to see what minor improvements are possible in existing policies.

In some ways this pessimistic view of the policy process is attractive. In the last section we saw how obscure the goals underlying modern agriculture have become. The easy route would be to seek improvements in small increments. However, if there is no moral underpinning to our actions, behavior becomes a matter of what is expedient at the moment. Without a guiding philosophy, man loses his claim to superiority over the animal kingdom. History gives many examples of how men, or nations, in a similar babble of discordant views looked at their problems with a new clarity, developed new policies, and followed those policies with actions which changed the world. If the policy analyst attempts to develop a global view, he may fail, but at least he will see individual parts of the problem in better perspective relative to the whole.

Of course the analyst will never have enough information on all the issues involved to achieve certainty in his recommendations. However, this should not be a deterrent, for the role of the analyst or student or researcher or adviser is not to make decisions but to improve the information or knowledge base upon which responsible legislators, administrators, and others who have decision making power can act. For example, a student would not be expected to be able to recommend a complete and consistent policy program for U.S. agriculture. He should be able to point out the relationships among policies; the likely cumulative effects; the inconsistencies; and the potential effects on producers, consumers, distributors, suppliers, international groups, and other parts of the network in which U.S. agriculture is embedded.

Even the fact that a holistic approach right now may be infeasible for politicians or unpalatable for voters cannot excuse the analyst from attempting to examine the total picture. Politicians and voting alliances change, often quite abruptly, and with them go programs which once seemed above challenge. The Sugar Act's demise in 1974 was just such an abrupt and unexpected event. So, in a sense, the analyst must take a timeless approach: The more rooted his analysis is in current events, the more rapidly it will become outmoded.

The Role of Government

Having said this, it is necessary to review briefly what the past and present have been, before discussing appropriate goals for future policy. A major issue is the role of government in agricultural policy. The 1970 and 1973 Agricultural Acts helped the U.S. government in the first half of the 1970s to reduce its involvement in price supports and production controls for agriculture. However, the growing importance of foreign conditions brought increases in other forms of government involvement in agricultural policy. Agriculture was a vital tool in the restoration of normal relations between the U.S. and the major Communist nations, Russia and Mainland China. Agriculture was at the center of international concerns over food shortages, development aid, and increased trade. Many of these issues could only be tackled by exchanges between governments. Domestically, concerns about inflation in general, and rising food prices in particular, brought concentrated union and consumer pressures for government controls on agricultural exports. Indeed, the net effect may have been a reduction in the involvement of the Department of Agriculture in agricultural affairs but a more than compensating increase in the involvement of the Departments of State, Treasury, Commerce, and others.

During his unsuccessful 1976 drive for re-election, President Ford appeared to restore the mantle of leadership in agricultural policy to the Department of Agriculture by appointing the secretary of agriculture to be chairman of a new Agricultural Policy Committee, an interagency group responsible for overseeing both domestic and international agricultural policy making. As concern about food shortages and inflation waned in 1976 and farm prices began to fall in the 1976 harvest period, it became likely that traditional concerns about falling farm incomes would come to the fore, thus giving back to the Department of Agriculture its traditional role. In October, loan rates for wheat were increased by 50 percent and for feed grains by 20 percent. Meat import quotas were imposed at the same time that the EEC was considering *permitting* imports because of scarcer world supplies. Milk supports were increased although stocks of most dairy products were rising.

At this same time Congress showed a renewed willingness to get back into thirties-style price support and production control programs at the first sign of distress in agriculture. This was apparent during the passage of the Emergency Farm Act of 1975, later vetoed by President Ford. Congress, like most legislative bodies, has a built-in bias toward the marginal increment approach. In agricultural policy, this means making policies for one commodity, one sector, or one area at a time (an approach best calculated to appeal to down-home voters), rather than taking a single approach to many interrelated problems. In general, congressmen or senators do not have the personal experience or staff aid to take a holistic view of agricultural policy. The committee structure, lobbying pressures, and legislative precedent reinforce the tendency to take the partial, short-range approach. Congress has also been inadequate in reviewing existing measures for their effectiveness, consistency, and additivity, so that despite decades of debate the nation does not have a comprehensive agricultural policy, but has, instead, a hodgepodge of inadequate and often contradictory measures. Like the executive branch, Congress, by its own floundering attempts at rescue, can become part of the drowning man's problem.

Nongovernment Influences

Farm organizations are in a better position than is Congress to offer new initiatives in farm policy. However, they have tended to look backwards, to see the situation as they would like it to be rather than as it is, to be divided and yet provincial in reconciling the good of farmers with the good of the nation. Perhaps, since they must achieve their policy goals through Congress, they have been forced into adopting the piecemeal approach which Congress prefers. They have learned from sad experience that it is not the broad declarations of policy but the fine print and legal clauses which affect the individual farmer's pocketbook. Yet farm organizations cannot be written off. For many centuries and in many countries the aroused farmer has been an occasional catalyst of great changes.

Rather surprisingly, it has been the business-oriented "think" groups, such as the Committee on Economic Development (CED) and the National Planning Association (NPA), which have taken the most holistic view of future agricultural policy. However, while their reports are written under the direction of distinguished economists, the exploitation of the reports is in the hands of the business-oriented trustees and staff. In interacting with Congress and the executive branch, these officers have much leeway in interpreting the economists' recommendations. For example, the CED report called "A New U.S. Farm Policy for Changing World Food Needs" uses such ambiguous terms as "unwanted surpluses," "extensive action of market forces," "a spirit of leadership and international cooperation on the part of the United States," and "the national interest in reasonably stable food prices for consumers and a steady flow of agricultural exports."

Where We Are Now

As well as being constrained by the leading characters involved in policy development and administration, future policy goals must take into account where we are now as a result of the legacy of past policies. Although intended to improve the income of small family farmers, past policy benefits have gone primarily to larger farmers and to landowners. Benefits have been unequally shared among producers of different commodities in different regions. Policies have frequently been inconsistent with each other or have continued after their original purpose was no longer valid. In a single year, farm fortunes are not equal; however, consistently over the years, the gap has widened between what are now known as commercial farmers and the rest—the farmers who cannot make a viable living from farming but cannot or will not leave farming. Among the rest, too, there is a gap between those who can earn income off the farm and those who cannot, either due to age, lack of skills, remote location, or lack of off-farm opportunities.

Farm labor—owner–operator, family, and hired help—has declined steadily since the early part of the twentieth century. However, the decline in numbers has halted and is not likely to fall sharply again unless agriculture runs into a severe depression. The more dramatic change taking place in farm labor is a change in quality. Farmers are becoming younger, better educated, and more knowledgeable about the complex system in which they operate. As farms become larger, farmers are purchasing more knowledge inputs, management and accounting services, pesticide and environmental consultants, weather and market information, and so on. Farmers are having to learn to work with and interpret results from computers, satellites, new means of telecommunication, etc. As a result, the people they employ must be trained in the agricultural sciences and other sciences or management fields. The last great leap forward in agricultural productivity relied heavily on cheap and plentiful water, energy, fertilizer, pest controls, and weed killers. Concerns about scarcity and the environmental impacts of the energy-intensive system will put considerable restraints on that approach in the future. Farmers will have to substitute knowledge (some of it not yet developed) in place of unavailable inputs. For example, in their pest management practices, farmers are extensively substituting monitoring to determine harmful levels of insect populations where spraying automatically by the calendar was formerly the practice. Both the farmer and his workers must retrain to operate under these limitations.

Much of the availability of the highly productive inputs in the past was due to the industrialization of the agricultural supply industry. In the future, agricultural supply services will have to grow alongside industry to provide the knowledge inputs needed. A major policy issue may arise over whether these knowledge inputs should be provided by subsidized public agencies such as the federal and state extension services or by private firms. Industrialization of agricultural processing, distribution, and to some extent production has also taken place. There is much more controversy over the extent of benefits which farmers or consumers have derived from these marketing changes contrasted with changes in agricultural supply, largely because marketing margins have shown a long-term tendency to rise faster than farm prices. However, the period of erratic price swings in the early 1970s has convinced both farmers and the marketing and distribution sector of their need for more knowledge inputs. We can expect a development of marketing information services on world, national, and commodity issues similar to those services on the supply side.

A further production issue will be the competition of other sectors of the economy for the inputs which agriculture monopolized for centuries. Nonowners of land have established their claim to control or limit the use of land which is the private property of the farmers. Development, potential as well as actual, for housing, highways, recreation, or open spaces tends to bid up land prices in select locations above the marginal value product from farming. At the same time, advances in technology have made deserts bloom and could conceivably increase the productivity of marginal land in ways not now dreamed of. The stock of productive farm land is not as fixed as was once thought, nor is it easily increased; neither is it any longer sacred to agriculture. Likewise, water is increasingly required for household consumption, hydroelectric or nuclear power plants, or for industrial uses. And agriculture must compete with other sectors of the economy for its steel, wood, fuel, machinery, and other scarce inputs over which it has not had a special claim.

Domestic and Export Markets

Domestic consumers, approaching 250 million by the end of the century and enjoying incomes above present levels, will continue to be the world's largest market for food and fiber. However, income elasticity (so our theory would suggest) is likely to decline even further, so that the market rate of growth will be small. Consumer concerns over diet, quality, wholesomeness, and safety are not likely to be dissipated for many years, given the unwillingness of processors and retailers to adapt unless legally compelled to do so. Consumers themselves have been under pressure to reduce their consumption of livestock products so that U.S. agriculture can devote more resources to growing grain for food deficit countries. Whether they will do so may depend on the frequency and extent of future famines overseas.

Fear of famine, rather than any assurance of continued strong world demand for grain, is also at the heart of renewed efforts to increase yields in U.S. agriculture. The National Resources Council has called for more basic research to bring about new yield breakthroughs. The type of technology required will have important effects. If future yield increases require a more capital-intensive agriculture, they may lead to consolidation and reduction in number of farms, displacement of established farmers, and perhaps further inroads of capital-rich conglomerates into agriculture. If the new technology is one best handled by owner–operators on smaller farms, the reverse could be true. In addition, yield increases without increased demand (which is by no means assured) will bring inevitable price declines and the bankruptcy of debt-heavy (mostly younger) farmers. The family farm's fate may hinge on the outcome of the work of a lone agricultural researcher.

As long as demand for U.S. farm products continues to depend heavily on foreign markets and as long as supply remains vulnerable to weather, pests, and disease, uncertainty will continue to be farm producers' largest problem. However, much work has been done in analyzing the frequency and sequence of occurrence of supply and demand disturbances. Very little in life is ever completely new. We can learn much from the past. We can do much to prepare for likely future events. This work needs to be intensified and made available to decision makers in all parts of the food and fiber system. The farmer in particular is still too frequently taken by surprise in situations which he should and could have anticipated.

International Issues

Even the international economy has an inner logic to its development. For example, the collapse of the Bretton Woods Agreement has not led to economic disorder. If anything, it has forced the advanced countries to take initiatives which they would not otherwise have taken. They have acknowledged the folly of overrapid increases in domestic money supply and of unilateral trade restrictions, even though changing the bad habits may prove difficult. The developing countries are aware of the bonds between the advanced countries in military, political, and economic affairs, for example, the desire of OECD member countries to maintain their economic leadership. The LDCs can only hope to promote their own interests by gaining a position of strength through cartels, as in oil, or through international agreements. As growing markets for the products and invested capital of advanced countries, LDCs can use this to gain advantages in trade, aid, and technical assistance. Wherever they see a position of strength emerging, they are likely to use it to further their aims.

The United States is in a very favorable position to improve its relations with advanced, centrally planned, and developing countries. For the foreseeable future, the U.S. will be the major grain reserve for both trade and aid. It also has a valuable domestic market to which it can grant increased access in return for offsetting benefits. It has the experience and resources to increase greatly its credit program for other countries. And it is the single greatest repository of the modern technology and technical knowledge for which other nations are clamoring.

Its position as the major world food reservoir carries risks as well as opportunities. The U.S. has been reluctant to build its own grain reserves or to press for an international buffer stock system. As a major exporter, it can gain from high prices when world production is short and little stock exists. Yet if it builds up its grain reserves, almost certainly government must become involved, the existence of large stocks can depress prices—as in the 1960s—and the release of stocks can be subjected to political pressures. Even if reserves are large, when famine strikes the value of the grain will rise and the nation may be reluctant to pay the higher cost of food aid, especially when it will lead to further increases in domestic food prices. In addition, the availability of large stocks and the prospect of food aid may deter certain LDCs from making the painful choices involved in bringing their population and food supplies into balance.

Ever since the Russian grain deal of 1972 awakened Americans to an awareness that food is not always and inevitably plentiful and cheap, the debate about food policy has grown in complexity. For simplicity, we will discuss only food grains such as wheat and rice. However, the great food debate is paralleled by similar concerns about livestock and livestock products, about feed grains tied to the livestock economy, and about overall calorie and protein availability.

One boundary of the debate involves the simple equation that total availabilities of food divided by population must exceed per capita biological needs for survival of all the earth's population. However, most analysts would suggest that if people are to produce more than they consume, their food needs must be substantially above the minimum needs for survival. Most recent studies reject the thesis of the Club of Rome reports that the world food situation in the foreseeable future will be near the disaster zone. In general, the world food situation will be in the realm of normal commercial concern, with occasional temporary shortages in specific regions. Those who go hungry are as likely to do so due to maldistribution of income within countries as to maldistribution of supplies among countries. These two issues, of course, are not independent. When supplies are short and prices are high, the poor are likely to go hungriest.

In the United States, the questions asked in the great food debate include the following. Can the U.S. meet its own and world deficit grain needs? How can it best do this? How large a food reserve should it hold? How much will it cost? Should we be concerned more about security of supplies or stability of price? Should sales remain in private hands or be controlled by a government agency? Should production be permitted to become as concentrated as sales? Can we meet production needs without exhausting available energy? Are price supports needed to ensure sufficient production?

Some of these questions have been answered in previous sections. Reasonable answers to the remaining issues can be provided only in light of the world supply and demand balance (Table 9.2). We have broken supply and demand into categories which, while a little unorthodox, do help to highlight the key issues. In any year, only enough commercial stocks will be held to meet normal convenience needs. Unless they wish to increase stocks for speculative purposes, commercial stockholders will clear above average production at below average prices. The full adjustment to changed supplies, however severe, will occur in one season. So, governments acting either singly or in concert will have to intervene if stocks are to be increased and the price decline reduced in that season. Of course, such increased stocks will add to supplies and depress prices in subsequent years. Any scheme to juggle reserves must also be concerned with the likely sequence of production from year to year and the resulting price effects. Stocks themselves are costly to carry. If they are allowed to build up excessively, they become both a depressant on the market and a drain on the funding agency. When that happens, the agency must then impose production controls. Should these controls be on all production or only on production for export sales?

Governments have devised many schemes for stimulating the latter while restraining the former. However, for an export-oriented country such as the U.S., production controls and/or price supports both tend to inhibit exports. Price supports can be extremely costly since they are open ended—that is, there is no clear limit to the volume which will require support.

Table 9.2 Annual World Food Supply and Demand Balances

Supply	*Demand*
Opening Stocks (commercial and government)	*Purchases* from home supplies
+	+
Production for domestic sale	*Purchases* from imports
+	+
Production for export sale	*Food Aid Needs*
+	+
Production for food aid	*Closing Stocks* (commercial and government)
TOTAL SUPPLY	TOTAL DEMAND

Finally, production for international aid can either be left to chance (that is, be a residual after other needs are met) or be specifically provided for out of reserves or by additional plantings. It too will involve trade-offs between security of supplies and freedom to produce, price to growers and cost to the aid agency.

On the demand side, purchases from home supplies are relatively easy to predict from country to country. For example, in the United States, domestic demand has been stable and relatively price inelastic in recent years. However, the other three items on the demand side are very uncertain. Both the EEC and the USSR aim to be self-sufficient in food grains but do enter the world market to make up any shortfalls in their own production. Their needs can dramatically alter the supply–demand balance. Food aid needs, too, are dependent on production swings in the developing countries. Even though, in general, these countries can meet their normal needs, shortfalls requiring aid can be very severe indeed. Demand for closing stock is heavily dependent on government decisions, which in turn are a mixture of economic and political motivations which will vary with changes in consumer and producer pressure, political ideologies, and parties in power.

Finally, overall demand may vary as a result of variations in its components. There is no reason why either the surpluses of the sixties or the shortages of the seventies should not be repeated. Policy must be flexible enough to deal with either extreme or with intermediate situations without causing further distortions in either supply or demand. Governments, either alone or in concert, cannot remove all the variability in supply or price. Perhaps a more reasonable target would be government measures which would handle the ranges that are most likely to be encountered.

Against this background, what can the U.S. role in food grain supply be? Clearly, the U.S. can meet its own needs, but it cannot alone meet any large or continuous deficit either among its paying customers or for food aid. U.S. consumers cannot be protected from rises in prices due to external demand without some form of export controls, which in turn penalize U.S. producers. However, in most years, for domestic requirements the United States would not need to keep food reserves. These are of much more importance to large importers such as Japan and other Southeast Asian countries. Any reserve scheme, to survive, must have the support of and possibly leadership from these importing countries. It must also have the support of occasional but substantial commercial buyers, like the EEC and USSR. There does not appear to be either the will or the international resources to provide large quantities of food aid on anything but a temporary basis, unless this can be linked in some manner with increased earnings from oil, minerals, raw materials, or other traded goods. It is clear that the U.S. should be willing to expand its production of low-cost food grains; it would in general be an efficient provider of such grain to the world. However, unless it is willing to permit access to its markets for agricultural products such as dairy products, wool, cotton, palm oil, etc., from other countries, it will find its grain markets artificially restrained. Of course, the EEC and the USSR and its allies must also open up their agricultural markets if the U.S. is to be willing to do so. There is a mistaken belief that a producer with lower average cost will capture all the market of a producer with higher average cost. This is not true. It will only undercut those producers who are at the margins of efficiency. These may switch to a more productive sector of agriculture or to the nonagricultural sector. For two hundred years, modern society has advanced by moving labor from less productive to more productive outlets. It is self-defeating deliberately to retain unproductive labor in agriculture, in the U.S. or elsewhere.

From this perspective, the great food debate is just a part of the overall debate about how world society wishes to organize the exploitation of its resources in the production and allocation of goods and services. Clearly, common international policies must be based on an international consensus of goals, beliefs, and values. Much of the recent stalemate in international debate among major power groups, between North and South, between East and West has arisen because too little effort has been expended on developing such a consensus. Americans must begin to think a little like Russians and Europeans a little like Africans if the great food debate is to produce anything other than empty rhetoric.

Pivotal Role of Knowledge

Of course, to resolve these dilemmas adequately, more knowledge will be needed. The USDA occupies a pivotal position in agricultural research, publication, demonstration, and education. Many would like to see the research, extension, and educational role of the USDA restored to its pre-1930s importance and a reduction of the resources eaten up in the bureaucratic exercise of standing still while appearing to be in motion. However, the quality of personnel needed for such an adjustment can be developed only over a decade or more. Investment in increased numbers of skilled people seems crucial to the continuing development, application, and adaptation of knowledge to agriculture in the U.S. and throughout the world.

The Poor—A Continuing Problem

One group of problems will not be resolved by technological advancement and may indeed be heightened—that is, the problem of the poor farmers, poor rural people, and poor urban people. Where a farmer is poor primarily because he lacks the resources and knowledge base to be otherwise, his problem becomes identical to that of the nonfarm poor. It may seem ironical to help the poor farmer with food stamps, since the program was originally intended as a boost to farm product demand and farm incomes. And indeed, one must question whether there is not a better way to help the poor than with food stamps. While they do boost real income and food expenditures, there is little evidence that they improve the nutritional content of the diets of the poor. Indeed, Hendrick S. Houthakker suggests that it is no accident that the major nutritional deficiencies in U.S. diets (calcium and vitamins A and C) are those supplied by milk, fruits, and vegetables, whose price is inflated and supply limited by government-aided programs. The USDA should not be asked to represent the conflicting interest of commercial agriculture and the poor. Given its established links with commercial agriculture, the poor are not likely to fare well. In a previous section we have argued that efforts to help the poor can be effective only if they attack the problems at the individual community and national levels simultaneously.

Goals for the Future

Based on the foregoing review, and in the absence of any deep philosophical underpinnings such as saving the world for capitalism, establishing American hegemony, or building world brotherhood, the goals which emerge for U.S. agriculture appear rather mundane:

1. Supply the food and fiber requirements of domestic and commercial export markets at the supply-demand equilibrium. Domestic needs are likely to change only slowly over time, export needs more erratically.

2. Maintain food and fiber emergency reserves at the level needed to meet the normal trade needs of commercial customers and the exceptional needs of countries with a food deficit. These reserves could only be released when world production in any year fell below prearranged levels.

3. Maintain a highly skilled core of commercial farmers and allow them as far as possible to respond to market signals.

4. Recognize the mutuality of interest between agriculture and other sectors of the U.S. economy. The nation needs an agriculture that is best for its citizens in total, not just for its farmers.

5. Recognize the mutuality of interest between U.S. agriculture and the agriculture of other nations. In a shrinking world, possibly a starving world, mountains of unsold butter and massacres of unsold chickens are morally unacceptable. Neither the U.S. nor the EEC can continue to protect inefficient producers.

6. Encourage technological innovation. Higher productivity may be crucial to world survival. Even if population and food and fiber needs do not become critical, the world can continue to benefit as it has for two centuries from release of resources not needed to provide food.

7. Treat rural poverty as a welfare, not an agricultural, problem.

We could be more general or more explicit about future goals for U.S. agriculture. You may have other preferences which you would wish to have included. The seven goals listed above arise naturally from the way I see U.S. agriculture. Whatever the goals finally agreed upon, however, they should form the basis for a consistent and comprehensive U.S. agricultural policy.

Key Words	Central Concepts
Blueprint for the future	Detailed outline of future plans for U.S. agriculture.
Global view	A look at all sides of an issue.
Piecemeal approach	In contrast to the global view, involves tackling small parts of a problem one at a time.
Knowledge inputs	Inputs which provide knowledge, or information, to the farm manager.
Food deficit countries	Countries in which demand for food exceeds supply. Sometimes applied to LDCs where the demand for minimum daily nutrient requirements exceeds supply.

QUESTIONS

1. Discuss the arguments for a piecemeal rather than a global approach to agricultural policy? Which most resembles current policy?
2. Suggest a guiding philosophy for U.S. economic and agricultural policy.
3. Document a policy decision of the past, in the United States or elsewhere, which changed the world.
4. What is the proper role of the policy analyst? Should the policy analyst take sides on issues?
5. In what ways do voting alliances change? Give examples.
6. Did the U.S. government in the 1970s increase or decrease its involvement in agriculture?
7. Can Congress develop a comprehensive policy for U.S. agriculture in the next decade?
8. Why are farm organizations less successful than nonfarm organizations in developing a holistic view of farm policy?
9. Discuss the role of knowledge inputs into the future of U.S. and world agriculture.
10. Can the present capital- and energy-intensive mode of U.S. agriculture survive?
11. What changes in supply and marketing services will the U.S. farmer require in the future?
12. Can agriculture compete successfully with nonfarm economic activities for its basic inputs?
13. How rapidly can we expect the U.S. domestic market for food to grow?
14. What are the likely benefits and hazards of increased productivity in U.S. agriculture?
15. Do the OECD countries and the LDCs have common and conflicting economic goals? Discuss.
16. Should the U.S. build grain reserves? How large should they be? How should they be acquired? By whom held? When released?

17. Should the USDA restore its former emphasis on research and education?
18. What goals would you suggest for U.S. agriculture in the 1980s?

A FRAMEWORK FOR FUTURE AGRICULTURAL POLICY

The goals discussed in the last section suggest a general framework for future U.S. agricultural policy. We need an agricultural policy which will serve all the citizens of the United States and all the peoples of the world, not select pressure groups at home and abroad. We need a highly productive agriculture, because the risks to the world of underproduction and of serious famine are so grave. We must remove as many barriers as possible, both in and out of agriculture, to release agriculture's full productive potential. We need a climate of enterprise which will encourage farmers to invest in new and improved techniques and at the same time provide a means of protecting farm businesses from unfavorable consequences of any risks they undertake in the national interest.

The following is a list of agricultural and other policy prescriptions for the future which would help to meet the goals outlined. Some of the proposals are common, some novel. The reader with a different set of goals may wish to offer alternatives.

1. The commodity orientation of present farm programs would be ended. Payments would no longer be made for planting or not planting a specific crop or producing milk or livestock products. Allotments, conserving bases, set-asides, and other quantity control devices would be phased out. Trade barriers on free movement of agricultural products would be ended.

2. Government would no longer be responsible for thirties-style price support or production control programs. Government would continue to administer those services which an atomistic and geographically scattered food industry cannot—market information, research, extension, grades and standards, health and safety, and regulation. However, where possible these services too should be financed and operated by agriculture itself.

3. As is now being done within the EEC, farmers would be ranked in terms of commercial viability based on quantity and quality of land, labor, capital, and managerial skills. Then from all farmers, a core of continuing

farmers would be chosen, preferably by a group dominated by farmers themselves. This core would give the hope for efficient and significant increases in productivity. The core would include both producers of geographically specialized crops and of crops which can be readily substituted for in many regions, such as, wheat.

4. Core farmers would be guaranteed a minimum income level based on their historical income level and their opportunity cost. We want to keep these "desirable" farmers in agriculture. The number of core farmers could be altered as circumstances changed. Because of their efficiency, core farmers would rarely need to call on the guarantee.

5. Provisions would be made for replacing "desirable" farmers who wished to leave agriculture because of old age, illness, or better economic alternatives elsewhere with "desirable" new entrants, again chosen on competitive criteria. Farmers falling below certain minimum standards could also be dropped from the class of core farmers.

6. Noncore farmers would be encouraged to leave farming. They would be eligible for aid in making the transition to nonfarm employment (retraining, job placement, compensation for capital losses, etc.).

7. Core farmers would be left essentially free to meet the relatively stable components of demand, for example, domestic demand for food or demand under long-term contracts. Over the long run, losses in one year will tend to be compensated for by gains in another year. Core farmers, with their scale and efficiency, are likely to need only minimal government payments in occasional years to meet their guaranteed income level.

8. However, where the government or an international agency wishes to stimulate supply to meet needs for domestic distribution, food aid, or government stockbuilding, this should be done initially by seeking tenders from core farmers. Thus each core farmer could, in advance of production, decide whether he wished to alter his crop mix or his total output level to meet these artificial, temporary, and highly variable needs. Perhaps the greatest cause of uncertainty in modern agriculture is production without any knowledge of overall prospective supply or demand. A system of forward contracting would bring greater certainty to the unstable portion of the agricultural market. If governments wish to call forth added production, they should be prepared to bid in advance for it.

9. Welfare programs, community development programs, and nutritional programs would no longer be part of agricultural policy but of national economic policy. If society wishes to transfer resources from one group to another, the transfer should be recognized as such. Welfare programs such as the food stamp program frequently fail to aid the poor or nutritionally deficient, give little boost to agricultural demand, and cost taxpayers dearly. True welfare programs are not likely to emerge as adjuncts of programs to boost demand for agricultural products.

10. Of vital importance in making agriculture freer and more efficient is (a) the simultaneous removal of uneconomic regulations, whether originally designed to protect farmers or railroads or consumers; (b) the promotion of competition in supply and marketing industries and services; (c) the prevention of discrimination, as with the provision of credit to small but efficient farmers; and (d) the extension to agriculture of the same bargaining rights as unions now possess.

This ten-point program would encourage a robust, self-renewing, progressive, independent and generally profitable agriculture. The core of highly productive farmers is already in existence. There really is no justification for attempts to contort economic laws to keep about 2 million marginal farmers producing marginally when the resources of land, capital, and manpower could be more profitably employed elsewhere. It is to the core farmers that the nation and the world must look for meeting their growing needs. Core farmers would be able to compete effectively with other sectors for their needed inputs and would not fear market competition for their output. It would be hoped, too, that at the first unfavorable sign, core farmers would be less eager to appeal for, and the citizens less eager to offer, the stifling handout from government. It is my belief that in the modern world, the types and levels of protection afforded to agriculture have become asinine. Governments rarely deliver what they promise. We must get out of the present foolish cycle of piling one failed policy upon another. One could go into greater detail about how such a system, revolving deliberately around core farmers, would work. However, that would be sufficient material for a further volume. Here, let us rest.

Key Words	Central Concepts
Policy prescription	A policy proposal aimed at remedying existing ills.
Commercial viability	The capability of yielding a return on investment in land, labor, and capital comparable to that in competing sectors of the economy.
Core farmers	Commercially viable farmers chosen on the basis of competitive criteria and guaranteed a basic income (just as an employee is guaranteed his salary) to stay in farming.

QUESTIONS

1. Should agricultural policy serve all of agriculture or all citizens? Is there a conflict?
2. What would be the advantages and disadvantages of a system of core farmers?
3. What specific criteria of commercial viability might one suggest?
4. How would the stock of core farmers be renewed?
5. How would core farmers be assured of stability yet stimulated to be more productive?
6. Should noncore farmers be encouraged to remain in production?
7. How would extraordinary demands created by national or international governments be linked with more normal market demands?
8. Why is "point ten" so critical to achievement of a continuously robust agricultural sector?
9. Would you add or take away any elements from the author's ten-point proposal?
10. Do you know more about U.S. agricultural policy now than when you began this book? If not, is the fault primarily yours or the author's?

ten

SUGGESTIONS FOR FURTHER READING

From a vast literature dealing with many aspects of U.S. agricultural policy, I have suggested a few readings which can give the interested reader deeper insights into the main topics discussed. Many of the most important contributions in the literature are written in complex mathematical or theoretical language or in technical journals not easily accessible to most readers. However, I hope that the more accessible readings suggested may stimulate the reader to acquire the mastery needed to understand the more technical works. It is appropriate at this point to repeat the warning that all studies of policy will be colored by the particular vested interests, value judgments, and biases of their writers. In policy studies, who says something and why may be as informative as what is said.

GENERAL SOURCES OF INFORMATION

Agricultural policy is often discussed in popular language in the economic and business sections of farm journals, major national and local newspapers, weekly news magazines such as *Time, Newsweek*, and *U.S. News and World Report*, and in business magazines such as *Business Week, Forbes*, and *Fortune*. The U.S. Department of Agriculture also issues popular commentaries including *Agricultural Outlook* (monthly), *Foreign Agriculture* (monthly), and a number of situation reports (quarterly). The Federal-State Cooperative Extension Service in many states issues regular reports on both general and commodity-oriented policies. They will be pleased to send you more details. The *OECD Observer* and the EC's *European Community* report on policy developments affecting their member countries.

Some basic sources of U.S. statistics for use in further study include the Censuses of Agriculture, Population, Distribution, and Transportation (held at approximately five-year intervals), the *Statistical Abstract, Agricultural Statistics*, and *Handbook of Agricultural Charts* (all annual) and monthlies such as *Agricultural Prices*, the *Social Security Bulletin*, and the *Federal Reserve Bulletin*. The OECD, European Community, and the United Nations (especially the Food and Agriculture Organization) issue many comparable statistical publications dealing with various aspects of agriculture in many countries.

Most technical publications on economic aspects of U.S. agricultural policies are found in the *American Journal of Agricultural Economics* (five issues per year), the *American Economic Review*, regional journals in agricultural economics, and in reports issued by the agricultural research centers of Land Grant universities.

SELECTED READINGS

Araji, A. A., and J. C. Roetheli. "Structural Trends in the Food Processing Industry in the Western Region," in *The U.S. Food Industry: Description of Structural Changes*, vol. 1, ed. Walter G. Heid, Jr., et al. Fort Collins, Colorado: Colorado State University Experiment Station, Technical Bulletin 129, 1975.

Black, John D. *Parity, Parity, Parity*. Cambridge, Mass.: The Harvard Committee on Research in the Social Sciences, 1942.

Clawson, Marion. "Historical Overview of Land-Use Planning in the United States," in *Environment: A New Focus for Land-Use Planning*, ed. Donald M. McAllister. Washington, D.C.: National Science Foundation, Rann Research Applied to National Needs, October 1973.

Willard W. Cochrane. "The Agricultural Treadmill," in *Farm Prices, Myth and Reality*. Minneapolis, Minnesota: University of Minnesota Press, 1958. Outlines the process by which technical improvements in agricultural fail to be translated into improved incomes.

——— *Farm Prices, Myth and Reality.* Minneapolis, Minnesota: University of Minnesota Press, 1958.

——— *Feast or Famine: The Uncertain World of Food and Agriculture and Its Policy Implications for the United States.* Washington, D.C.: National Planning Association, February 1974. Discusses alternative goals and policies.

——— *The City Man's Guide to the Farm Problem.* New York: McGraw-Hill Book Company, 1966. Chapter 1 discusses the developing economic structure of U.S. agriculture.

Cochrane, Willard W., and Mary E. Ryan. *American Farm Policy 1948–73.* Minneapolis, Minnesota: University of Minnesota Press, 1976.

Committee on Economic Development. *A New U.S. Farm Policy for Changing World Food Needs.* New York: Committee on Economic Development, October 1974. Also discusses alternative goals and policies.

Earle, Wendell, and John Hughes. *Operating Results of Food Chains, 1971–72.* Ithaca, New York: Cornell University, 1973.

Economic Report of the President. Washington, D.C.: U.S. Government Printing Office (annual). Reviews recent economic events and government plans. Contains many useful statistical tables.

Executive Office of the President. Office of Management and Budget. *The Budget of the United States Government.* Washington, D.C.: U.S. Government Printing Office (annual).

Fox, Karl A., "Agricultural Policy in an Urban Society." *American Journal of Agricultural Economics,* 50:5, pp. 1135–48. Discusses the breakdown of rural communities and their replacement by urban poles of influence.

Galbraith, John K. *American Capitalism.* Boston, Mass.: Houghton Mifflin Company, 1952. Describes the noncompetitive nature and resulting behavior of much of the U.S. economy.

George, P. S., and G. A. King. *Consumer Demand for Food Commodities in the United States with Projections to 1980.* Berkeley, California: Giannini Foundation Monograph No. 26, March 1971. A very detailed analysis of demand for food commodities at farm and retail levels.

Greig, W. Smith. "A Description of Structural Trends in the Food Processing Industry in the U.S.," in *The U.S. Food Industry: Description of Structural Changes,* vol. 1, ed. Walter G. Heid, Jr., et al. Fort Collins, Colorado: Colorado State University Experiment Station, Technical Bulletin 129, 1975.

Gulley, James L. *Beliefs and Values in American Farming.* Washington, D.C.: USDA Economic Research Service, ERS-558, August 1974. A survey of the historical roots of present beliefs and values in U.S. agriculture.

Handy, Charles R., and Daniel I. Padberg. "A Model of Competitive Behavior in Food Industries." *American Journal of Agricultural Economics,* 53, no. 2, 182–90.

Hardin, Charles M. *Food and Fiber in the Nation's Politics.* Washington, D.C.: National Advisory Commission on Food and Fiber, vol. 3, August 1967. An excellent historical and philosophical analysis.

Hathaway, Dale E. *Government and Agriculture.* New York: The Macmillan Company, 1963. Chapter 4 explains the classical exposition of the theory developed by Glenn L. Johnson, and chapter 7 explains the role and powers of Congress in agricultural policy formation. See also the *Congressional Record* and *Congressional Staff Directory.*

Heid, W. G., Jr., et al. ed. *The U.S. Food Industry: Description of Structural Changes*, vol. 1, Fort Collins, Colorado: Colorado State University Experiment Station, Technical Bulletin 129, 1975.

Houthakker, Hendrik S. "Do We Need a National Food Policy?" *American Journal of Agricultural Economics*, 58, no. 2, 259–69.

Johnston, Richard S. "Some Structural Changes in the Food Service Industry," in *The U.S. Food Industry: Description of Structural Changes*, vol. 1, ed. Walter G. Heid, Jr., et al. Fort Collins, Colorado: Colorado State University Experiment Station, Technical Bulletin 129, 1975.

Keynes, John M. *The General Theory of Employment, Interest and Money*, First Harbinger Edition, New York: Harcourt, Brace and World, Inc., 1964.

Le Bovit, Corinne. *The Impact of Some Demographic Changes on U.S. Food Consumption, 1965–75 and 1975–90.* Washington, D.C.: USDA, Economic Research Service, National Food Situation, NFS-156, May 1976, pp. 25–29.

Mayer, Leo V. "Estimated Net Costs of PL480 Food Aid with Three Alternative U.S. Farm Programs," *American Journal of Agricultural Economics*, 54:1, pp. 41–50. Points out that net costs are less than the cost of Commodity Credit Corporation storage operations.

McCune, Wesley. *Who's Behind Our Farm Policy?* New York: Praeger, 1956. Dated, but still a useful antidote to aseptic textbooks. For contrast, read the annual reports of major foundations.

Mansfield, Harvey C. "The Congress and Economic Policy," in *The Congress and America's Future*, ed. David B. Truman. Englewood Cliffs, New Jersey: Prentice-Hall, Inc., 1965.

Meadows, Donella H., et al. *The Limits to Growth.* New York: Universe Books, 1972. A pioneering simulation study of the pressures of economic and population growth on earth's scarce resources. While the pessimistic conclusions of the study have been challenged, its general thesis of stress on the earth's resources is widely accepted.

Mesarovic, Mihajlo, and Eduard Pestel. *Mankind at the Turning Point.* New York: Reader's Digest Press, 1974.

Monroe, Wilbur F. *International Trade Policy in Transition.* Lexington, Massachussets: D. C. Heath and Company, 1975. Discusses recent major changes in U.S. trade policy and their relationship to changed world economic conditions.

National Advisory Commission on Food and Fiber. *Food and Fiber for the Future.* Washington, D.C.: Government Printing Office, July 1967.

National Research Council, World Food and Nutrition Study. *Enhancement of Food Production for the United States.* Washington, D.C.: National Academy of Sciences, 1975.

National Research Council, World Food and Nutrition Study. *Interim Report.* Washington, D.C.: National Academy of Sciences, 1975.

Neustadt, Richard E. *Presidential Power, the Politics of Leadership.* New York: John Wiley and Sons, 1960.

Nicholls, W. H. "Southern Tradition and Regional Progress: A Perspective from the 1970's," *American Journal of Agricultural Economics*, 54:5, pp. 736–45.

OECD. "DAC Members' Development Assistance in 1974." *OECD Observer*, no. 76, July/August 1975, pp. 33–36.

Paarlberg, Don. *American Farm Policy.* New York: John Wiley and Sons, 1964.

Paddock, William, and Elizabeth Paddock. *We Don't Know How.* Ames, Iowa: Iowa State University Press, 1973. A provocative critique of U.S. and other programs of aid and technical assistance to developing countries.

President's National Advisory Commission on Rural Poverty. *Rural Poverty in the United States.* Washington, D.C.: Government Printing Office, 1968.

———. *The People Left Behind.* Washington, D.C.: Government Printing Office, September 1967. A popular version of the Commission's full report on rural poverty in the mid-1960s.

President's Science Advisory Committee. *The World Food Problem*, vol. I. Washington, D.C.: Government Printing Office, May 1967.

Progressive Grocer. "Annual Survey of the Grocery Industry." New York. April issues.

Projector, Dorothy S., and Gertrude S. Weiss. *Survey of Financial Characteristics of Consumers.* Washington, D.C.: Board of Governors of the Federal Reserve System, August 1966.

Rasmussen, Wayne D., Gladys L. Baker, and James S. Ward. *A Short History of Agricultural Adjustment, 1933-75.* Washington, D.C.: USDA, Economic Research Service, Agriculture Information Bulletin No. 391, March 1976.

Raup, Philip M. *Nature and Extent of the Expansion of Corporations in American Agriculture.* St. Paul, Minnesota: University of Minnesota Institute of Agriculture, Staff Paper P75-8, April 1975.

Reimund, Donn A. *Farming and Agribusiness Activities of Large Multiunit Firms.* Washington, D.C.: USDA, Economic Research Service, ERS-591, March 1975.

Reynolds, T. M., E. O. Heady, and D. D. Mitchell. "Alternative Futures for American Agricultural Structures, Policies, Income, Employment, and Exports: A Recursive Simulation." Ames: Iowa: Iowa State University, CARD Report 56, 1975. Future scenarios.

Robinson, Joan. "The Second Crisis of Economic Theory," *The American Economic Review*, 62:2, pp. 1–10. The Keynesian revolution and its present implications, as seen by a friend and colleague of Keynes.

Ruttan, Vernon W., ed. *Agricultural Policy in an Affluent Society.* New York: W. W. Norton and Company, Inc., 1969.

Schultz, Theodore W. *Agriculture in an Unstable Economy.* New York: McGraw-Hill Book Co., 1945.

_______ *Redirecting Farm Policy*. New York: The Macmillan Company, 1943. A cogent critique of 1930s agricultural policies with suggestions for change.

_______ *The Economic Organization of Agriculture*. New York: McGraw-Hill Book Co., 1953.

_______ *Transforming Traditional Agriculture*. New Haven, Connecticut: Yale University Press, 1964.

Schultze, Charles L. *The Distribution of Farm Subsidies*. Washington, D.C.: The Brookings Institution, 1971.

Stigler, George B. "The Economist Plays with Blocs." *American Economic Review*, May 1974, pp. 7–14. Holds an opposite viewpoint to J. K. Galbraith.

Talbot, Ross B., and Don F. Hadwiger. *The Policy Process in American Agriculture*. San Francisco: Chandler Publishing Co. Examines the motivations of farmers and farm organization in historical and institutional contexts.

Thoman, Richard S., and Edgar C. Conkling. *Geography of International Trade*. Englewood Cliffs, New Jersey: Prentice-Hall, Inc., 1967.

Toffler, Alvin. *The Eco-spasm Report*. New York: Bantam Books, 1975.

Tolley, G. S. "Management Entry into U.S. Agriculture," *American Journal of Agricultural Economics*, 52:4, pp. 485–93.

Tweeten, Luther. *Foundations of Farm Policy*. Lincoln, Nebraska: University of Nebraska Press, 1970.

Tweeten, Luther, and James Plaxico. "U.S. Policies for Food and Agriculture in an Unstable World," *American Journal of Agricultural Economics*, 56:2, pp. 364-71. Discusses the desirable goals of U.S. agricultural policy and how near the 1973 act goes toward achieving them.

U.S. Department of Agriculture. *Agricultural Outlook*. Washington, D.C.: Economic Research Service (monthly).

_______ *Balance Sheet of the Farming Sector, 1975*. Washington, D.C.: Economic Research Service, Agriculture Information Bulletin No. 389, September 1975.

_______ *Developments in Marketing Spreads for Agricultural Products in 1975*. Washington, D.C.: Economic Research Service, Agricultural Economic Report No. 328, March 1976.

_______ *Economic Tables*. Washington, D.C.: Economic Research Service, ERS-559, August 1974.

_______ *1975 Handbook of Agricultural Charts*. Washington, D.C.: Agriculture Handbook No. 491, 1975.

_______ *The World Food Situation and Prospects to 1985*. Washington, D.C.: Economic Research Service, Foreign Agricultural Economic Report No. 98, December 1974. Suggests that world food supplies will in general be adequate for normal needs but that occasional or localized shortages may occur.

U.S. Department of Commerce. *Characteristics of the Population Below the Poverty Level: 1974*. Washington, D.C.: Bureau of the Census, Current

Population Reports, P-60, no. 102, January 1976.

——— "The Input–Output Structure of the U.S. Economy: 1967." *Survey of Current Business* 54, no. 2, 24–56.

U.S. Department of Health, Education and Welfare. *Social Security Programs Throughout the World, 1975.* Washington, D.C.: Social Security Administration, Research Report No. 48, December 1975.

University of Illinois. *Who Will Control U.S. Agriculture?* Urbana, Illinois: Cooperative Extension Service, Special Publication 28, 1975.

Van Dress, Michael G., and William H. Freund. *The Food Service Industry.* Washington, D.C.: USDA, Marketing Economics Division, Economic Research Service, Statistical Bulletin No. 416, February 1968.

Wentworth, Edna C., and Dena K. Motley. *Resources after Retirement.* Monograph No. 34, Office of Research and Statistics Research Reports, Social Security Administration, Washington, D.C.: U.S. Government Printing Office, 1970.

Wilcox, Walter W., W. W. Cochrane, and Robert W. Herdt. *Economics of American Agriculture.* Englewood Cliffs, New Jersey: Prentice-Hall, Inc., 1974.

Yeh, Chung J. "Prices, Farm Outputs and Income Projections under Alternative Assumed Demand and Supply Conditions," *American Journal of Agricultural Economics,* 58, no. 4, 703–11.

index

D

E

G

H

I

J

K

L

M

Y